Maritime Capital

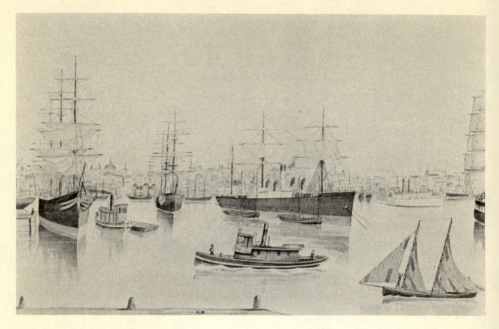

A painting of Saint John harbour, late nineteenth century, by E.H. Russell. Several stages in marine technology appear: sailing ships, a steel-hulled auxiliary steamer, a side-wheeler, and steam tugs. Dalhousie University Archives

Maritime Capital

The Shipping Industry in Atlantic Canada, 1820–1914

ERIC W. SAGER

with

GERALD E. PANTING

McGill-Queen's University Press
Montreal & Kingston • London • Buffalo

Legal deposit fourth quarter 1990
Bibliothèque nationale du Québec

Printed in Canada on acid-free paper

This book has been published
with the help of a grant from the
Social Science Federation of Canada,
using funds provided by the
Social Sciences and Humanities
Research Council of Canada.

Canadian Cataloguing in Publication Data

Sager, Eric W., 1946–
    Maritime capital, the shipping industry in
    Atlantic Canada, 1820-1914

    Includes bibliographical references.
    ISBN 0-7735-0764-7
    1. Shipbuilding industry—Maritime Provinces—
    History—19th century.
    2. Shipping—Maritime Provinces—
    History—19th century.
    3. Maritime Provinces—Economic conditions—To 1867.
    4. Maritime Provinces—Economic conditions—1867–1918.
    I. Panting, Gerald.   II. Title.
    HE635.Z7A84 1990   338.4'562382'009715   C90-090216-7

This text was set in 10/12 Baskerville
by Q Composition Inc., Etobicoke, Ontario

In memory of
David George Alexander
1939–1980

Contents

Illustrative Material

MAPS

TABLES

PLATES

Following page xviii

Acknowledgments

This book is the work of two members of the Atlantic Canada Shipping Project. The interpretation is ours alone, but the book is also the result of a collaborative effort, over more than a decade, involving a team of researchers and several institutions. We acknowledge first the ideal of collaborative research, realized in practice more often by those in the social or natural sciences than by historians, but fundamental to the project and a necessity for any who would tackle so vast a subject.

The Atlantic Canada Shipping Project was conceived by three members of the Maritime History Group at Memorial University of Newfoundland: the late David Alexander, the late Keith Matthews, and Gerry Panting. Keith Matthews chaired the group, and he was largely responsible for initiating the transfer of British Imperial Crew Agreements from the Registrar of Shipping and Seamen in the United Kingdom to Memorial University. In the effort to find a home for these documents, Keith was assisted by Robin Craig, then of University College, London; by the late Ron Seary, former head of the Department of English at Memorial University; and by the late Stephen, Lord Taylor of Harlow, president of Memorial University at the time. Keith Matthews was the principal creator of the great maritime archive at Memorial, called initially the Archive of the Maritime History Group, and since 1986 the Maritime History Archive.

The Atlantic Canada Shipping Project, based on that archive, was funded from 1976 to 1979 by the Canada Council and subsequently to 1982 by the Social Sciences and Humanities Research Council of Canada. Memorial University, the home of the project, also gave generous support. We are particularly indebted to two of its presidents, M.O. Morgan and Leslie Harris, and to the late James A.

Tague, head of its Department of History during the project. We give sincere thanks to our many other friends and colleagues at Memorial.

We in the project are indebted also to many present and former members and employees of the Maritime History Group and its successor organizations at Memorial University, the Maritime Studies Research Unit and the Maritime History Archive. Our research assistants were B.A. (Sandy) Balcom, Janet Bartlett, Terry Bishop-Stirling (now a member of the History Department at Memorial University), Olga Prentice (Olga Ilich of Richmond, British Columbia), Roberta Thomas, and Heather Wareham (who now heads the Maritime History Archive at Memorial University).

Much of the data entry for the project was done by a hard-working staff. Of these, Ivy Dodge, Paula Marshall, and Rose Slaney remain with the staff of the archive. Others were Catherine Brennan, Alyson Carter, Barbara Chapman, Margaret Gulliver, Doris King, June Knight, Rita O'Keefe, Hilary Rifkin, Lorraine Rogers, Geraldine Starkes, Mary Walsh, and Irene Whitfield. Assistant professors (research) were Lewis R. Fischer, Rosemary Ommer, and Eric W. Sager.

T.W. Bussey, now director of Memorial University's Computing Services, designed the project's data entry system. Greg Bennett and Craig Slaney did much of the programming. We received help with SPSS and with the statistics from Alan Cornish, Ruth Cornish, and Jake Knoppers. At the University of Victoria, Michael Keating and Laura Proctor helped with later stages of the computer work.

Conferences were a vital part of the Atlantic Canada Shipping Project, and we thank all who came to our six meetings. Robin Craig was our principal guide and mentor throughout, generously sharing his time, his knowledge, and his hospitality. Phil Buckner gave cogent advice, and we learned much from the work of T.W. Acheson. Douglass C. North and Peter McClelland compelled us to rethink our entire approach. We learned from many others at those conferences, and we thank especially Peter N. Davies, Ralph Davis, Judith Fingard, James M. Gilmour, Richard Goss, Basil Greenhill, C. Knick Harley, James K. Hiller, Niels Jannasch, Walter Kresse, Larry McCann, Campbell McMurray, Helge Nordvik, Sarah Palmer, Stuart Pierson, Richard Rice, Jeffrey Safford, David Sutherland, Patricia Thornton, Hugh Whalen, David Williams, and Graeme Wynn.

We are indebted to many archives and museums in Canada and Britain, and especially to the staffs of the Baker Library (Boston, Massachusetts), the Dalhousie University Archives, the Legislative Library of Nova Scotia, the Maritime Museum of the Atlantic (Halifax), the National Maritime Museum (Greenwich), the New Brunswick Archives, the New Brunswick Museum, the Provincial Archives of Newfoundland and Labrador, the Public Archives of Nova Scotia, the Public Archives of Prince Edward Island, and the Yarmouth County Museum.

More has been learned than they realize from colleagues at the University of Victoria and from the graduate students in history at that university. Valuable help was given by Christine Godfrey, Robert MacDonnell, and Christopher Roberts in Victoria and by John Noble and Suzanne Zeller in Toronto. Paul Fox, principal of Erindale Campus, University of Toronto, granted Sager the leave of absence that allowed him to return to Memorial in 1981–2. Further research funding and travel assistance were provided by the University of Victoria and the Social Sciences and Humanities Research Council.

Several people have given advice on specific matters or read parts of the manuscript of the present book and we thank particularly Harald Hamre, Rod Hay, Kris Inwood, Rosemary Langhout, Eric Lawson, Larry McCann, Helge Nordvik, Lauritz Pettersen, and, once again, Robin Craig. We are grateful to David Frank for showing us his material on steel shipbuilding. Ian McKay read the entire manuscript for us, and we thank also two anonymous assessors.

Stuart Daniel of Victoria did the maps and graphs. We are grateful to the University of Victoria and Memorial University for providing funds for the cartographic work. Publication was supported by a grant from the Social Science Federation of Canada. The authors and readers of this book owe much to our copy-editor, John Parry of Toronto.

This is *our* book, and we both take responsibility, but Panting provided the core of chapters 4 and 7 and the huge research files containing our evidence on major shipowners; Sager contributed the rest and, for the sake of consistency, the prose style.

The intellectual driving force in the Atlantic Canada Shipping Project from 1976 until his death in 1980 was David Alexander, a British Columbian who began his university education thirty years ago at Victoria College, now the University of Victoria. The project was inspired by David's vision and by questions that are still pertinent, many years after he posed them for us:

It was not to the credit of eastern Canada that their shipping industry developed in the first place, but it is equally not to their discredit that it disappeared. Yet today in Atlantic Canada we are entering a political and economic situation in which we are going to have to go to work, and it is unlikely that we can continue to depend on the income guarantees we have had in the past. If what happened in eastern Canada was an inevitable result of technological change, the present and future prospects for the region look dismal ... The issue is more than an academic one for us, and even more than a strictly historical one ...

We cannot know what this book might have been, had David survived to share in writing it. What we offer here is our modest thanks to him.

Eric W. Sager
Victoria

Gerry Panting
St John's

Right and overleaf Crew agreement of the *Africa* of Windsor, Nova Scotia.

Eng. 1.

Executed in Twenty Pages.

* Any Erasure, Interlineation, or Alteration in this Agreement will be void unless attested by some Superintendent of a Mercantile Marine Office, Officer of Customs, Consul, or Vice-Consul, to be made with the consent of the persons interested.

R. G. & R. O. REGISTERED 22 JUN. 94

AGREEMENT AND ACCOUNT OF CREW.

FOREIGN-GOING SHIP.

Issued by the Board of Trade, August, 1891, in pursuance of 17 & 18 Vic. c. 104

The term "Foreign-going Ship" means every Ship employed in trading or going between some place or places in the United Kingdom and some place or places situate beyond the Coasts of the United Kingdom, the Islands of Guernsey, Jersey, Sark, Alderney, and Man, and the Continent of Europe, between the River Elbe and Brest inclusive.

Name of Ship.	Official No.	Port of Registry.	Port No. and Date of Register.	Registered Tonnage. Gross.	Registered Tonnage. Net.	Nominal Horse Power of Engines (if any).
"Africa"	100734	Windsor N.S.	July 1893	—	679	—

REGISTERED MANAGING OWNER.

Name.	Address. (State No. of House, Street, and Town.)	No. of Seamen for whom accommodation is certified (30 & 31 Vict. c. 124.)	FOR PARTICULARS AS TO LOAD LINE, SEE LAST PAGE.
E. Churchill & Sons	Hantsport N.S.		

Scale of Provisions to be allowed and served out to the Crew during the Voyage, in addition to the daily issue of Lime and Lemon Juice and Sugar or other antiscorbutics in any case required by 30th and 31st Vict., c. 124, s. 4.

	Bread lb.	Beef lb.	Pork lb.	Tinned Meats lb.	Soup and Bouilli pint.	Preserved Potatoes lb.	Compressed or Preserved Vegetables lb.	Flour lb.	Peas pint.	Rice lb.	Tea oz.	Coffee oz.	Sugar oz.	Molasses oz.	Water qts.
Sunday	1	1½													
Monday	1		1¼					½			⅛	½	2	0	3
Tuesday	1	1½							⅓		Daily				
Wednesday	1		1¼												
Thursday	1	1½						½	⅓						
Friday	1		1¼												
Saturday	1	1½						½	⅓						

Note.—In any case an equal quantity of Fresh Meat or Fresh Vegetables may, at the option of the Master, be served out in lieu of the Salted or Tinned Meats or Preserved or Compressed Vegetables named in the above scale.

SUBSTITUTES.

at the master's option

The Several Persons whose names are hereto subscribed, and whose descriptions are contained on the other side or sides, and of whom are engaged as Sailors, hereby agree to serve on board the said Ship in the several capacities expressed against their respective Names, on a voyage from[1]

Hantsport to Parrsboro thence to U.K. or Continent of Europe, thence to any ports or places within the limits of 75 degrees North and 60 degrees South Latitude, to and fro for a period not to exceed twelve Calender Months final port of discharge to be in the United States or Dominion of Canada

And the Crew agree to conduct themselves in an orderly, faithful, honest and sober manner, and to be at all times diligent in their respective Duties, and to be obedient to the lawful commands of the said Master, or of any Person who shall lawfully succeed him, and of their Superior Officers, in everything relating to the said Ship and the Stores and Cargo thereof, whether on board, in boats, or on shore; in consideration of which Services to be duly performed, the said Master hereby agrees to pay to the said Crew as Wages the sums against their names respectively expressed, and to supply them with provisions according to the above Scale. And it is hereby agreed, That any Embezzlement or wilful or negligent Destruction of any part of the Ship's Cargo or Stores shall be made good to the Owner out of the Wages of the Person guilty of the same: And if any Person enters himself as qualified for a duty which he proves incompetent to perform, his Wages shall be reduced in proportion to his incompetency: And it is also agreed, That the Regulations authorized by the Board of Trade, which are printed herein and numbered[2]

are adopted by the parties hereto, and shall be considered as embodied in this Agreement: And it is also agreed, That if any Member of the Crew considers himself to be aggrieved by any breach of the Agreement or otherwise, he shall represent the same to the Master or Officer in charge of the Ship in a quiet and orderly manner, who shall thereupon take such steps as the case may require; And it is also stipulated that the Seamen shall receive the advances of wages entered herein against their names: And it is also agreed, That[3]

The Ship to be considered fully maned with nine hands all told, all over that number Considered Extra, No cash advanced abroad or liberty allowed but at the masters option

* The authority of the Owner or Agent for the allotments mentioned within is in my possession.

{ *Superintendent, Officer of Customs, or Consular Officer.*

* This is to be signed if such an authority has been produced, and to be scored across in ink if it has not.

In Witness whereof the said Parties have subscribed their Names on the other Side or Sides hereof on the days against their respective Signatures mentioned.

Signed by W. Davison Master,

on the 13 day of July 1893.

Date of Commencement of Voyage.	Port at which Voyage commenced.	Date of Termination of Voyage. (These Columns to be filled up at the end of the Voyage.)	Port at which Voyage terminated.	Date of Delivery of Lists to Superintendent.	I hereby declare to the truth of the Entries in this Agreement and Account of Crew, &c.
13 July 1893	Hantsport N.S.	4/6/94	Cardiff	11/6/94	W. Davison Master.

[1] Here the Voyage is to be described, and the places named at which the Ship is to touch, or, if that cannot be done, the general nature and probable length of the Voyage is to be stated.
[2] Here are to be inserted the Numbers of any of the Regulations for preserving discipline issued by the Board of Trade, and printed on the last page hereof, which the parties agree to adopt.
[3] Here any other stipulations may be inserted to which the parties agree, and which are not contrary to Law.

N.B.—This Form must not be unstitched. No leaves may be taken out of it, and none may be added or substituted. Care should be taken at the time of Engagement that a sufficiently large Form is used. If more men are engaged during the voyage than the number for whom signatures are provided in this Form, an additional Form Eng. 1 should be obtained and used.

W B & L (251ss)—7687—1500-8-91

Twenty Pages.

PARTICULARS OF ENGAGEMENT.

Reference No.	SIGNATURES OF CREW.	Year of birth.	Town or County where born.	If in the Reserve, No. of Commission or R. V. 2.	Ship in which he last served, and Year of Discharge therefrom.		Date and Place of signing this Agreement.		In what capacity engaged, and if Master, Mate, or Engineer,* No. of Certificate.	Time at which he is to be on board.
					Year.	State Name and Official No. or Port she belonged to.	Date.	Place.		
	1	2	3	4	5	6	7	8	9	10
1	W. Davison *Master to sign first.*	44	Hantsport			"Chester"	13/7/93	Hantsport	C. C. *Master.*	
2	P Beganson	25	Wilmerson			Lacinia	26/7/93	Parrsboro	3925 male	Vona
3	Burton Davison	32	Hantsport			Quebec	14/7/93	Parrsboro	2nd Mate	do
4	Edward Lang	30	Sweeden			Am. Bkt	19/7/93	Hantsport	Cook & Steward	14/7/93
5	Edward Coalfleet	56	Hantsport			"Loanda"	14/7/93	Do	A. B.	14/7/93
6	Wellington Beganson	17	Mt Denson N.S.			St Paul	14/7/93	Do	A.B	14/7/93
7	Thomas Hilgrove	19	Parrsboro N.S.			"Bahama"	27/7/93	Parrsboro	A. B	29/7/93
8	William Megratt	20	do			"Adelaide"	27/7/93	Do	A. B	29/7/93
9	James R. Milton	23	"			"Harry"	31/7/93	"	A. B	2/8/93
10	Robie Graham	17	Horton			"Loanda"	14/7/93	Hantsport	O.S.	14/7/93
11	Levi Patterson	17	Falmouth			Quebec	14/7/93	Parrsboro	O.S	Vona
12										
13										
14										
15										
16										
17										
18										
19										
20										

* Engineers not employed on the Propelling Engines and Boilers

† If any Member of the Crew enters Her Majesty's Service, the Name of the Queen's Ship into which he enters is to be stated under the head of "Cause of leaving"

(257 aa)

		PARTICULARS OF DISCHARGE, &c., To be filled in by the Master upon the Discharge, Death or Desertion of any Member of his Crew.					RELEASE (late M).		

Amount of Wages per Week or Calendar Month.	Advances made in the United Kingdom if not more than One Month's Wages, conditional on going to Sea.	Other Advances, not being conditional on the Seaman's going to Sea from the United Kingdom.	Amount of Weekly or Monthly Allotment.	Signature or Initials of Official before whom the Seaman is engaged.	Date.	Place.	Cause.†	Balance of Wages paid on Discharge.	We, the undersigned Members of the Crew of this Ship, do hereby release this Ship, and the Master and Owner or Owners thereof, from all Claims for Wages, or otherwise in respect of this Voyage, and I, the Master, do hereby release the said undersigned Members of the Crew from all claims in respect of the said Voyage. Signatures of Master and Crew (each to be on the Line on which he be signed in Col. 1).	Signature or Initials of Official before whom the Balance of Wages was paid and Release signed.	Reference No.
11	12	13	14	15	16	17	18	19	20	21	
				J. M. Lewis	13/6/94	Cdf	Dis		W. Davison		1
40.00				E. Pulley	12/6/94	Cardiff	Dis	59 7 4	P Boyann		2
30.00				E.G	11/6/94	Cdf	Disch	3. 11. 1	Burton Davison		3
35.00				M.L	4/6/94	Cdf	d..d	58. 13 1	Edward Lang		4
20.00				M.L	30/5/94	Cardiff	Disch	41. 2. 10	Edward Woolflat		5
20.00				M.L	30/5/94	do	do	32. 1	Wellington Boyann		6
20.00	10.00			E.G	28/6/94	do	do	25 4	Thomas Hilgrove		7
20.00				E.G	28/6/94	do	do	26 5 2	William Megavu		8
18.00	10.00			E.G	28/6/94	do	do	19 14	James B Milton		9
15.00				M.L	28/5/94	do	do	16 00	J.P.S. Graham		10
15.00				E.G	28/6/94	do	do	14 6	Levi Patterson		11
											12
											13
											14
											15
											16
											17
											18
											19
											20

should be described as Engine Drivers here and in Div. I.
the Ship," thus, "H.M.S. Revenge;" and the other Causes of leaving the Ship should be briefly stated thus, "Discharged," "Deserted," "Left Sick," "Died."

Twenty Pages.

The *Strathern* of Maitland, Nova Scotia. Built in 1892, she was one of the last of the large ocean-going barques built in the Maritimes. Dalhouse University Archives

Right Schooners loading lumber from flatcars in Liverpool, Nova Scotia, c. 1912. Hector MacLeod, Liverpool, Nova Scotia

Crew of the ship *Agnes Sutherland* in San Francisco in 1878. Nova Scotia Museum

Halifax Drydock, c. 1890. The drydock was used for the repair of Royal navy and merchant vessels. Public Archives of Nova Scotia

This ship *Marlborough*, 1,383 gross tons, built at Hantsport, Nova Scotia, in 1863.
Note that the vessel carried double topsails and the house flag of the owner, Ezra
Churchill, at the top of the main mast. Public Archives of Nova Scotia

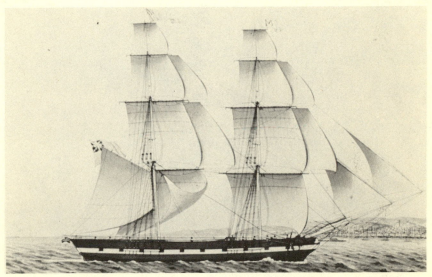

The brig *James*, built at Ship Harbour, Nova Scotia, in 1826. With square sails on both masts, the brig was a common ocean-going rig in this period. Nova Scotia Museum, Halifax

Maritime Capital

CHAPTER ONE

Sailing Ships and Regional History

The story of the shipbuilding and shipping industries of Atlantic Canada has been written before. Among our parents and grand-parents were many who loved to read about the old sailing ships and many who mourned the lost industry of "wooden ships and iron men," a lament that began with Frederick William Wallace in the 1920s.[1] The golden age of sail was a source of pride for a people whose region was in decline. And in the passing of the sailing fleets there was consolation: the decline of the shipping industry was the inevitable result of iron, steel and steam, technological forces that lay beyond the control of the region and its people.

A later generation should not allow academic condescension or whiggish faith in the progress of our discipline to deny the merit of this older understanding of the sailing ship industry. Wallace gave us our first extended chronicles of those sailing vessels, and in *Roving Fisherman* he gave us one of our finest first-hand accounts.[2] He has had many followers – popular historians, memorialists, novelists, and keepers of the visual record.[3] Many truths abide, thanks to their labours. The shipping industry was indeed a magnificent achieve-ment – a story not of modest regional success but of successful partici-pation in the international markets of nineteenth-century capitalism. The industry still serves to remind us that Maritimers and Newfound-landers were capable of great things, before and after the "shabby dignity" that Confederation and dependence bequeathed to the region in the twentieth century.[4] In these chronicles there is also frequent testimony to the labour of the thousands who created and worked those ships, and there are reminders that they were not "iron men" at all, but flesh and blood, and women as well as men. And if today we think that a technological explanation for the industry's decline may be simplistic and self-defeating, we might concede that it is preferable to self-pity or a fruitless search for scapegoats in central Canada.

As the twentieth century draws to a close, our understanding of the argosies of the age of sail is changing, and it is unlikely that there will be a single or shared understanding.[5] Many things have changed: the historical discipline itself, absorbing methods and theory from related human sciences; explanations for regional disparities and differential patterns of economic development, acquiring new sophistication and diversity; and the region itself, at least in needs and expectations. Only the stark evidence of disparity and dependence remains, and its persistence may also influence our explanation: whatever happened to the shipping industry of Atlantic Canada did not occur in a short time, as a single catastrophic event, but as part of a structure possessing its own stability and durability, constraining economic development today, as it did a century ago.

Situating the rise and decline of shipping and shipbuilding in a longer time frame is a difficult task, not least because the decline of these industries was very rapid. In 1880, with 1.3 million tons on its shipping registries, Canada may have had the fourth largest merchant marine in the world, after Britain, the United States, and Norway. Official figures sometimes invite scepticism, and the high ranking of Canada's merchant marine was questioned at the time; but there remains no doubt that this was a relatively large merchant marine at the height of the age of sail.[6] This merchant marine was also concentrated in eastern Canada. If we include Newfoundland's tonnage, by 1880 no less than 73 per cent of all British North American shipping was registered in three Canadian provinces and one British colony: Nova Scotia, New Brunswick, Prince Edward Island, and Newfoundland. In the three decades that followed, Canadian shipowning declined, in both absolute and relative terms, and by 1910 Canada's merchant marine was tenth or eleventh in the world. This overall decline was almost entirely the result of what happened in the Maritime provinces of Canada, because elsewhere – especially in Ontario and in British Columbia – shipowning increased.[7]

Shipowning and shipbuilding in the Maritimes did not simply decline – these industries collapsed. By 1900 the local fleets were a third of their size a mere two decades earlier. Readers may object that our measure of domestically owned shipping capital may be imperfect and may exaggerate the decline that occurred, since we rely on ship registries and official figures of tonnage on registry in the region. Tonnage owned in the region but registered elsewhere is therefore unknown. There were always those who held shares in vessels registered in Britain, for instance – we simply do not know how such ownership changed over time. Our conclusion about the collapse of the industry is likely to remain unchallenged, however. Until the end of the nineteenth century there was still a strong relationship between location of owners and location of registry, and there was no compelling incentive to register vessels in one part of the empire rather than another. Thus William Thomson registered several British-built steamers in Saint John, and Newfoundland's British-built coastal steamers found their way onto the St John's registry books. Our examination of the probate and other records of shipowners indicates no great movement toward British or foreign-flag vessels. Certainly contemporaries did not dispute the idea that a collapse had occurred.

The collapse to which we refer, however, was not simply that of regionally based shipowning businesses. What collapsed were two related industries – shipbuilding and shipowning – both of which had once been linked to the business of shipping goods in the region's export and import trades. All three parts of this transportation complex collapsed together. In the two decades after 1879 shipbuilding output in the three Maritime provinces declined at an average *annual* rate of 13 per cent![8] By the end of the century shipbuilding in the region meant little more than production of small wooden coasters and fishing craft. When Canadian shipbuilding boomed again in the First World War, almost all deep-sea tonnage, whether wooden or steel, naval or mercantile, was built in other Canadian provinces. Well before the war the Canadian Atlantic carrying trades had been taken over by British or foreign vessels. In the mid-1870s about 28 per cent of sea-going tonnage entering and clearing Canadian ports was Canadian-registered; by 1904 the proportion had fallen to 12 per cent.

Given these parameters of decline, it is still tempting to write the history of an event, imprisoned within a short time span, to be explained "by making play, factitiously or not, with those 'causes' and 'effects' so dear to the historians of yore."[9] And surely only technological obsolescence could explain so sudden an event?

This question we must answer with a resounding negative and hope that our answer will be heard even by those who never read this book. Of course the transition from sail to steam, and from wood to iron, must be part of our story. But a technological explanation for the collapse of the shipping complex of Atlantic Canada is unacceptable. Such an explanation lacks a convincing historical logic, and it brings nothing of value to our understanding of the Atlantic provinces in their past and future. It bears a message of despair – that economic change is determined by inexorable forces of technology and markets that lie ultimately beyond human agency and control, and beyond the control of those living in the region.

The technological "explanation" merely evades explanation. It leaves unanswered two obvious questions. First, if survival in the shipowning business required investment in iron steamships, then why did Maritimers not buy many more such vessels, as shipowners elsewhere were doing? Second, if survival in shipowning depended critically on local production of ships, then why did Maritimers not build more iron steamships? These are the questions that remain to be answered. Simple answers do not exist.

However reluctantly and however modestly, we historians must turn to the work of other scholars in search of method or theory to guide us. We have no choice but to do this, for history is a discipline that is informed and structured by theory, even if some historians try to ignore that fact; and any history that closes itself off from other disciplines is self-impaired. By guiding our reasoning from the particular to the general, theory tells us what we know. By making apparent that which it cannot explain, theory may guide us to the areas of human experience that we must still explore. The results will be acceptable as history, of course, only if theory and jargon-free language serve to clarify rather than obscure the meaning and structure that we seek in the evidence of the past. For this reason, and as a courtesy to our readers, we include in our endnotes brief definitions of terms that may be complex or unfamiliar.

There are those who would derive an approach from the vast pool of neo-classical economic theory and its reservoirs of regional development theory. At the level of industries, this body of theory offers a model that explains how resources are allocated to alternative uses through the operation of markets and a price system. With industries such as shipping, shipowning, and shipbuilding, we are necessarily concerned with international markets, since ocean-going ships and their services were exchanged in such markets. Here the critical concept is called comparative advantage, which derives ultimately from David Ricardo's law of comparative costs.

This law suggests that trade between countries will take place where cost differences occur. Thus if wheat is relatively cheap in Canada, and ships are relatively cheap in Britain, it is likely that Canada will specialize in wheat and Britain in ships, and a mutually beneficial exchange will occur. However, such mutually beneficial exchange may still occur, even if both commodities can be produced more cheaply in one country. Thus it might still benefit Canada to specialize in wheat and to exchange wheat for ships from Britain, even if ships could be produced cheaply in Canada.

This is the framework that Peter McClelland and others have commended to us, in the context of a "location of industry" problem.[10] In this framework an explanation for the decline of shipping in Atlantic Canada requires an answer to the following question: what advantages encouraged Britons or Norwegians to specialize in the exchange of shipping services, or of ships built on their shores, and what advantages encouraged Canadians, including Maritimers, to specialize in other commodities or services? This procedure makes our problem manageable, for essentially we must plot simple supply curves, and to do this we must know cost structures. We should then seek to discover the costs of operating (or building) ships in Britain and Norway and the costs of operating (or building) ships in Maritime Canada. Then we should examine how relative costs changed with a critical shift in technology – the transition to iron and steam. If we discover a change in relative costs, affording greater comparative advantage to Britain or Norway, we have gone a long distance toward explaining the decline of the shipping complex in Canada. Furthermore, were we to add evidence on profits or rates of return in shipping and in landward industries in Canada in the late nineteenth century, and were we to discover a decline in returns in shipping compared with returns in other industries, we should move even closer to an explanation for the movement of capital away from shipping. Of course, behind a change in comparative advantage may lie a different distribution of resources in Canada compared to Britain or Norway, and this too becomes part of the explanation.

About such an approach much more could be said, and only the ignorant would deny its merits. In this book we present evidence on costs and on profits, and we acknowledge some of the specific advantages to shipbuilding and shipowning in other countries. Our story might then be told as follows. In the first half of the nineteenth century, the Atlantic colonists assembled the inputs of a shipbuilding industry: shipyard labour with its specific skills; the capital required to establish such shipyards, with their specific technologies and supply networks; and the resources, among them the nearby supply of timber which was so critical to the region's comparative advantage in shipbuilding and shipowning. This comparative advantage was reflected in the relatively low prices of most colonial-built tonnage.[11]

Having assembled the basic inputs in shipbuilding, the colonists found that the returns to each of these inputs, and to the ships themselves, varied considerably over time, especially with changes in international shipping markets – the supply of shipping and the demand for shipping services in these markets. The inputs had to change, especially in the last three decades of the century, and survival in the markets required substitution – more iron and less wood, more steam-engines and less sail, and different skills embodied in labour. The costs of substitution appear to have been relatively high in Canada, and this is reflected in the price difference between British-built and Canadian-built steamship tonnage in the early twentieth century. With the costs of substitution so high, the neo-classical principles of maximization and "opportunity cost" predict the outcome – movement of capital away from shipbuilding and shipowning altogether and into arenas having very different equations of costs and comparative advantage.[12]

The story told in this way could be powerful, and for many it would be persuasive – but it would not be complete. There is a great deal of evidence that this model will not contain. First, consider the business of shipowning. If the costs of substituting iron for wood or steam for sail were so high in the Maritimes, then shipowners had other means of substitution: they could simply purchase British-built steamships rather than building their own.

The same point applies to other elements in the cost structure of shipowning: all inputs were purchased in international markets to which all nations had access. Where ships could not be purchased freely between nations, but were subject to import duty, as in France, the state often gave subsidies to shipbuilders and shipowners in order to compensate for the disadvantage of the duty. Labour costs varied from one place to another, but most tramp ships competing in the same trades had to hire labour in the same ports. Even the advantage afforded Norwegian shipowners by the low wages paid to Norwegian sailors has recently been cast in doubt.[13] Of course, the decline in freight rates in international shipping markets affected rates of return and stimulated substitution – but this does not take us any closer to understanding why some engaged in substitution and others quit altogether.

Nor was there a failure on the demand side that might account for the Maritime Canadian withdrawal. With a steep decline in freight rates and relatively slow growth in international trade, perhaps some sellers of shipping services must be forced out of business, and fewer (perhaps larger) sellers will survive in fewer locations. But we must take care what we infer from falling freight rates. In the decades after 1814 freight rates for timber from British North America fell dramatically and almost continuously, but investment in shipping grew rapidly.

We must not infer from a decline in freight rates that demand for

Graph 1.1
Sea-Going Tonnage Entering and Clearing All Canadian Ports,
1876–1910

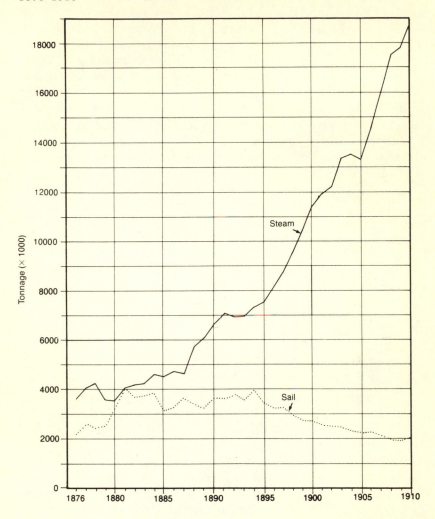

Source: Canada *Sessional Papers*, 1911, XLV, no. 6, 80–1. The graph indicates the sum
of all tonnage entering and clearing.

shipping was declining or that any suppliers at all will disappear.
Between 1880 and 1900, world demand for shipping and world
tonnage grew by about 1 per cent a year, despite the steep decline in
freight rates. In Canadian ports, demand for ocean-going shipping
grew steadily (Graph 1.1). Even the demand for sailing ships held up

longer than we might have expected – the decline in demand for sailing tonnage followed more than a decade *after* the collapse of the sailing ship industry in Atlantic Canada had begun.

In Canadian ports demand doubled in two decades. In the same two decades the shipping complex in the Maritimes collapsed. With more tonnage, growing demand, and cost structures differing only marginally between national operators in international markets, it remains to be explained why shipowners in one Canadian region withdrew.

But of course we have hardly approached the limits of what the neo-classical model can tell us. As we have already noted, even if costs in shipowning were roughly equal, and even if they were lower in Canada, comparative advantage might dictate that Canada specialize in wheat and purchase a growing volume of shipping services from Britain. It is not very difficult to show that this specialization occurred.

But still our questions are not answered, because they relate to three Canadian provinces that possessed no great advantages in the production of wheat. The exchange equations must include not two but at least three geopolitical units – Canada, its Maritime provinces, and Britain – and a range of commodities and services produced in each. Why, for instance, did not the Maritime provinces exchange shipping services for wheat or other products with central Canada, thereby absorbing much of the central Canadian demand for shipping? The exchange relations are now three-sided ones and are necessarily very complex.

It might be possible to solve such equations and to prove that comparative cost structures dictated a shift of capital away from shipowning in the Maritimes, but for one further complication. There is at least one critical factor or historical condition that the model does not contain. This factor is the state – a series of institutions, largely exogenous to the neo-classical model, which had a crucial effect on costs and opportunities in each country. One of the great and abiding lessons of maritime history is the recurring effect of state policy on comparative advantage. We need hardly refer to the role of the British state in the era of the Navigation Acts. In the period of Canada's decline as a maritime power, Japanese investors built shipping and shipbuilding industries with the encouragement of state protection.[14] Even if we did prove that in some measurable sense comparative advantages in eastern Canada lay outside shipping, we should still be compelled to ask why this was so, and why the state did little or nothing about it.

Even if we were to say that comparative advantages in the Maritimes dictated exchange of other products with central Canada, we should be little further ahead. It is entirely possible that state policy induced investment in industries for which comparative advantages did not exist. Indeed, in the Canadian context it is quite likely that this did occur, precisely because state protection or subsidy was given often in areas where the initial capital or infrastructure costs were so high as to deter private investment. Thus we know that after 1900 Maritimers put more capital into railways, steel, and textiles than they did into ships. This may have been the result not of comparative costs or comparative advantage at all but of an exogenous set of tariffs and infrastructure investments introduced by the state.

One other factor that the neo-classical model does not easily admit is the effect of information and culture on choice.[15] Comparative costs explain the location of industry only to the extent that information and knowledge are held constant, exerting no differential impact on the utility functions or expectations of investors in different places. The neo-classical economist must protect his or her model with the qualification that all other things are equal, including the distribution or costs of information, and this ceteris paribus assumption allows the model to retain predictive force.

How far such assumptions impair economic analysis is a matter of debate.[16] But surely in historical explanation such assumptions are likely to be fatal. There is every reason to assume that the flow of information, filtered through the complex fabric of culture, was different for investors in the Maritimes in the 1880s than it was in the 1840s, and different in Britain or Norway than it was in Canada. It remains possible that investment choices, or the movement of capital, may reflect such differences rather than the investors' "rational" analysis of opportunity costs.[17]

So far our discussion of the comparative advantage model relates to shipowning. The shipbuilding industry raises another problem which is even more damaging to the comparative cost approach. We cannot solve the exchange equations described above for shipbuilding, because it is not possible to solve equations in which several variables remain unknown.

As a simple example, let us take the possible exchange of ships and manufactured consumer goods between central Canada and the Maritimes. We can suppose that production costs appear, for the sake of simplicity, as follows (in man-hours per unit of output): for the Maritimes: consumer goods, 12, and ships, 10; for central Canada: consumer goods, 8, and ships, 9. Central Canada "exports" to the Maritimes one unit of consumer goods and "imports" in return 12/10 units of ships (which it may then use to ship wheat to Britain, for instance). If central Canada had invested eight man-hours in ships rather than in consumer goods, it would have produced only 8/9 units of shipping; central Canada has gained from this trade by the difference (12/10 − 8/9).

The advantage to central Canada, and the mutual benefits to both trading partners, may be estimated only if we know the production costs in each cell of the table. Unfortunately these are not known, and they cannot be known. There are no production costs for ocean-going steamships in the Maritime provinces in the entire period between the 1860s and 1914, because the industry did not exist. It is no answer to say that the industry never located in the region because production costs there were too high. We do not know what the production costs might have been. The best contemporary estimates were that Nova Scotia possessed all the necessary advantages for steel shipbuilding except skilled labour. G.B. Hunter, managing director of Swan and Hunter, the British shipbuilding company, confidently declared that steel ships could be built as cheaply in Nova Scotia as elsewhere.[18] We do know that when steel ships were built in Halifax at the end of the First World War, costs were not significantly higher than elsewhere in Canada.[19]

Cost estimates based on the short production runs of the post-war Halifax Shipyards are of little use, however. First, the post-war costs were much higher than any pre-war costs would have been. Second, the cost of producing the first ships was very different from the cost of subsequent ships in the same location, as shipbuilders knew: "Our experience has shown ... that the cost of construction on the tenth vessel as compared with the first as far as the actual direct labor is concerned was cut nearly in half. This was the result of keeping the same men working over and over again on the same parts of each individual vessel."[20] We do not know what the pre-war production costs of ten or twenty steel vessels would have been in Nova Scotia: the decision not to invest in this industry was taken long before the economies of longer production runs were realized and long before real costs were known.

Comparative cost analysis offers little help in explaining the regional distribution of steel shipbuilding within Canada by the 1910s. A shipyard capable of producing 10,000-ton steamships would presumably locate where the following conditions existed: proximity to developed coal resources and an iron or steel industry; proximity to plants capable of producing steel plate or to the sources of steel plate in the eastern United States or Britain; proximity to major markets for shipping services, either coastal or international; availability of the necessary skilled labour or of a cheap labour force capable of acquiring necessary skills; existing managerial experience in either shipbuilding or shipowning; the presence of governments willing to offer bonuses and tax relief.

The best prediction would be that steel shipbuilding would locate in eastern Canada, including Nova Scotia, where all these conditions existed and where municipal and provincial governments had agreed to bonus steel shipbuilding by 1902. By 1920, however, Nova Scotia had only 14 per cent of all Canadian steel shipbuilding capacity. The province having the largest shipyard capacity was British Columbia, with 34 per cent of the nation's production capacity. British Columbia was the province located furthest from the major markets and having the highest pre-war construction costs.[21] Comparative cost analysis does not explain this outcome.

Is it possible to refine the model so as to take into account known conditions of production in Atlantic Canada? Perhaps the staple approach offers such refinement. Staple theory holds that the pace and nature of economic growth in a country or region are determined by the characteristics of its staple product. The peculiar resource endowments and the unusual land-capital ratio of new regions or colonial frontiers allow people to produce something for which there is demand, especially in metropolitan markets. This pulls in factors from elsewhere, and there is a predictable pattern of growth. Economic development will occur as a process of diversification around the staple or export base. Shipbuilding and shipowning arise, therefore, from the production of the staple, as inputs in the production of fish or timber, for instance; or they arise as forward linkages from the staple, using timber as the prime input in shipbuilding, for instance. It follows that the decline of shipbuilding and shipowning will be the result of changes in the "production function" of the staple or the decline of staple dependence.[22]

The staple approach is appealing in the context of colonies that depended on the export of bulky raw materials across oceans. Our earlier experiment with this model satisfied few readers, however.[23] For one thing, the staple model requires a focus on raw material production which may distort our portrait of the colonial economy. A staple economy is assumed to be characterized by high ratios of land or resources to capital; it is surprising, therefore, to discover that the colonial economy most dependent on exports of a low-value staple – Newfoundland – was the colony with the largest per capita stock of capital (Table 1.1).

A very large item in the colonial capital stock was, of course, ships. Part of the problem with the staple approach is that the production function of the staple explains little about ships. Both timber and fish

Table 1.1

Economic Indicators, British North American Colonies, c. 1812

Colony	Per Capita Value (Pounds Sterling)		
	Output	Exports	Capital Stock
Upper and Lower Canada	24	1	27
New Brunswick	32	12	38
Nova Scotia	26	6	59
Cape Breton	23	3	79
Prince Edward Island	43	23	159
Newfoundland	59	39	368

Sources: P. Colquhoun, *A Treatise on the Wealth, Power and Resources of the British Empire, in Every Quarter of the World Including the East Indies* (New York, 1965), cited in Steven D. Antler, "The Capitalist Underdevelopment of Nineteenth Century Newfoundland," in Robert J. Brym and R. James Sacouman, eds., *Underdevelopment and Social Movements in Atlantic Canada* (Toronto: New Hogtown Press, 1979), 181. Output includes that of the fisheries.

required ships, of course, and so production of these staples may explain a growing colonial demand for ships. "Theory and history," wrote Mel Watkins, "suggest that the most important example of backward linkage is the building of transport systems for collection of the staple, for that can have further and powerful spread effects."[24] But this does not help in any way to explain the source of supply of the transport system or the location of shipbuilding. It is entirely possible that the country importing the staple may provide the entire transport system, and so there may be no transportation linkage at all in the staple-producing frontier. Whether or not a transportation linkage appears depends on conditions outside the staple model, such as the effects of war or tariff structures imposed by the metropolitan countries.

The staple model usually asks us to assume that in the early stages of development the export of unprocessed or semi-processed raw materials is predominant. "The closer we approach the first economic stirrings of the region, the greater the likelihood that the product of primary activity will be exported in unprocessed form."[25] But what about the colony that develops a secondary manufacturing sector early in its history and then loses that industry, becoming more dependent on staples over time? This is precisely what happened to Prince Edward Island. In the mid-1820s this small, relatively new colony was certainly export-dependent, but no less than 80 per cent of those exports consisted of manufactured products![26] The principal export was, of course, ships, and to preserve his or her model the staple theorist must counter that such ships were staples, which is to rob the word staple of its meaning.[27] Colonial-built sailing ships, even when they received much of their outfit in Britain, were not unfinished or semi-finished raw materials. They were manufactured products.

Of course the staple trades generated both demand for ships and many of the raw materials used in ship construction. Without these "linkages," the shipping industry would have been much smaller than it became. Staple production was a necessary condition for the growth of shipowning, but not a sufficient condition. Observing the rapid growth of shipowning in the Maritimes in the 1860s and 1870s, we reach the limits of what the staple approach can tell us: if ships were a type of linkage from the staple trades, then why should shipowning grow so rapidly when the old staple trades faltered? And what connection can be made between staples and the decline of shipowning and shipbuilding?

It is difficult to show that the Atlantic region as a whole lacked the resources necessary to make the transition to iron steamships, and all the more difficult when Nova Scotia acquired an iron and steel complex. The region possessed coal, iron ore, capital, a labour "surplus," and long experience in ship construction and management. Eventually the quality of local coal may have contributed to higher costs of certain inputs and relatively low productivity, as it appears to have done in the Nova Scotia steel industry.[28] But steel plate is only a small portion of the total cost of a steel-hulled steamship, and in any case the decision against large-scale shipbuilding in the region was taken before any such weakness in the local resources was known. A plant for the manufacture of steel plate for ships was not built in Nova Scotia until after the First World War.

In Atlantic Canada, as in Ontario, the staple approach has long since lost much of its persuasive force.[29] It does not help to explain the growth and timing of manufacturing and service sectors. It tends to assign undue priority to the nature of a region's resource base and the constraints imposed by that base. Furthermore, there is no a priori reason for believing that resource-poor regions are inevitably doomed to backwardness. There are regions and countries that overcome natural and geographic deficiencies by the manner in which they organize production. This being so, it is very difficult, perhaps impossible, to isolate resource inadequacy as an independent variable. It is, furthermore, unhelpful to do so, since the argument offers no guide to human action, either in the past or in the future. If our automobile runs out of gasoline and we fail to reach our destination, the mishap has a human cause, however much we may blame the vehicle for its shortage of fuel.

The staple approach, and its more sophisticated offshoot, export-base theory, will continue to find defenders, especially among those who study earlier stages in our history. But the decline of the shipping industries occurred after those stages. The export-base approach is useful "for a *part* of our history," Douglass North insisted. At a certain point the staple economy reaches a limit to extensive growth, or an "equilibrium," where "you have an equation between the opportunity cost of capital in a particular export industry and in other economic activities." At this point, "you arrive at the end of what export-base theory can tell us."[30]

Having said this, North then offered a telling qualification: in the course of its growth, the export base may have altered the economy in ways that affected subsequent development. Specifically, the economy structured around export-based growth may have altered the region's factor endowments, particularly its "human capital," as well as the role of government and the pattern of government investment. No more useful suggestions have been offered us from the direction of neo-classical economics. But this wise counsel directs us away from the staple approach and export-base theory: important as staples may have been, a region's endowment of skills, the historical conditions that generated those skills, and the role of the state cannot be explained simply as by-products of staples and their production function.

Wooden sailing ships were never merely the dependent offspring of timber and fish. They were part of the development of commercial capitalism on a colonial frontier. The reproduction of commercial capital began within the framework of British mercantilism. Such obvious, but scarcely trite observations point toward another literature on regional economic development – that vast body of work dealing with development in other former colonies of Europe, particularly those in Latin America, Africa, and Asia.[31] This literature is relevant to our study, and to Atlantic Canada, because it deals with relationships between colonizers and colonies, with the intrusion of capital into pre-capitalist economies, and with the recurring question about whether integration into an international capitalist economy entails relative stagnation or sustained growth and diversification.

There is no need to summarize a complex literature, itself rooted in conflicting bodies of theory. From parts of that literature, and from the related work of several Canadian scholars, we draw a hypothesis, and no more. The hypothesis is that the shipping industry was part of a specific mercantilist structure of exploitation of labour and resources on a colonial frontier. Although deep-sea sailing ships were proto-industrial workplaces using wage labour, they served the interests of merchant capital and contributed to the dominance and survival of merchants in the economy of Atlantic Canada. Ships were essential to mercantile control of markets and to merchant profits for the first three-quarters of the nineteenth century.

Why then did the shipping industries decline thereafter? One factor was international: falling rates of return in wooden sailing ships encouraged the shift of capital into new shipping technologies or away from ships altogether. But this condition, although necessary to explain why Maritimers chose the second of these alternatives, cannot be sufficient. The sufficient conditions lie in the pattern and direction of the industrial transition in the region. That pattern was determined by a specific historical conjuncture: the gradual and uneven integration of economic and social structures, inherited from the region's mercantile past, into the Canadian Confederation. Within this pattern a regional merchant marine became redundant.

It is important that we not attempt to claim too much here. Our dependent variable, in most of what follows, is the shipping industry, in its rise and decline. Those who want an answer to the bigger question about relatively slow economic development in Atlantic Canada will not find a complete answer in the study of one or two industries, however important they may have been. But of course the relationship between shipping and the economic and social structures of which it was part will be reciprocal. At a certain point the shipping industry itself becomes an independent variable: what did possession of such a large shipping sector mean for the region? Certainly the transition to industrial capitalism in this region was slow and incomplete, at least by comparison to that in central Canada between Confederation and the 1920s. Did the shipping industries have anything to do with this?

It would be easier to answer this question if we had a satisfactory general explanation for the region's slow industrial transition. Unfortunately we do not. Comparisons with central Canada remain difficult because historians of Ontario and Quebec have done more to describe the industrial revolution that occurred in those provinces than to explain it.[32] At a certain point the emphasis on the allegedly weak resource base or locational disadvantages of the Maritime provinces becomes reductionist and question-begging. Certainly any explanation that ignores the social organization of production will be incomplete. Important as it is, this subject – the social relations of production in Atlantic Canadian industries – remains largely uncharted territory, and we admit that our own reconnaissance is tentative and incomplete.

T.W. Acheson has suggested that the industrialization of the Maritimes under the National Policy may have been limited by economic and social structures inherited from the era of merchant dominance.[33] Ian McKay has suggested that "a major key to Maritime regional underdevelopment is to be found in the nature of the region's links to the world capitalist economy in the period of merchant's capital (c. 1750–1870), which focused development in dependent export enclaves, undermined the socio-economic potential for integrated and balanced growth, and retarded the development of a home market."[34]

And where merchant domination through control of markets was so complete, it may be that non-capitalist production was particularly durable: various forms of petty commodity production remained extensive, and so the social relations of production that developed within agriculture and other primary production in the Maritimes discouraged the substitution of capital for labour and worked against a more complete transition to industrial capitalism.[35]

It is consistent with our hypothesis that the sailing ship industries have a place in such explanations, however tentative, of the long-term structure of economic development. To the extent that locally owned and locally built fleets helped to establish and to preserve merchant dominance, petty commodity production, and even non-capitalist social relations, the shipping industries contributed to a relatively slow transition to industrial capitalism.

The rest of what follows is no more than a modest rendering of evidence that may bear on this hypothesis about the connections between shipping and colonial merchant capital. In presenting this evidence, we are no longer playing with the "causes" of an event but seeking instead the necessary and sufficient conditions of a merchant marine, in its rise and decline. We are not solving a "location of industry" problem, because shipping did not rise and fall in a zero-sum game where the number of ships and the number of shipowning locations were limited by ceilings of demand or comparative advantage. We are studying not a single industry but a marine complex, with all its social and cultural underpinnings.

It is worth thinking again about ships and their functions, which are always more than simply economic, in the narrow sense. A ship is a vehicle, an instrument of production in transportation, and its first function is to produce and sell a change of location. This is productive activity: in neo-classical economics, the change of location

adds value to a commodity by taking it to market; in Marxist economics, the transportation industry effects a real circulation or movement
of commodities, transforming them into use-values and exchange-
values.[36]

In the British North American colonies, ships were part of the
production and circulation of timber, fish, farm output, and many
other colonial products. The economic function cannot be separated
from its social conditions, for whoever owned ships also controlled
the circulation of goods and took a share in the control of exchange
mechanisms and prices. Ships were essential to the production and
distribution of fish and timber and to the circulation of imported
commodities. Whoever owned or controlled the ships held proportionate control over the surplus generated. To the extent that ships
became part of the realization of "surplus value" in a system of wage
labour, they were capital, and a particularly important type of capital
in export-dependent colonies.[37] Shipping capital came first from
Britain; eventually it would become the capital of colonial merchants.

To begin in this way is to leave open to us the insights of post-
dependency writing about development in other former colonies.
One such insight is that capital, as it enters societies in which pre-
capitalist production is dominant, does not everywhere act as a solvent of those pre-capitalist "modes of production."[38] Of course we
are aware that parallels with Latin America or India cannot be carried
too far, and we know that the pre-capitalist production systems of
native peoples in the Maritimes had long since been weakened or
marginalized. There was no "Asiatic" mode of production here, and
no complex "articulation" of modes of production of the kind that
some Marxist scholars have found in Latin America.

But there is still a point to be drawn from studies of commercial
capital in other contexts. The expanding capitalist sector – in mining,
in sawmilling, or in shipping – may yield many small exchanges with
rural smallholders, thereby sustaining the peasant proprietor or the
small family farm. Industrial capitalism cannot become dominant
until labour is freed from the means of production; but where merchants may capture economic surplus through control of exchange
relations and price mechanisms, they may have little incentive to
expropriate the smallholders and so to create a class of propertyless
wage labourers.

Merchant's capital, by itself, is not sufficient to generate a process
of development toward industrial capitalism: "The independent and
predominant development of capital as merchant's capital is tanta-
mount to the non-subjection of production to capital, and hence to
capital developing on the basis of an alien social mode of production

which is also independent of it. The independent development of merchant's capital, therefore, stands in inverse proportion to the general economic development of society."[39] The interaction of imported capital and the regional social formation may limit the extension of capitalism, despite the existence of commodity circulation, profit-making activity, and even technical innovation.[40]

A further insight is that imported capital may bring its own cultural forms, which may then interact with the host society to yield a pattern of expectations and investment specific to that interaction. Two long passages from a study of mining in Peru illustrate our point: both echo the experience of regional development in Atlantic Canada; more important, they challenge us by their sophisticated integration of social, cultural, and economic forces. Replace "mining" with "shipping" and we might be in Nova Scotia in the third quarter of the nineteenth century:

the movement of labour between agriculture and mining reinforced the predominant pattern of smallholder farming of low productivity. In this context capital accumulated through trade, transport or savings on mine wages was not likely to be invested in developing and consolidating agricultural or industrial production at the local level. Instead, investments were channelled into transport and trading activities and into improving the social infrastructure of localities by building schools, water and electricity systems and by providing health facilities and new public buildings. Although these activities created work at the local level and improved the general standard of living, they also shifted the focus of village life towards external opportunities and urban status criteria, such as education, modern styles of dress, and modern household accoutrements.[41]

In the Maritime provinces, as we shall see, shipowners invested heavily in the social infrastructure of their port towns. The external opportunities and "modern" criteria came increasingly from the landward centres of an industrializing Canada.

Although it is possible to refer to the merchants of Atlantic Canada as a class, the pattern of exploitation on the colonial frontier may have slowed development of class within the region. Very often, in Peru, a nascent bourgeoisie had the character of a series of élites, located in townships throughout the region, each élite competing with the others:

The regional economy evolved as a loosely integrated one in which different and, at times, conflicting economic rationalities coexisted amongst different sectors of the population. Hence, we find in the agricultural sphere, capitalist farmers, peasant entrepreneurs and smallholders dependent on communal resources. In the urban/industrial sphere, large-scale capitalist enterprises were often administered by foreigners and manned by workers who retained rights to land and returned regularly to their villages ... The transformations that occurred in the central highlands were partial ones in that they did not result in the complete integration and rationalization of the economy at a regional level. Thus, small-scale enterprise in farming, commerce and industry survived and proliferated alongside the growth of large-scale capitalist mining operations. This structure was basically a dualistic one ... This dualistic structure was not based on the separation of economic sectors, but rather on the pattern of exchanges and interdependencies between them. The large-scale mining enterprise benefited from cheap labour and supplies subsidized by peasant agriculture; this limited the consolidation of landholdings and the expansion of agricultural production. It also hindered the development of an industrial proletariat since even the unionized mine workers retained links with their villages and had land there ... In the absence of a strong local political organization controlled by the regionally important business class and linked to nationally powerful classes, regional government remained weak ... No clear class hegemony developed [in the region] ... This political and social fact is crucial to understanding the subsequent economic development of the region.[42]

This is very like what happened in the Maritime provinces of Canada, and perhaps in Newfoundland as well – or so this book proceeds to argue. If it works, the approach allows us to perceive anew the complex interactions between merchant capital and its host society. The approach assumes a historical distinction between merchant and industrial capital, although the links and overlap between the two were extensive, and they began even in shipping. The fundamental business of merchant capital is exchange, or the buying and selling of commodities, typically without direct control over the labour process.

Merchants' capital is often dependent on the class of independent producers or others who control labour and the tools of production, even though merchants may at the same time dominate those producers.[43] Transportation, unlike exchange, can alter the value of commodities and is part of the production process; for this reason some theorists say that transportation is not really merchant activity.[44] In Atlantic Canada, however, shipping was subordinated to merchant capital, even when shipping was part of the process of producing staples. The ship itself was often a commodity in the circuit of merchant capital; very often the merchant interest was mainly in the exchange of commodities carried by the ship.

Shipping was, therefore, a cautious mercantile venture into the final stage of a production process of which the merchant-shipowner saw little. This maritime capital was very important in the British North American colonies because of the costs of transporting bulky commodities, often of low unit value, over great distances. Well into the nineteenth century, merchant capital stimulated commodity production and made profits by controlling markets rather than by revolutionizing production processes. It follows that merchants did not control everything: in subsistence farming, fishing, and other non-wage work, families struggled to be independent, and they often succeeded.

This book is about a particular branch of that merchant capital which many scholars have studied in other North American contexts.[45] In adding to a substantial literature we do not suggest that "maritime capital" was a distinct mode of production; the term merely draws attention to a commercial capitalism that was, in the British Atlantic colonies, heavily oriented toward overseas trade, marine transportation, fishing, and other seaward activity. And our approach differs from the "international systems" perspective of R.T. Naylor, with its over-emphasis on the transformative power of exchange relations and market mechanisms imposed from Europe.

Although we emphasize here the conservative nature and "Janus face" of merchant capital, and although we see the shipping industry growing in the context of British mercantilism, we cannot assign a "determining role" throughout to "the ebb and flow of imperial history."[46] The globalist perspective misses too much of the specific colonial and regional evolution of production systems and social relations and may even lead, for instance, to the misleading conclusion that by 1860 economic power in New Brunswick still resided with shipbrokers in Liverpool and London.[47] It is precisely this kind of procrustean bed that we seek to avoid, as we search for meaning in the vast empirical base that we have inherited from the Atlantic Canada Shipping Project.

For all these reasons this approach to regional development does not take us away from ships and shipowners but toward them, for ships were never merely technological artefacts operating independent of society and culture. The conclusions from economic anthropology cited above flexibly integrate culture and class in the explanation for regional economic change. If there is to be such a synthesis for Atlantic Canada, the maritime capital of merchant shipowners must have a place in the synthesis.

CHAPTER TWO

Rise of an Enclave Industry

Long before the industrial revolution came to the northern half of North America, colonists were building and owning ships along the eastern shores of the continent. The earliest records of European activity along these coasts tell of the discovery of great timber forests. Norsemen used the forest resources and may have been the first Europeans to build boats on these shores. By the sixteenth century Basque whalers built boats in Labrador, and we do not know how many fishermen from many European nations used the timber of Newfoundland to build fishing boats. The first recorded shipbuilding occurred in the Maritimes in 1606 – two small vessels at Port Royal. Shipbuilding for both military and commercial purposes took place in New France. By the early eighteenth century builders in Newfoundland were producing craft for use in the Atlantic crossing to England.[1] In the same half-century, many other settlers were building boats and small decked vessels along both the Atlantic and the Gulf shores.

By the eighteenth century, shipbuilding was still a pre-industrial craft, undertaken mainly to meet the need of settlers for coastal transportation and for fishing vessels. Demand for such craft was clearly related to patterns of settlement and resource exploitation, and there was as yet little separation between the builders and the owners of vessels. Farmers and fishermen and their sons built small craft for their own use and worked the vessels themselves.

Resources and staple exports, important as they were, would not by themselves give rise to a shipbuilding industry. Shipbuilding as a manufacturing industry awaited the nineteenth century. Shipbuilding depended, above all, on the combined impact of European wars, British economic development, and British policies: it grew as much from these as it did from the forests of eastern Canada. Following establishment of Halifax in 1749, Governor Cornwallis gave an early hint of trends to follow when he set a bounty of ten shillings per ton on newly built vessels and encouraged the growth of local shipping to carry goods to and from the West Indies.[2]

Behind this modest protection lay a much longer tradition which British Americans inherited. The Navigation Acts were the core of a system of imperial protection in which shipbuilding was born. The 'Charta Maritima' of 1660 gave trade between Britain and her colonies exclusively to British shipping. An act of 1696 confined colonial trade to English shipping, defined as ships built in the British Isles and English possessions in Asia, Africa, or America.[3] By such acts, two basic principles had been established: colonial trade was confined to English ships, and colonial ships were English. The Act of General Registry of 1786, which set up the system of vessel registration for British ships, repeated these principles in the grandiloquent language of its preamble: "Whereas the wealth and strength of this kingdom, and the prosperity and safety of every part of the British Empire, greatly depend on the encouragement given to shipping and navigation; and whereas it is proper that the advantages hitherto given by the legislature to ships wholly owned and navigated by his Majesty's subjects should from henceforth be confined to ships wholly built and fitted out in his Majesty's dominions ... "

The Registry Act excluded foreign ships from the privileges of British shipping.[4] The provision that restricted British registry to vessels wholly built in some part of the British dominions was not repealed until 1849.[5]

This protection alone was not sufficient to create a major shipbuilding industry, because the supply of vessels from the mother country was more than adequate to meet the needs of transportation across the Atlantic for much of the eighteenth century. But the Navigation Acts encouraged small and scattered shipbuilding operations that met the demand from specific trades, particularly from the growing trade in provisions and lumber with the British West Indies. In the Maritimes this pre-industrial craft of shipbuilding became a continuous economic activity by the 1780s. In 1769, 1770, and 1771 only three or four sloops and schooners were built in each year.[6] By the end of the American revolutionary wars, a few dozen new vessels were being launched into Nova Scotian waters each year (see Table 2.1).

The growth of shipbuilding in the Maritimes represented by these figures had occurred very largely in the 1780s, as a response to wartime demand, to opportunities in the West Indies carrying trade, and to the arrival of the Loyalists. The latter group brought shipbuild-

Table 2.1
Colonial Shipping in 1787–8

	Built in 1787		Registered as of Sept. 1788	
	Number	Tonnage	Number	Tonnage
Newfoundland	22	1,767	90	6,390
Nova Scotia	33	1,951	233	15,273
New Brunswick	10	909	41	3,306
Quebec	16	786	88	4,637
St John's (Prince Edward Island)	2	221	–	–

Source: Public Record Office, Customs 17.

ing expertise, combined with the ambition to pursue mercantile opportunities which many perceived their former colonial neigh-bours to have forfeited by revolution.

The industry remained small, however, as the annual figures on shipbuilding indicate. But there was very respectable growth in ton-nage on registry in the Atlantic colonies, as Graph 2.1 suggests. Official figures of tonnage on registry must be treated with some suspicion: they do not always reflect tonnage actually retained by owners within the region, and many vessels were likely to have been transferred to ownership elsewhere before the registry was changed. Nevertheless the data are useful in suggesting a general trend and the timing of periods of growth in local ownership. The growth in the 1780s and 1790s was led mainly by Nova Scotia, related largely to expansion in the carrying trade to the British West Indies, from which the rebel colonies were at first excluded.

Although there was a relaxing of the Navigation Acts as they applied to the United States in the 1790s and afterward, the West Indies carrying trade was further stimulated by other government actions. These included Nova Scotian fishing bounties and the American embargo of December 1807, which prohibited American trade with the West Indies. Nova Scotian merchants and shipowners faced reduced competition in the West Indies trades.[7] Total tonnage clear-ing Nova Scotia for the British West Indies increased by more than four times between 1805 and 1814.[8]

The importance of the West Indies trades is no surprise. The total tonnage required was not insubstantial. Between 1788 and 1792 many more ships and a larger volume of tonnage cleared Nova

Graph 2.1
Tonnage on Registry by Colony, 1788–1820

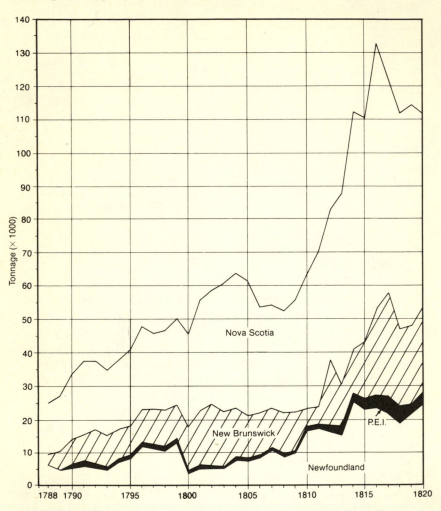

Sources: Public Record Office Customs 17, for 1788–1806, and PRO Board of Trade series 162, 1807–70; Richard E. Rice, "The Rise of Shipbuilding in British North America, 1787–1855" (PHD thesis, University of Liverpool, 1978), Appendix B

Scotia and New Brunswick for the West Indies than for the United Kingdom. Not until the early nineteenth century did the volume of tonnage clearing for the United Kingdom exceed the tonnage clearing for the West Indies.[9] Most of the ships embarking for the West

Indies were engaged in bilateral trading, returning directly to the Maritimes, sometimes stopping in the United States en route.[10]

While many of the commodities exported from British North America were carried in vessels owned and registered in the United Kingdom, British owners were less likely to supply tonnage for the Maritimes – West Indies trades. For one thing, demand for tonnage on the eastward passage from British North America to the United Kingdom was growing very rapidly in the first decade of the nineteenth century – much more rapidly than demand for tonnage on the westward passage. Between 1800 and 1808 the eastward passage from Nova Scotia and New Brunswick accounted for 39 per cent more tonnage than did the westward passage.[11] Thus vessels crossing the Atlantic were more likely to return directly to the United Kingdom with a cargo of timber than to load for the West Indies.

In these circumstances, merchant-exporters in the Maritimes supplied their own West Indian tonnage, while continuing to rely heavily on United Kingdom – registered tonnage for the North Atlantic route.[12] To the extent that Maritimers engaged in bilateral rather than triangular trades, they followed the pattern of eighteenth-century American shipowners.[13] The evidence on ownership of tonnage employed in various trade routes is incomplete, but such evidence as we do possess suggests that during and after the Napoleonic Wars the majority of vessels moving between the colonies and the West Indies were owned in the North American colonies. In 1808 and 1809, for instance, about 60 per cent of vessels clearing Saint John for the West Indies were registered in Saint John.[14] In 1821, 88 per cent of all tonnage entering Halifax from the West Indies was owned in Nova Scotia.[15]

The West Indies trade was a major stimulus to shipbuilding and shipowning in the Maritimes. Natural advantages by themselves did not create this stimulus. The stimulus came from wartime conditions in which increased demand for shipping was not matched by a stable supply of either British or US tonnage. For shipping, as for the staple trades, "the commercial welfare of the Maritime Provinces after 1783 was determined by the course of Anglo-American diplomacy."[16]

The overall growth in tonnage on registry in the Atlantic colonies was also related to the growth of permanent settlement in Newfoundland and of a resident fishery. These influences are not to be underestimated: after all, official figures suggest that in most years between 1810 and 1816 there was as much tonnage on registry in Newfoundland as in New Brunswick. Tonnage registered in New Brunswick was a smaller proportion of the regional total in 1815 than it had been at the beginning of the Napoleonic Wars. Such evidence reminds us that the New Brunswick timber trade was not the only stimulus to shipbuilding in the region.

In Nova Scotia, coastal shipping and fishing were scarcely less important than in Newfoundland. The Loyalists brought not only shipbuilding skills but an entirely new pattern of coastal settlement. Increasing volumes of imported goods were trans-shipped at Halifax and other entrepôts and carried to outport communities in small sloops and schooners. Coastal trading, often illicit, continued between the colonies and the eastern United States. It is impossible to estimate the proportion of locally registered tonnage employed in these coastal trades, but most vessels registered in the Maritimes before 1820 were small, designed and rigged for coastal trading rather than for sale in Britain. The difference between vessels remaining on registry in the Maritimes and vessels *built* there suggests the importance of small vessels for local owners: vessels remaining on registry in the colonies were on average much smaller than vessels built locally. Between 1800 and 1815 the average tonnage of vessels on registry was between 69 and 75 tons; the average tonnage of vessels newly built was over 100 tons in most years, and the average tonnage of vessels built in New Brunswick was 168 tons.[17]

The West Indies and the coasting trades created a significant demand for carrying capacity. Shipbuilding and shipowning in the Maritimes began with these trades. But there is a great deal that cannot be explained by reference to these trades. For one thing, shipbuilding in the Maritimes grew more quickly than did tonnage on registry in the long period from 1795 to the end of the Napoleonic Wars (the growth rate for shipbuilding output was 3.0 per cent a year, while tonnage on registry grew by 2.3 per cent a year). Ship-builders were not building simply for local markets in British North America. To the list of external stimulae we must add another factor: the sustained growth of British demand for shipping tonnage in international, colonial, and home trades.

The export trade in ships was at first much more important in Lower Canada than in the Maritimes. Between 1795 and 1806, 63 per cent of tonnage newly registered in Quebec was transferred to English or Scottish ownership or was registered initially by English or Scottish owners.[18] The proportion was certainly much lower in the Maritimes, although incomplete runs of vessel registries rule out precise comparisons. Registries for Prince Edward Island do exist, however, and they indicate that while two-thirds of the tonnage newly registered there between 1795 and 1806 was later transferred to outside registry, an insignificant amount – about 6 per cent – was transferred to the United Kingdom. The first market for Prince Edward Island's shipbuilders was within British North America.[19] Large-scale export of ships did not begin, in fact, until after the Napoleonic Wars.

It is easy to demonstrate that most shipbuilding output before the 1820s was required to replace tonnage on registry in the Maritimes. From the analysis of existing registries we know that the average life of vessels built before 1820 was ten years. Graph 2.2 shows the tonnage that would have been on registry in the Maritime colonies, excluding Newfoundland, if no "leakage" had occurred; that is, all newly built tonnage is assumed to have remained for ten years on local registry. The graph also shows the official estimates of tonnage actually retained on local registry.

This is an exercise in speculation, and both time series must be read as estimates, partly because there is no way to take into account vessels imported from outside the region. The import of vessels certainly occurred, although on a small scale, and the registration of prizes captured in war helps to explain why fleets were larger at the end of the Napoleonic Wars than local shipbuilding output would have allowed, even if all vessels had remained in the region.

The graph does not allow a precise measure of the volume of tonnage transferred from the region, but it does show when the transfer of vessels became substantial. It was not until the 1820s that local shipbuilding output far exceeded local consumption. By the 1820s the shipbuilding industry had a life of its own. For the next four decades it would remain a much larger industry than local markets and local demand would by themselves have sustained. Just as shipowning in the Maritimes was the creation of exogenous forces – protection, war-induced demand, and the recurring exclusion of American tonnage from colonial trades – so too was shipbuilding stimulated and sustained by exogenous demand, from the heavily protected British market.

Between 1815 and 1860 more than 2.2 million tons of shipping was built in the three Maritime provinces. In the same years more than 800,000 tons was built in Upper and Lower Canada. By comparison total sailing ship tonnage built and first registered in the United Kingdom in these forty-five years amounted to 5.2 million tons.[20] British North America had become one of the world's major ship-building centres. Much of the output was absorbed by the British market: about half of all tonnage built in the Maritimes in these years ended up on registry in the United Kingdom. Table 2.2 shows the proportion of newly registered tonnage in the major ports in the

Graph 2.2

Estimated Actual and Potential Fleet Size, Maritime Provinces, 1796–1829

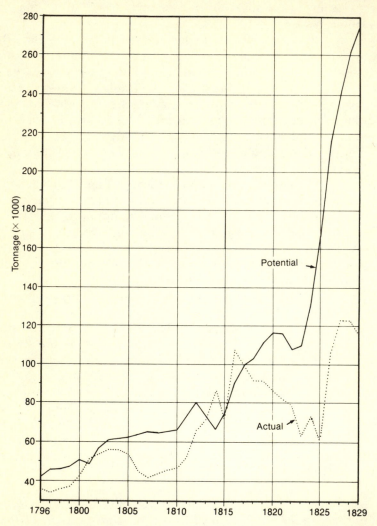

Sources: Richard Rice, "Measuring British Dominance of Shipbuilding in the 'Maritimes,' 1787–1890," in Keith Matthews and Gerald Panting, eds., *Ships and Shipbuilding in the North Atlantic Region* (St. Johns: Maritime History Group 1978), Appendix 1; Public Record Office Customs 17 and Board of Trade Series 162 Plantation Registries. The vessels newly built in each year are arbitrarily assigned a life of ten years.

Table 2.2
Tonnage Transferred to United Kingdom Registry, 1820–69

Port	1820s	1830s	1840s	1850s	1860s
Saint John					
Tonnage	85,540	108,770	191,360	309,260	151,596
% of total	68	64	76	76	43
Halifax					
Tonnage	17,964	39,753	41,532	18,171	16,963
% of total	25	35	37	27	15
Yarmouth					
Tonnage			7,116	15,571	14,924
% of total			15	28	14
Windsor					
Tonnage				13,941	16,505
% of total				36	20
Pictou					
Tonnage			47,063	54,272	14,444
% of total			69	57	27
Miramichi					
Tonnage		33,799	49,028	88,068	85,885
% of total		90	92	91	81
Charlottetown					
Tonnage	40,829	53,896	107,831	145,337	168,676
% of total	69	58	67	70	70

Source: Board of Trade series 107/108 vessel registries.
Note: Percentages are gross tonnage transferred as a portion of newly registered tonnage. "Decade" indicates time of first registry, not of transfer.

Maritimes that was transferred to registry in the United Kingdom. In other smaller ports of registry not included here, especially those in Nova Scotia, the export of ships to Britain was much less important (in Sydney, for instance, only 11 per cent of tonnage). In Newfoundland, local shipbuilding was linked closely to the local market, and Newfoundland was a net importer of shipping tonnage for most of the nineteenth century. But in ports of registry located in major shipbuilding areas – Saint John, Miramichi, Charlottetown – shipbuilding was a manufacturing industry very closely tied to the "home" market across the Atlantic.

Shipbuilding was a British industry with a large part of its productive capacity located in British North America. Britain was dependent on shipbuilding in British North America for several reasons. First, it was the world's largest national market for shipping services in the nineteenth century. In 1820 Britain and its colonies possessed no less than 38 per cent of world shipping under sail.[21] Over the next quarter-century demand for tonnage to and from ports in the United Kingdom grew at an annual rate of close to 4 per cent;[22] at the same time output from shipyards increased at only 1.8 per cent a year.[23] Between 1820 and 1850, tonnage on registry in the United Kingdom grew at a mere 1.1 per cent a year.[24] This meant that the nation's share of all world tonnage was declining and that a declining share of the demand for carrying capacity in colonial and foreign trades to and from Britain was met by builders and owners in the United Kingdom. Part of the new demand was met by an increase in foreign tonnage employed in the foreign carrying trade to and from the United Kingdom.[25] Far more important, however, tonnage built and/or registered in the colonies was expanding and answered much of the total British demand for carrying capacity in the last decades of the Navigation Acts and for a few decades after their repeal.

By mid-century, Britain's colonies accounted for almost half of all new tonnage being built in the empire (see Graph 2.3). The colonies also became shipowning centres: in 1815 they accounted for less than 8 per cent of all tonnage in the empire; by 1846 they had over 16 per cent. The colonies in British North America were by far the most important in terms of tonnage built and registered: by 1846 they accounted for 64 per cent of all tonnage on colonial registries.

Colonial-built vessels entered the British carrying trades, whether or not they were on registry in the United Kingdom. But many colonial vessels were sold to owners in Britain and so found their way onto the United Kingdom's registries, until by 1846 almost 20 per cent of all tonnage on registry in Britain had been built in the colonies. The major suppliers of tonnage for owners in the United Kingdom were builders in Lower Canada and the Maritimes, as Table 2.3 suggests. Vessels of all sizes and rigs were transferred to registry in England, Scotland, and Ireland. Canadians and New Brunswickers tended to build and sell large sailing vessels. Builders in Prince Edward Island and Newfoundland specialized in much smaller craft. The major purchasers were in Liverpool, Scotland, and Ireland; London and east coast shipowners were much less interested in colonial vessels (see Map. 2.1). Although London had by far the largest amount of shipping on its registries, Liverpool took more than three times as much colonial tonnage. Scottish and Irish ports were particularly dependent on vessels built in British North America.

There were many factors that contributed to the demand for colonial-built vessels. The relatively low cost of colonial tonnage was

Graph 2.3

Tonnage Built in the United Kingdom and the Colonies, 1814–51

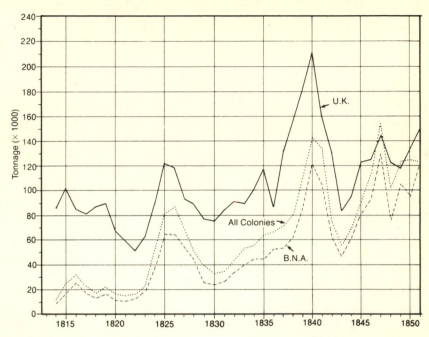

Sources: Mitchell and Deane, *Abstract of British Historical Statistics*, Transport 2; R.S. Craig, "British Shipping and British North American Shipbuilding in the Early Nineteenth Century, with Special Reference to Prince Edward Island," in H.E.S. Fisher, ed., *The Southwest and the Sea* (Exeter, 1968), Table 3; Rice, "The Rise of Shipbuilding," Appendix A. "B.N.A." includes Newfoundland. The "U.K." figures are for all ships built and first registered in the United Kingdom.

certainly a major factor. Another was the preference shown for particular types of craft for use in specific trades. Liverpool owners required tonnage for the timber and cotton trades, and the relatively cheap colonial vessels were well suited to these trades, or so their owners believed. Where shipowners and merchants were most committed to trade with India and the East Indies, or where English or Scottish builders could supply a large volume of relatively cheap tonnage, as in Sunderland, the interest in colonial vessels was weakest.[26]

Whatever the reasons for British investment in colonial vessels, the British "home" market clearly had a significant impact on the pattern of shipbuilding in the Maritimes. Since over 50 per cent of tonnage built in the Maritimes ended up on registry in the United Kingdom, it is no surprise to find a close correlation between annual shipbuilding

Table 2.3
British North America–Built Ships on Registry in the United Kingdom, 1846

Colony	No.	Tons	% of British North American Tonnage on Registry in United Kingdom
Canada	326	154,930	28.3
New Brunswick	608	228,368	41.7
Nova Scotia	417	103,319	18.8
Prince Edward Island	311	56,079	10.2
Newfoundland	63	5,631	1.0
Total	1,725	548,327	100

Source: "Return of the Gross Number and Tonnage of Colonial-Built Vessels Registered at Each of the Ports of the United Kingdom," Parliamentary Papers, 1847, LX, 311.

output in the Maritimes and annual output in Britain. There is a strong positive correlation ($r = + 0.84$) between tonnage built in British North America and tonnage built and first registered in the United Kingdom between 1814 and 1850.[27] The correlation is particularly strong between tonnage built in New Brunswick and United Kingdom – built tonnage, and the relationship strengthens in the 1830s and 1840s. The correlation with Prince Edward Island is not so strong: builders there also specialized in producing small tonnage for owners in Newfoundland and the Maritimes, and these markets often followed a different pattern than the British.

Several years ago Robin Craig suggested that the response by builders in the Maritimes to British demand was delayed by about a year, because of the seasonal nature of shipbuilding in the Maritimes and the slow transmission of market news westward.[28] If we look at the most sensitive measure of correlation between time series – the correlation between annual changes in the data – there does appear to be a lagged response, but only up to about 1830. After 1830 the correlation is stronger if shipyard output for the Maritimes is not lagged.[29]

There could be many reasons for the closer correlation after 1830, including more prompt official reporting of tonnage built in the Maritimes. The point is, however, that shipbuilding in the Maritimes was closely synchronized with trends in the British market, and the coincidence is not accidental. Either shipyards in the Maritimes were producing tonnage on contract for British owners, or they were

Map 2.1
British North America–Built Tonnage on Registry in United Kingdom Ports,
1846

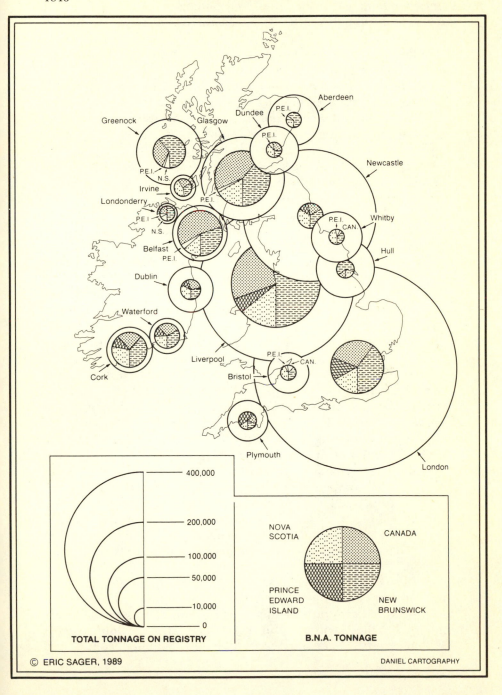

Greenock

Glasgow

Dundee

P.E.I.

Aberdeen

P.E.I.

Newcastle

P.E.I.

N.S.

Irvine

Londonderry

P.E.I

P.E.I.

N.S.

Belfast

P.E.I.

P.E.I.

CAN

Whitby

Hull

Dublin

Waterford

Cork

Liverpool

Bristol

P.E.I.

CAN.

Plymouth

London

TOTAL TONNAGE ON REGISTRY

400,000

200,000

100,000

50,000

10,000

0

NOVA
SCOTIA

CANADA

PRINCE
EDWARD
ISLAND

NEW
BRUNSWICK

B.N.A. TONNAGE

© ERIC SAGER, 1989

DANIEL CARTOGRAPHY

hoping for a quick speculative sale when prices in the United Kingdom were high. Even when tonnage remained on registry in the Maritimes, builders were often responding to the same market demand for shipping services that influenced builders and owners in the United Kingdom.

So long as the Navigation Acts remained in force, colonial shipbuilders enjoyed preferential access to the British market for ships. This protection was not the modest intrusion of preferential tariffs: it simply excluded foreign-built tonnage from the privilege of British registry, except for tonnage captured in war. In these circumstances a British manufacturing industry was transplanted across the Atlantic.

But there was more to the story of protection than this. Among the advantages to shipbuilding in the Maritimes was the opportunity to carry a cargo on the passage to the United Kingdom prior to the sale of the vessel. This was a very considerable advantage, and it is one reason why so many ships built of colonial timber were assembled in the Maritimes rather than in the United Kingdom. The freight cost of pine from the Maritimes to the United Kingdom in the 1820's fluctuated between 35 and 45 shillings per load; this represented between 40 and 50 per cent of the c.i.f. price of the timber in Britain (the c.i.f. price is the purchase price of the goods including the cost of insurance and freight). The timber exporter was a major purchaser of shipping services, and freight was a large proportion of his operating costs. This cost represented a substantial potential revenue to the shipbuilder. If, for instance, a 300-ton vessel were sold in the Liverpool market for 3,000 pounds sterling, the same vessel might earn a gross revenue of 600 pounds from the timber freight on the passage to Liverpool.

The homeward freight was a type of bounty to the shipbuilder. In 1844 G.F. Young, chair of the General Shipowners' Society in Britain, argued that the colonial shipbuilder enjoyed two principal advantages over his competitors in the United Kingdom: savings in construction from building the ship at the place where the construction material was produced and the guaranteed freight on the homeward passage. Young argued that "these combined advantages operate as a direct bounty on colonial shipbuilding, amounting to from £3 to £4 per ton."[30]

This was certainly an exaggeration, because Young had not taken into account either the voyage costs of the homeward passage or the costs of other inputs in ship construction, many of which were imported to the Maritimes. But there was an effective bounty to the shipbuilder in the homeward cargo of about 15 shillings to one pound sterling per ton, or 10 per cent of the selling price of a vessel in Liverpool. Another benefit to the colonial builder lay in the British tariff structure: whereas most colonial products were subject to a tariff on entry to the United Kingdom (albeit in some cases a modest preferential duty), ships were a manufactured product subject to no duty at all. Attempts by shipbuilding interests in the United Kingdom to persuade government to levy a duty on colonial ships failed.

The timber trade was not the only stimulus to shipbuilding in the Maritimes, and its importance must not be exaggerated. As we have seen, both shipbuilding and shipowning were expanding before the rapid growth of the timber trade during the Napoleonic Wars. When combined with the apparatus of protection for both timber and ships, however, the timber trade offered a specific inducement to locate both shipbuilding and shipowning on the western side of the Atlantic. Since timber was a commodity of high freight costs relative to its value, the timber exporter had good reason to become a shipowner. Carrying his own timber in his own vessels meant that the merchant could more easily absorb freight costs, or even write them off altogether when a vessel had paid for itself. The timber merchant had a vested interest in lowering his freight costs by guaranteeing his supply of shipping.

This was all the more important in a staple trade in which price fluctuations could be very steep. A stable supply of shipping was not easily guaranteed in the era of sailing ships, even when freight rates were experiencing a gradual long-term decline. During the nineteenth century the supply of shipping was highly inelastic in response to short-term changes in demand.[31] It was difficult to accelerate sailing ship output: the gains to be had from accelerating sailing speeds or turn-around in port were limited, and the delay between the ordering and receipt of newly built tonnage was considerable. This meant that increases in demand for shipping were reflected in rapid and even disproportionate increases in freight rates.

The timber exporter could avoid the risk of high freight charges by maintaining local output in shipbuilding: a regular supply of tonnage from local shipyards would stabilize freight costs. A related solution was to become a shipowner onself and to maintain sufficient tonnage in one's possession to compensate for any short-term supply problems – or merely while awaiting a better selling price for the vessel in the British market.[32]

Keeping a vessel for more than a single passage entailed risks, of course. Freight earnings on the westward passage were uncertain, for instance, and many vessels cleared the United Kingdom for British North America in ballast (in 1845 and 1846, for instance, over 60 per cent of tonnage).[33] Keeping vessels in one's own hands meant running the risk of poor earnings from the vessel when freight rates fell. In addition, the loss rate in the timber trade was high. But the presence of two options helped to minimize risk and encourage investment in ships: either one could retain tonnage to transport one's own goods or one could sell tonnage in Britain.

A further stimulus to shipbuilding came from the sheer volume of carrying capacity demanded by the timber trade. When the timber trade began its rapid growth after 1807, this growth coincided with massive British hiring of shipping for war-related transport and a steep increase in freight rates.[34] The timber trade meant a sudden increase in tonnage required for the eastward passage, in particular from New Brunswick to Britain (see Graph 2.4).

By the end of the Napoleonic Wars, the tonnage moving between New Brunswick and the United Kingdom was greater even than the tonnage from Canada to Britain. The timber trade was the single reason for this sudden increase in shipping activity. Since timber was the major bulk commodity being shipped from New Brunswick, the correlation between loads of timber exported and tonnage clearing for the United Kingdom is virtually perfect.[35] The correlation between loads of timber imported into Britain from British North America and shipping tonnage entering Britain from the same source is also remarkably close. Even if we correlate annual changes in the two time series over a long period – from 1800 to 1849 – the resulting coefficient is $+0.94$.

If we assume that this is a relationship between an independent variable (timber exports) and a dependent variable (shipping tonnage employed), then no less than 88 per cent of changes in tonnage employed on the eastward route were the result of changes in the volume of timber exports. The result if partly a statistical illusion, because other commodities, such as grain, often followed a similar pattern to timber and exercised an independent influence on the demand for shipping. But timber was more important than any other export in determining the massive increase in demand for tonnage in British North American ports after 1807.

Not until the world wars of the twentieth century would Canadian Atlantic ports witness another such expansion in shipping activity. Tonnage clearing for the United Kingdom increased at an annual rate of over 16 per cent between 1805 and 1819 and continued to grow through the first half of the century: the long-term growth rate from 1800 to 1849 is 7.4 per cent a year.[36]

There as a critical difference, however, between the expansion of shipping activity in the early nineteenth century and anything that

Graph 2.4

Tonnage Entering Great Britain from British North America, 1800–19

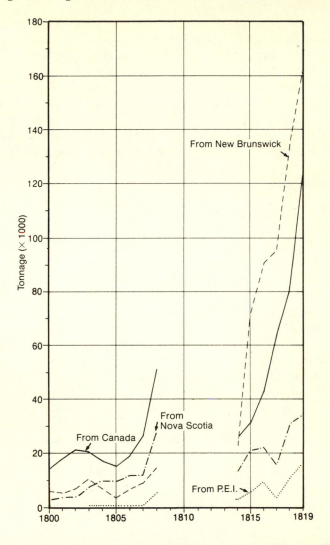

Sources: Gerald S. Graham, *Sea Power and British North America 1783-1820* (Cambridge, Mass., 1941), Appendix C (to 1815); Lords Select Committee on Foreign Trade Relative to Timber, *Parliamentary Papers*, 1820, III, 469.

happened in the twentieth century. The great shipping boom of the 1800s and 1810s occurred within the context of British mercantilism: both timber and shipping enjoyed forms of protection that would never be repeated. Foreign ships were excluded altogether from the British North America – United Kingdom passage – even though the demand for tonnage could not be met from suppliers of shipping in the United Kingdom. The result was an unprecedented stimulus to shipbuilding in British North America, particularly in New Brunswick and Quebec. While timber exports increased in volume by more than eight times between 1806 and 1811, shipyard output in New Brunswick increased by thirteen times in the same five years, and shipbuilding output increased by more than six times in Quebec. The relationship between newly built tonnage and timber exports continued after the Napoleonic War, as Graph 2.5 suggests.[37]

How important was imperial protection to the rise of timber and shipbuilding? It is impossible to measure the relationships exactly, but imperial protection was certainly critical to the high growth rates in shipyard output. We must remember that there were other potential sources of shipping tonnage for the routes between the colonies and the United Kingdom, apart from colonial shipyards. In the absence of the Navigation Acts, much of the demand would have been met by non-colonial shipowners. In trades not covered by the Navigation Acts, for instance, foreign tonnage increased its share of carrying capacity entering the United Kingdom.[38] British and other non-American tonnage increased its share of tonnage entering US ports in the decades after 1815, even though the US mercantile marine was growing rapidly. It would have taken only a small diversion of British and American tonnage from US trades to replace all British North America – built tonnage used in the British North America – United Kingdom trades in the 1830s.[39]

There is no simple way to measure the effectiveness of the Navigation Acts, but we know what happened when these acts were repealed: large amounts of foreign tonnage immediately entered the trades between British North America and Britain (Graph 2.6). As early as 1853, almost 23 per cent of the tonnage entering Britain from British North America was foreign.[40] Repeal also affected British demand for colonial vessels, as owners in the United Kingdom purchased and put on British registry a substantial amount of foreign-built tonnage. By 1854 such foreign purchases totalled 97,641 tons – nearly equivalent to the total shipbuilding output of Nova Scotia and New Brunswick in that year.[41]

Timber exporters depended on colonial-built vessels, and the two

Graph 2.5
United Kingdom Timber Imports from British North America and New
Tonnage Built in Quebec and the Maritimes, 1806–49

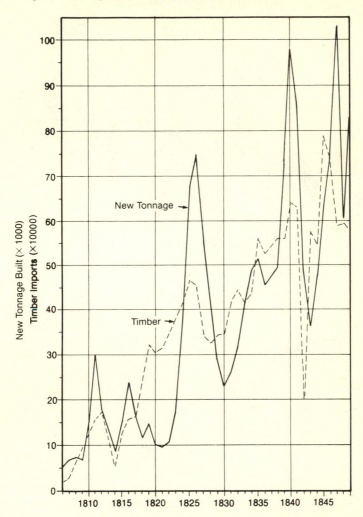

Sources: Estimates of the total number of loads of timber imported into the United
Kingdom from British colonies in America by the inspector general of imports and
exports, *Parliamentary papers*, 1828, XIX, 568; Peter McClelland, "The New Brunswick
Economy in the Nineteenth Century" (PHD thesis, Harvard University 1966), for
timber loads after 1827; Rice, "Measuring British Dominance," Appendix I.

Graph 2.6
British and Foreign Tonnage Entering United Kingdom Ports from
British North America, 1848–65

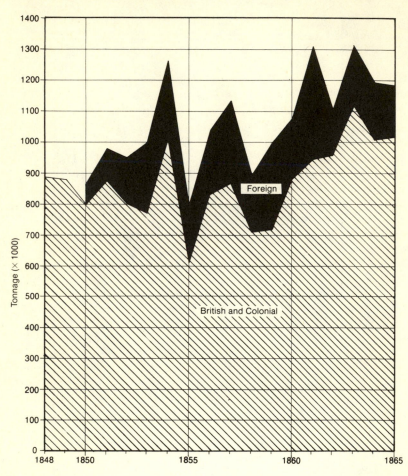

Source: Shipping returns in British *Parliamentary Papers*.

industries became mutually self-supporting. Colonial politicians
understood the connection between timber duties and local shipowning, and they cited the shipowning interest when arguing that preferential duties be maintained:

Should the Ministry still persevere in their endeavours to alter the relative
rates of duty payable on colonial and foreign timber and deals, the most
strenuous exertions must be directed to defeat a measure so ruinous in its

consequences as it cannot fail to prove, if carried into effect, both to the shipowners and the North American colonies. When we compare the immense amount of tonnage at present [1832] employed in the North American colonial timber trade, with that which would be required should the prohibitory measures of the Ministry be adopted, we are persuaded that at least four-fifths would be thrown out of employment.[42]

This was something of an exaggeration. Nevertheless, by the mid-1830s colonial-built vessels accounted for between 46 and 53 per cent of the tonnage clearing Canada and New Brunswick for Britain, according to Richard Rice.[43] The supply of locally built tonnage succeeded in lowering the freight costs of timber in the long run (see Graph 2.7).

This decline in freight rates was one reason why North American timber remained competitive with Baltic timber in the British market. The freight cost of timber from the Baltic was much less than the freight cost from Quebec or New Brunswick. In the early 1820s, for instance, when the timber freight rate from New Brunswick varied from 40 to 50 shillings per load, the freight cost from Memel to Britain varied from 21 to 27 shillings per load. Any significant change in this differential could affect the difference in selling price between Baltic and North American timber in the British market.

The preferential duty never eliminated Baltic competition in the British market. In the early 1840s, for instance, the Baltic accounted for almost 20 per cent of timber, about 50 per cent of deals and deal ends, and 45 per cent of sawn lumber imported into Britain.[44] Between 1817 and 1820 the freight differential between New Brunswick and Memel timber was about 25 shillings per load, and this represented between a quarter and a third of the selling price.[45] Any narrowing of this differential would contribute to the lower selling price of colonial timber, and the differential in fact fell to between 13 and 18 shillings per load in the 1820s and 1830s.

A useful measure of the importance of freight costs in the delivered price of a commodity is the freight factor, calculated as follows:

freight factor = freight / c.i.f. value × 100

The freight factors in Graph 2.8 suggest the critical importance of freight costs in colonial timber and the relatively steep decline in freight costs for colonial timber as a proportion of the final selling price.

Important as the freight differentials may have been, they were less significant than preferential duties in affording colonial timber a

Graph 2.7
Timber Freight Rates from New Brunswick and Quebec to Britain
(Shillings per Load), 1810–49

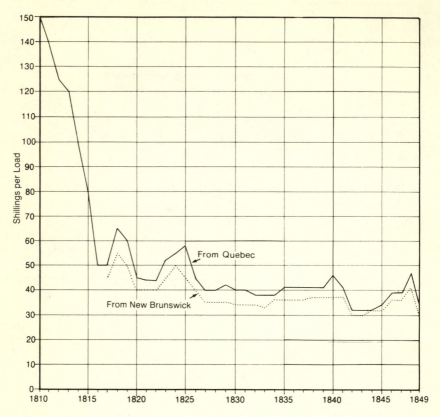

Sources: These are Douglass North's timber freight indices, compiled mainly from the
following reports in British *Parliamentary Papers*: 1820, III (Lords Select Committee on
the Timber Trade); 1833, VI (Select Committee on Manufactures, Commerce and
Shipping); 1835, XIX (Select Committee on Timber Duties); 1844, VIII (Select Committee on British Shipping); and 1847, X (Select Committee on Navigation Laws). The
indices appear also in McClelland, "The New Brunswick Economy," Table XXVI,
93–5; and Douglass C. North, "Ocean Freight Rates and Economic Development
1750–1913." *Journal of Economic History*, 18, no. 4 (December 1958), 553.

comparative advantage over Baltic timber. For most of the period
between 1820 and 1842 the tariff structure afforded New Brunswick
timber a differential of 45 shillings per load compared to Prussian
timber. With the gradual reduction of this differential and its elimination in 1860, Baltic timber, deals, and sawn lumber recovered their
predominant share of the British market.[46]

Graph 2.8
Freight Factors for Quebec Yellow Pine and Baltic Fir Timber, 1812–46

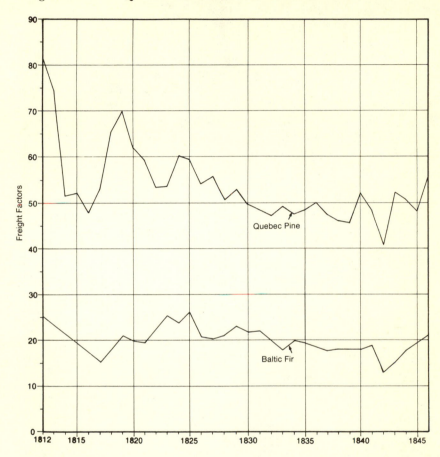

Sources: Quebec yellow pine prices from McClelland, "The New Brunswick Economy," Table xxx, 102; Quebec freight rates from Graph 2.6 (above); Baltic fir freight factor from Douglass C. North, "The Role of Transportation in the Economic Development of North America," in *Les Grandes Voies Maritimes dans le monde XV–XIX siècles* (Paris, 1965), Table 3, 240-1.

In the absence of preferential duties, there might still have been a colonial timber trade, and it is impossible to know how much the tariff structure contributed to the growth of this staple trade. But there is no doubt that shipbuilding and shipowning grew within the framework of a system of colonial protection. Without this protection, the growth of merchant shipping in the Maritimes would have been determined largely by the growth of coastal and West Indies trades.

Colonial shipbuilding enjoyed three distinct forms of protection. It benefited from the protection of preferential duties on colonial commodities shipped to Britain and to other colonies. It benefited from the Navigation Acts, which excluded foreign shipping from the most important colonial trade routes. And colonial shipbuilders enjoyed unusually privileged access to the British market: they sold a manufactured product that was subject to no duty at all. Shipbuilding and shipowning in the Maritimes arose from this endowment of natural resources and British protection.

The shipbuilding industry of the early decades of the nineteenth century had many of the characteristics of an enclave industry. It depended in large part on capital and markets in the mother country and on materials and labour imported from there. It grew within the closed and protected commercial system of a transoceanic empire. Like the timber trade described by Graeme Wynn, shipbuilding was "a gigantic bandalore," its movements tied to the staple trade and the British market to which it was linked.[47] After the mercantilist system was dismantled, it remained to be seen whether the colonies or the new Canadian Dominion would erect a comparable navigation system, based on their own commercial and strategic needs. In the half-century after Confederation, an inherited enclave industry would either extend its domestic roots – or collapse.

CHAPTER THREE

Colonial Argosy

Shipping is a service industry, and ships are waterborne containers that perform the service of transportation. Demand for this service may come from a variety of sources, and ships may carry many things, including people, goods, and information. Although ships built in the northern half of North America very often carried passengers, especially in the westward passage across the North Atlantic, their primary function was to carry goods. In carrying goods, ships become part of the costs of production in the goods-producing sectors of the economy.

In both neo-classical and Marxist economic analysis, transportation has a dual role: it is an independent branch of production and at the same time part of the production process in other industries. For the user, transport is the link between the sources of raw material, the processing location, and markets. Producers use transportation to assemble raw materials and to distribute products to markets: thus transportation is part of the creation of utility or use value and part of the production process.[1]

In the economic history of Atlantic Canada, shipping must first be understood from the perspective of its users. Only if we conceive of ships in this way, as inputs in processes of production and distribution, is it possible to understand why investment in ships should increase in the decades after 1815, at the same time as freight rates were falling. The steep and continuing decline in freight rates would appear to suggest a growing supply of carrying capacity relative to demand, and it would indicate falling rates of return, unless a very significant growth in vessel productivity was occurring.

In such circumstances neo-classical theory would predict a decline in investment and a movement of capital into industries having higher rates of return. As we have seen, however, both shipbuilding and shipowning expanded even as freight rates fell, because the decline in freight rates reflected much more than an increasing supply of tonnage. It reflected also a decline in the costs of production and distribution in economies depending on international trade.[2] Declining freight rates may indicate real productivity gains in industries that transportation serves, and in these gains lie the incentive behind continuing investment in ships.

In British North America the owners and users of ships included the producers of staples – the fishermen in their schooners, the lumbermen in their wood-boats, and the coastal mariners who took agricultural produce to markets or to entrepôts. The users of ships also included merchant capitalists who resided in Britain or in the colonies. The merchants used ships to import goods, to transport goods from regional entrepôts to outports, and to export staple products. These primary producers and merchant capitalists all had a vested interest in low freight costs. Their use of ships in production and distribution came from a prior interest in trade goods and from the primary function of the merchant capitalist – to "buy cheap and sell dear." Lowering freight costs was one means toward profit in trade, and for this reason merchants sought unceasingly to guarantee their supply of shipping.

Of course a region's demand for shipping can be met in more than one way. What took place in Atlantic Canada from the late eighteenth to the mid-nineteenth century was somewhat unusual in the context of British economic history. In Atlantic Canada the merchant capitalist was very often the supplier of his own ships: he was both trader and shipowner. This was true even of the timber exporter who sold both ships and their cargoes in Britain: however brief his ownership of the vessel, he was still a shipowner. In the Maritimes the consumer of ships, the shipowner, was also sometimes a producer of ships – a shipbuilder. Shipbuilding was often part of an integrated mercantile operation that comprised staple trading, importing, wholesaling, retailing, and the manufacture of ships.

In this integration of activities the colonial merchant firm resisted a more common tendency toward specialization in the British Industrial Revolution. In the late eighteenth and early nineteenth centuries owners of ships and owners of freight became increasingly separated.[3] In Atlantic Canada, specialist shipowners – those whose single or principal economic activity was owning ships in which to carry other people's goods – were relatively rare, even by the third-quarter of the nineteenth century.

Why were the functions of shipowning and trade so often united in the same merchant firm? Historians of the British timber trade have noted the same overlap among Liverpool timber importers: between 1820 and 1850 the number of major timber merchants who were also substantial shipowners increased.[4] The explanation for this trend, itself contrary to the dominant British movement toward specialization, relates to the nature of the cargo. David Williams follows Ralph Davis, who argued in the context of eighteenth-century shipowning that bulky commodities having low unit value and high freight costs tended to encourage shipowning by the owner of the commodity.[5] This was the most efficient way for the importer to minimize the high costs of transportation.

As Davis noted, however, particular trades require particular explanations. For Atlantic Canada it is tempting to repeat a simple staple explanation. Timber and fish, natural products having low unit value, did not promise high freight returns to their carriers and so did not attract enough tonnage away from more lucrative British trades. Furthermore, the plentiful supply of timber encouraged the building of ships locally. This is only part of what happened, however.

The rest of the story concerns the nature of mercantile activity on a resource frontier. On such a frontier there is a relative abundance of resources but a relative scarcity of labour and capital. This often leads to proliferation of small units of production and independent pre-capitalist commodity producers. By a variety of methods, however, merchants gradually assumed greater control over economic output, even where they did not directly control the process of production. Merchants used the timber licensing system to concentrate control of timber output; they used the truck system to accumulate the economic surplus in the fisheries; government encouraged the concentration of landholdings through regulation of prices and land granting.[6]

No less important to merchants' profits, however, was their control of output in the system of distribution and exchange and their control of imported goods and supplies. There was little to prevent smallholders from building their own small vessels, given ready access to timber and the presence of the necessary skills among many immigrants. Timber was often transported in very small vessels, after all. Planters in Newfoundland and extended fishing families in Nova Scotia could carry fish to West Indies markets in their own vessels. For merchants the acquisition of shipping meant greater control, not only over the output of staple industries but also over all imports into the colonies. To some extent this could be guaranteed through the use of tonnage chartered from shipowners elsewhere, and colonial merchants certainly had better access to shipping markets than did the small timber trader, the fisherman, or the farmer.

But acquiring one's own tonnage, in addition to whatever one might charter, had several potential advantages. Not only did vessels reduce one's dependence on a volatile freight market; they also allowed an accumulation of control by capital at the point of exchange and distribution. Ships were producer goods, inputs in both commodity production and in distribution. They were a form of capital that many merchants owned, in order to secure control of output and distribution on the colonial frontier.

It follows that the ships built and owned in Atlantic Canada were adapted to these purposes. As inputs in staple export trades, they were designed to carry particular commodities. Of course there were limits to vessel design and technology: there was no unique British North American ship, because the technology was inherited from elsewhere in America or from Britain. There were, however, indigenous adaptations of vessel technology that followed from the primary function of ships, which was to provide British and colonial merchants with inputs in particular trades as cheaply as possible.

Map 3.1 indicates certain general characteristics of the fleets built and owned (however briefly, in many instances) in Atlantic Canada.[7] Note first the dominance of sailing vessels throughout the region. Only 4.8 per cent of all tonnage was propelled by steam-engines, and most steamers were auxiliary steamers, carrying a full suit of sails. The overwhelming majority of vessels up to 1914 were built with wooden frames and planking in their hulls, topsides, and decks. A great deal of iron was used in many wooden-hulled vessels, and the industrial revolution did not pass by these fleets, but Atlantic Canadian shipowners were participating in the last stages of a pre-industrial technology. A major reason for the continuing preference for the technology of wood and sail was its relative cheapness: it meant a relatively small initial capital outlay for the purchaser.

Although there were characteristics common to all fleets, there was a degree of specialization in the major ports of registry, reflecting the differing uses of shipping from one port to another. For most of the nineteenth century the fleet registered in Saint John was larger than any other. Of the 5.3 million tons newly registered in the nine major ports in Map 3.1, 34 per cent was registered in Saint John. Saint John shipowners specialized in larger ocean-going vessels,[8] particularly in three-masted vessels rigged as ships. This was the classic square-rigged vessel, with sails suspended from yards carried at right angles to the line of the hull. The square sail took the wind from one side only but allowed for maximum forward propulsion when the wind

Map 3.1
Tonnage Newly Registered in Major Ports by Rig, to 1914

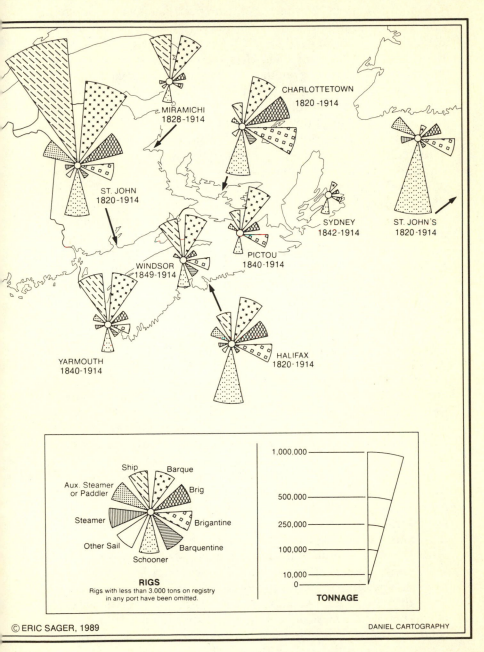

DANIEL CARTOGRAPHY

was aft, or on the quarter, as happened most often on long ocean voyages.

Nothing shows more dramatically the specialization in ocean-going trades than the size of the fleet of square-rigged ships registered in Saint John. There were 911 such vessels registered in the port between 1820 and 1914. By themselves these vessels were a larger fleet than any other in the region: their total tonnage was greater than that of all vessels built and registered in Prince Edward Island in the same ninety-five years. Saint John shipowners also placed on their registry the largest number of three-masted barques (766, about as many as appeared in Yarmouth, Halifax, and Windsor added together).

Right from the beginning, specialization in ocean-going vessels was apparent. The more common ocean-going craft of the early nineteenth century was the brig, a two-masted vessel that carried square sails on both her main and fore masts. The Saint John registry saw a very large fleet of brigs, especially in the 1820s, when brigs alone accounted for half of all new tonnage registered. The dominance of the square-rigged craft in Saint John reflected the importance of the timber trade and of the passage to the United Kingdom.

Newfoundland had fleets very unlike Saint John's. Their different structure would seem to defy any attempt at a region-wide analysis of shipping. There were building constraints: the smaller timber along most of Newfoundland's coastline discouraged the building of large ocean-going vessels. But more important were the conditions imposed by local trades in which vessels were used. Newfoundlanders in the nineteenth century acquired large numbers of schooners: on their one set of registry books in St John's they put more schooner tonnage than was acquired by all vessel registrants in Halifax, Yarmouth, and Windsor combined. No less than 60 per cent of all tonnage registered in St John's between 1820 and 1914 lay under the decks of schooners.

The schooner was the product of a long evolution in the design of coastal vessels in Europe and North America. In British North America the rig would be adapted for use in dangerous northern waters and along very lengthy coastlines. The result was a variety of schooners – some adapted for fishing, some for local coasting trades, some for the seal hunt, and others for long-distance voyages to the West Indies and South America. The schooner in British North America was usually a two-masted vessel, carrying fore and aft sails on both masts. The fore and aft sail was suspended on gaffs and booms behind the mast and could be quickly manoeuvred to take the wind from either side of the sail. Most sailhandling could be done by men standing on the deck of the vessel.

This rig was especially useful when working a vessel along sharply indented coastlines, in highly variable winds, and in cold temperatures, where ropes and canvas were often frozen and difficult to handle. The schooner used in long-distance coasting often carried one or more square topsails to give additional forward propulsion when the wind was from aft. This small two-masted schooner with square topsails was particularly common in Newfoundland in the nineteenth century and was quite different from the sleek fishing schooners of the *Bluenose* era in our own century.

The importance of vessels as factors of production is further suggested by the presence of steamers and auxiliary steamers on the Newfoundland registry. The fleet of steam-powered vessels registered in Newfoundland, most of them owned in St John's, was proportionately larger than anywhere else in the Atlantic colonies. Steam-powered tonnage was 12.7 per cent of all tonnage registered between 1820 and 1914 (by comparison only 5 per cent of new tonnage in Saint John was accounted for by steamers or auxiliary steamers). There was a single major reason for the relatively numerous steamers in St John's: most were purchased for use in the seal hunt, where they were more productive than sail-powered vessels. The steamers displaced both sailing vessels and labour in the last three decades of the nineteenth century. They were part of a social transformation of sealing that saw a new era of conflict between capital and labour in the industry.[9] The seal hunt encouraged other changes in wooden vessels, apart from the introduction of steam. The need for strength in the hull, in order to survive in the ice floes at the "front," meant that many wooden vessels carried unusually thick planking and many sealing vessels were sheathed in iron.

Specialization never went so far in the Maritimes as it did in Newfoundland, despite the relative size of the ocean-going square-riggers in Saint John. In each of the major ports of the Maritime provinces there was a range of vessel types, from the small, single-masted sloop to the large ocean-going square-rigger. Just as there was no division of labour between shipowner and shipper, so there was limited division of labour among ports. Even Saint John had a very large fleet of small schooners, for use in coasting, in short runs to the United States, or in West Indies trades. Proportionately, however, the schooner was much more important in Halifax, the major port of registry for Nova Scotia in the first half of the nineteenth century.

The Halifax registry reflected the pattern of investment by shipowners in much of eastern Nova Scotia. Here owners specialized in vessels for use in fishing, in the local coastal trades, and in the West Indies trades. Over 87 per cent of vessels registered in Halifax carried

one or more fore and aft sails, and whatever their rig, vessels tended
to be smaller than elsewhere. This reflected the smaller timber on
the eastern shores of Nova Scotia and the fact that a large hull was
not a prime consideration either in fishing or in coastal passages
passages between the entrepôt and small outports. The smaller hull
also minimized the initial capital investment and left much of the
labour of coastal commodity distribution to small owners – master
mariners and outporters themselves.

In ports from which a large proportion of tonnage was transferred
to ownership and registry in Britain (see Table 2.2), it is not surprising
to find a relatively large proportion of ocean-going vessels. This is
particularly evident in Saint John and Miramichi; in the latter port
82 per cent of new tonnage was accounted for by barques or ships.
Builders in Prince Edward Island certainly produced a large number
of ocean-going vessels, but they tended to specialize in medium-sized
craft, and there was a remarkably even distribution of tonnage among
schooners, brigantines, brigs, and barques. The island colony was a
great shipyard in the Gulf, producing tonnage for local owners and
for owners in Britain and in Newfoundland.

Much more remarkable than regional variation in vessel types was
the change in these fleets over time. The pre-industrial ship was
not a simple machine but an evolving technology that reflected the
changing demands of particular trades and the demands that owners
made of builders. All export trades became more capital-intensive
over the nineteenth century, and technological changes in shipping
were part of this trend. In lumbering, ton-timber gave way to sawn
lumber; in fishing, the dorry was joined by the bank schooner, which
eventually acquired an internal combustion engine for auxiliary
power; reapers and mowers and harvesting equipment appeared in
agriculture.

In much of staple production in the Maritimes, particularly in
agriculture, technological change was limited in the nineteenth century. But productivity gains at the transportation end of staple production were possible, even where the vehicle remained a pre-
industrial technology of wood and canvas. In many staple trades,
falling rates of return stimulated the search for productivity gains.
In shipping this search meant replacing labour with technology and
increasing the size of vessels without proportionate increases in
labour.

The rig of a sailing vessel was not fixed but variable, and changes
in sail plan offered some room for improved performance. Among
ocean-going bulk carriers, the most important secular change saw

Table 3.1
Average Tonnage of New Vessels by Rig and Decade

Decade	Schooner	Brigantine	Brig	Barque	Ship	All Vessels
1820s	52	114	208	358	397	105
1840s	53	111	182	438	775	154
1860s	56	180	237	468	1,026	226
1870s	47	215	281	695	1,252	255
1880s	59	246	258	959	1,607	161
1890s	56	234	–	934	2,002	106
1900–14	54	233	–	659	–	98

Source: Board of Trade series 107/108 vessel registries.
Note: These are averages of all newly registered vessels in Charlottetown, Halifax, Miramichi, Pictou, Saint John, St John's, Windsor, and Yarmouth.

the shifts from two to three masts and from the brig to the barque or ship rig. There were many other changes in sail plan and in the operation of sail in the nineteenth century. But more important than a vessels' rig was her hull size, or carrying capacity. A ship was a container, after all, and the volume of cargo carried was usually critical to productivity. Increasing the hull size did not proportionately increase purchase price or operating costs. The large barque or ship usually cost less per ton than the smaller brigantine or schooner. Within certain limits it was possible to expand the size of a hull without increasing the number of masts or sails, and so labour requirements did not increase as hull size increased.

In all major fleets in Atlantic Canada the average size of vessels increased, at least until the 1870s. In the 1820s new vessels on the Saint John registry had an average tonnage of 172 (old measurement); by the 1850s, although the method of tonnage measurement had changed, the average vessel was more than twice as large. In Yarmouth in the 1840s (the port had its own registry only from 1840) new vessels were only 94 tons on average; by the 1870s new vessels were 522 tons on average, and allowing for the change in methods of measurement, the real change in hull capacity was over 500 per cent in only three decades.[10] Table 3.1 shows the average tonnages of all vessels newly registered in eight ports of registry in Atlantic Canada. The decades in which tonnage measurement changes took place are omitted. The change in measurement rules in 1854 meant that the actual change in hull size after 1854 was greater than these figures suggest, particularly among smaller vessels. The change in capacity was especially impressive in the three-masted vessels, the barque, and the ship. The average for all vessels is something of a

Table 3.2
Average Dimensions (Feet) of All New Vessels
Built in the 1810s and the 1850s (Saint John
Registry)

Dimension	1810s	1850s	% change
Length	59.3	117.8	+99
Breadth	18.2	25.9	+42
Depth	8.1	14.1	+74

Source: Board of Trade series 107/108 vessel registries for
Saint John. For the 1810s the number of cases was 234; for
the 1850s, 951.

statistical abstraction, but it does indicate the continuing numerical preponderance of small coastal and fishing vessels.

The change in tonnage is a crude measure of the change in carrying capacity, since tonnage (particularly after 1836) was a measure of cubic feet under the upper deck divided by 100.[11] For most readers the change in the external dimensions of vessels will have more meaning. The gains in carrying capacity in British North American vessels were achieved mainly by lengthening and deepening the hulls of vessels. Table 3.2 shows the change in registered dimensions of vessels built in the 1810s and 1850s and registered in Saint John. The gains in capacity were more easily achieved in three-masted vessels, as Figure 3.1 suggests. The schooner and the brigantine of the 1880s were different from their predecessors, but the change in dimensions was much greater in the barque and the ship.

The greater depth of hull in the barque and the ship by the 1880s is especially striking. Maritime historians have often referred to the effect of old measurement (pre-1836) tonnage measures in encouraging builders to deepen the hulls of vessels (the old formula did not include depth of hull, and so very deep vessels had a carrying capacity that was not reflected in their stated tonnage and very often their port charges were thereby minimized). After 1836, however, Canadian barques and ships lost nothing of their depth. The Saint John barques of the 1880s were in fact deeper in relation to their length than were the barques of the 1820s.

In other ports the changes were even more dramatic, and in Yarmouth, the changes in the last half of the nineteenth century were particularly impressive. The average new barque of the 1880s was 196 feet in length, whereas its predecessor of the 1840s was 104 feet in length. In the same four decades the average Yarmouth ship had almost trebled in capacity.[12]

Figure 3.1
Average Dimensions of Vessels by Rig in Selected Decades (Saint John
Registry)

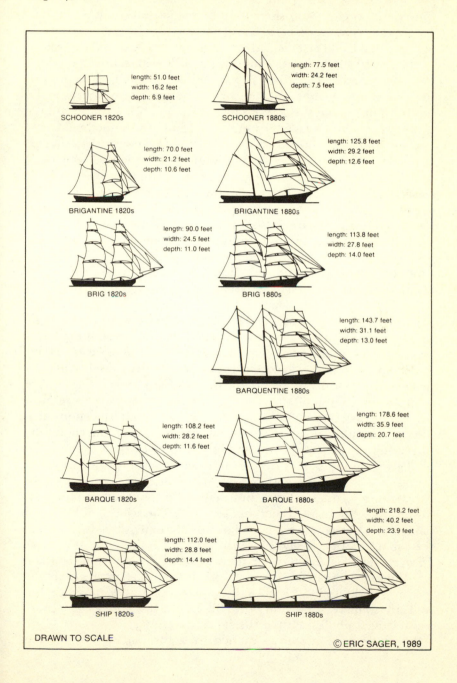

length: 51.0 feet
width: 16.2 feet
depth: 6.9 feet

SCHOONER 1820s

length: 77.5 feet
width: 24.2 feet
depth: 7.5 feet

SCHOONER 1880s

length: 70.0 feet
width: 21.2 feet
depth: 10.6 feet

BRIGANTINE 1820s

length: 125.8 feet
width: 29.2 feet
depth: 12.6 feet

BRIGANTINE 1880s

length: 90.0 feet
width: 24.5 feet
depth: 11.0 feet

BRIG 1820s

length: 113.8 feet
width: 27.8 feet
depth: 14.0 feet

BRIG 1880s

length: 143.7 feet
width: 31.1 feet
depth: 13.0 feet

BARQUENTINE 1880s

length: 108.2 feet
width: 28.2 feet
depth: 11.6 feet

BARQUE 1820s

length: 178.6 feet
width: 35.9 feet
depth: 20.7 feet

BARQUE 1880s

length: 218.2 feet
width: 40.2 feet
depth: 23.9 feet

length: 112.0 feet
width: 28.8 feet
depth: 14.4 feet

SHIP 1820s

SHIP 1880s

DRAWN TO SCALE

© ERIC SAGER, 1989

As the figures suggest, there was a relationship between the rig and the tonnage class of vessels. Most schooners were under 100 tons (77 per cent in the Saint John fleet; 94 per cent in the Halifax and Yarmouth fleets).[13] Most ships were in the 500–999 or 1,000–1,499-ranges. The connection between rig and tonnage is related to the size of vessel that could be efficiently propelled by each sail plan. A vessel of 100 to 110 feet in length could be propelled efficiently enough by the sails carried on two masts. But as hulls lengthened, more propulsive power was sought, and the first response was to increase the height of masts and the size of sails.

But this change entailed increases in labour and sometimes a cost in seaworthiness: higher masts meant extra caps and trestle-trees and extra weight aloft; they also meant separately fidded masts which had to be taken down in heavy weather, to reduce windage aloft, and this required extra labour. The two-masted brig usually supplemented her propulsive power by carrying studding-sails (pronounced "stunsails"). These are square sails set from booms extending beyond the yards, so that they appear as extensions of the square sail. These were usually fine-weather sails, used for extra driving power when the wind was abaft the beam. But studding-sails also required extra labour, and they could easily blanket, or keep the wind out of other sails.[14]

For such reasons vessels of 110 feet and more were increasingly fitted with three masts: the same area of canvas could be spread over three shorter masts and there was usually no increase in labour requirement. It was also found that much larger vessels could be propelled with canvas spread on three sails. If three masts were desirable in a vessel of 300 tons, they could also work a vessel with five times that capacity. Along with changes in construction techniques, the shift to three masts was an important prerequisite for the increasing capacity of the ocean-going sailing vessel.

The increasing size of deep-sea vessels affected performance in several ways. Builders and owners may not have had a scientific explanation for these effects, but they did notice them.[15] Hull size, for instance, affects the speed of the vessel. The science of hydrodynamics tells us that the top speed of a displacement hull is related to the square root of the length of the hull. Thus the great *William D. Lawrence* (262 feet in length), built at Maitland, Nova Scotia, in 1874, was theoretically capable of much greater speed than the small 80-foot brig of the 1820s.[16] Part of the explanation is that an increase in hull size so increases stability that the larger vessel may carry more sail relative to hull size than the smaller vessel.

The total area of canvas carried by a three-masted vessel was increased in two ways, as Figure 3.1 indicates. First, the number of yards and sails on each mast increased over time, until by the 1880s a square-rigged ship might carry seven separate sails on each of her three masts (foremast, main-mast, and mizzen-mast). Above the mainsail (also called the course) were the lower and the upper top-sails; above these might be the lower and upper topgallants (although such "double topgallants" were not common); above these might be the royal, and a few vessels carried skysails above the royal. The second means of increasing sail area was to add staysails, the sails suspended between the masts. The late-nineteenth-century square-rigger might also carry four jib sails, the sails set on stays between the foremast and the jib-boom.

When the size and the number of masts and yards increased, so also may have the labour required to set, reef, and furl sails. For a number of reasons, however, labour inputs did not increase in step with the increases in hull size or sail area. Shipbuilders in the Maritimes knew the concerns of their cost-conscious clients; an increasing proportion of shipyard output went on contract to local shipowners, particularly after mid-century, and very often the shipbuilder was himself a shipowner. And the merchant-shipowner was rarely a mere portfolio investor who knew little about the vehicle he purchased. The shipowner was very often a "practical" man who had been sea in his youth. Samuel Cunard and the Killams of Yarmouth were not the only men whose fathers sent them to sea as master of their vessels, to learn the business of merchant seafaring. The merchants of the Maritime colonies did not hesitate to quibble with their shipbuilders, or with Lloyds surveyors, over every aspect of a vessel during construction and survey, and in doing so they often reveal a thorough knowledge of the technical aspects of ship construction and ship handling at sea.

In the great barques and ships of the third quarter of the century, we see sails increasing in number much more than in average size. Beginning in the 1850s, the topsail was turned into two sails, following the inventions of two American ship masters, Robert Forbes and Frederick Howes. The yard of the upper topsail could be raised or lowered from the deck, and the sail furled much more quickly. The increasing use of staysails gave the square-rigger some of the advantages associated with fore and aft sails. Speed in a sailing vessel came not simply from maximizing the area of canvas that could take the wind when "running" with the wind astern or on the quarter. Speed also required that a vessel be "weatherly": capable of sailing "close-hauled," or as close as possible into the wind. In general, vessels carrying fore and aft sails were more weatherly than vessels carrying

only square sail (although weather conditions and the nature of prevailing winds on different trade routes affect general performance).[17]
The addition of staysails meant increasing the area of fore and aft sail
in a square-rigger, and it added to the area of sail that caught the
wind when sailing close-hauled or with the wind on the beam. At
certain points of sailing, these sails would catch the wind that the
square sails allowed to escape.[18]

Improvements in standing and running rigging, and new smooth-
running blocks with patent sheaves, also eased the labour in sailhandling. By the 1840s and 1850s wire standing rigging replaced
hemp and manila in larger vessels, making it easier to set up the
rigging (remove the slack from shrouds and stays). The patent windlass eased the work of raising anchors, and by the late nineteenth
century the donkey engine had appeared to assist in hoisting cargo
and sometimes even yards. Spars became lighter, and cotton sail
improved in quality. Such changes improved performance and passage times without comparable increases in labour; they also made
the industry more capital-intensive, even in the era of wood and sail.

In designing their vessels, builders sought the best compromise
among speed, seaworthiness, and carrying capacity. The famous clipper ships of the 1850s and 1860s often sacrificed cargo capacity in
order to maximize sailing speed. Clippers were built in the Maritimes – James Smith's *Marco Polo*, built at Saint John in 1851, is the
best known.[19] But Atlantic Canadian shipowners did not sacrifice
carrying capacity to speed, and the extremely slender clipper was a
rarity.

Nevertheless, the qualities of hull design that tended toward speed
were known: these included sharpness in the hull as it entered the
water; a long hull that was hollow at the bow; sheer lines to reduce
wave-making resistance; a minimum of roughness or foulness in the
vessel's bottom; and a low ratio of vessel weight or displacement
to rig size.[20] Canadian softwoods enjoyed the advantage of good
buoyancy, an important advantage when carrying bulky cargoes. By
the third quarter of the century, if not before, the copper sheathing
fitted to the hulls of vessels was replaced regularly to avoid accumulation of barnacles and other causes of fouling.

But it is also clear that builders paid considerable attention to the
configuration of hulls. Smaller vessels in the first decades of the
century tended to be squat, broad-beamed, and round in the bow.
This was true of coastal schooners for most of the century, particularly
of schooners designed to carry timber. The Saint John "wood boat"
was such a craft, often appearing to be almost as wide as she was long.

The giant timber vessels *Baron of Renfrew* and *Columbus*, built in Quebec in the 1820s, suggested the extremes to which a few owners were prepared to go in sacrificing seaworthiness to carrying capacity in the broad-beamed timber carrier.[21]

By mid-century, however, the growing proportion of sawn lumber and mixed cargoes carried by New Brunswick vessels facilitated stowage and encouraged the building of sharper bows. And as Table 3.3 suggests, there was a marked trend toward longer, finer hulls, even if Canadian builders avoided the very narrow lines of the "extreme" clippers built in the United States. The trend was particularly marked in vessels of 500 tons and more: the vessel measuring thirty feet in breadth had gained no less than thirty feet in length from bow to stern between the 1820s and the 1850s. By the 1850s, in fact, the length-breadth ratio of the *Marco Polo* (5.07) was close to the average for large vessels registered in that decade. In three decades there had been a very substantial change in hull design. The change after the 1850s was slight, and in smaller vessels there was even a return to greater breadth.

If there was a trade-off between speed and carrying capacity in specific aspects of hull design, nevertheless these two desiderata were closely related, since they came from the same desire for vessel productivity. The search for speed did not come from the need to transport perishable cargoes quickly; rather the shipowner wanted to maximize the volume of revenue-earning cargo that could be carried within a given period of time – either a season of the year or the lifetime of the vessel itself. Most of the cargoes carried by British North American vessels, at least in the first half of the century, were available on a seasonal basis, and speed was critical to the number of passages that could be made in a season. By the 1830s shipowners were pressing masters and sailors into three voyages with timber in a season, and the winter passage with high deck-loads became a notorious destroyer of ships and men.[22]

Faster passages meant greater carrying capacity, but there were limits to the gains from faster sailing or quicker turn-around. There were theoretically no limits, however, to the number of years that a vessel could spend plying the same route. Thus another way to maximize tonnage use was to increase the service life of the vessel and so to improve one's chances of amortizing the investment and earning profits on either the vessel or its cargoes.

It is easy to show that a modest increase in service life could achieve the same result as a significant change in sailing speeds. If a ship made an average of 2.5 North Atlantic voyages a year over a ten-year

Table 3.3
Ratio of Length to Breadth by Tonnage Class and Decade (All Vessels Newly Registered in Saint John and Halifax)

| | Tonnage Class | | | | |
Decade	10–99	100–249	250–499	500–999	1,000 +
1820s	3.14	3.43	3.77	4.01	–
1830s	3.31	3.62	3.97	4.34	–
1840s	3.50	3.99	4.45	4.70	4.82
1850s	3.56	4.05	4.72	5.01	5.23
1860s	3.19	3.79	4.43	4.74	4.95
1870s	3.18	3.67	4.28	4.71	5.18
1880s	3.07	3.50	4.43	4.81	5.39

Source: Board of Trade series 107/108 vessel registries.

lifetime, to increase the number of voyages to three a year would require very considerable effort and increased risk of disaster at sea. The same result – a total of thirty instead of twenty-five voyages – was achieved by increasing the service life of the vessel to twelve years.

For this aspect of performance, however, the British North American vessel was severely criticized in the early nineteenth century. Many British shipowners shared the belief that these vessels suffered extraordinarily rapid depreciation, although the language used was often more picturesque. "I should be very sorry to go to sea in the best of them," said the London shipowner Joseph Somes: "I call them coffins."[23] H.C. Chapman, a Liverpool merchant, said: "I did not know which was the most dangerous thing, a colonial ship or a race-horse," and one wonders whether the comparison was a reference to speed as well as risk.[24] G.F. Young, in a letter to W.E. Gladstone at the Board of Trade in 1844, insisted that "North American colonial ships rank in quality with the most inferior in the world" and that these "inefficiently-built ships" were responsible for a very large share of the losses of British ships at sea.[25]

These were not disinterested opinions, of course. They reflect the complaint of many British shipbuilders that imported colonial ships had caused the glut in the markets in the early 1840s and the steep drop in prices for all tonnage. Shipbuilders in London and elsewhere were using the poor reputation of colonial-built vessels to buttress their argument for a protective tariff at a time of depression in their industry.

The reputation of colonial vessels for being short-lived is not so easily dismissed, however. Much earlier in the century, colonial vessels were suspect on two main grounds: first, their softwood hulls deteriorated rapidly and were subject to "dry rot"; second, and compounding this problem, were deficiencies in construction, particularly the use of improperly seasoned timber.[26] What we know of the life expectancies of British and colonial vessels suggests that colonial vessels were indeed short-lived. Vessels built in New Brunswick in the 1820s and registered in Saint John lasted, on average, a mere seven years.[27]

There is no denying the extent of the tragedy and misery inflicted on thousands of men by the ruthless competition of merchants and masters in the timber trade. But it is more difficult to arrive at a firm conclusion about the quality of colonial vessels from the evidence of losses at sea. The Select Committee on Shipwrecks of Timber Ships in 1839 concluded that "there is as large a proportion of A1 and good ships lost, as of old and inferior ones; thus proving beyond a doubt, that the loss is occasioned by other causes than the frailty of the vessels themselves."[28] However, the evidence presented to that committee (and analysed by Richard Rice) suggests that vessels built in Canada and New Brunswick were more likely to be lost at sea than were British vessels in the North Atlantic passage (Table 3.4). And the average age of British North American vessels on this trade route was less than half that of vessels built in the United Kingdom.[29]

There was a real problem of longevity for colonial vessels, which the timber trade merely exacerbated. The Select Committee followed the opinion of most experts, that the cause of heavy losses in the timber trade was improper stowage and the carrying of heavy deckloads. These practices were clearly both common and risky, but for colonial-built vessels they were especially dangerous because of the kind of strain put on a softwood vessel by the timber cargo, especially if the vessel were not well fastened. The timber put considerable strain on the knee-fastenings and the joints of the ship, and bolts were easily loosened in softwood; thus a softwood vessel was likely to be severely strained aloft, quickly waterlogged, and thereby rendered unmanageable by her small and over-worked crews.[30] To some extent the poor reputation of colonial-built vessels was undeserved, because so many of them were employed in a dangerous trade in which both vessels and men were abused by fiercely competitive owners and masters. But softwood vessels were relatively short-lived, whatever the trade in which they were employed.

Serious as these problems were, especially for those who worked in this industry, the reputation of colonial vessels must also be set in a broader perspective. What difference did the short lives of these

Table 3.4

Vessels Lost on the British North America–United Kingdom Passage in 1836 and 1838

Year	Place Built	No. of Vessels Clearing	No. of vessels Lost	% Lost
1836	British North America	704	28	4.0
	United Kingdom	1,063	25	2.4
1838	British North America	767	43	5.6
	United Kingdom	968	37	3.8

Sources: Select Committee on Shipwrecks of Timber Ships, *Parliamentary Papers*, 1839, IX, 351ff; Richard Rice, "The Rise of Shipbuilding in British North America, 1787–1855," PHD thesis, University of Liverpool, 1978, 140.

vessels make to their owners, and to the viability of the industry? The short life of the softwood vessel was, for the merchant shipowner, a problem of rapid depreciation and high risk. In the context of the economy as a whole, these were problems of high capital consumption. Capital goods were created and then rapidly consumed in the process of production. Capital consumption occurs, of course, in all industries. In twentieth-century capitalist economies this means that net capital formation is less than gross capital formation by a considerable margin: net domestic capital formation is likely to be about 60 per cent of gross capital formation; thus capital consumption is 40 per cent of gross capital formation.

By these standards, shipping was subject to high rates of capital consumption, even in the United Kingdom. Using tonnage as our measure of physical capital, it is possible to compare net with gross investment in shipping in the United Kingdom. Even though net investment (annual changes in total tonnage on registry) was inflated by the importation of colonial-built vessels, net investment was only 45 per cent of gross investment in the 1830s and 1840s, and the proportion was a mere 26 per cent if the 1820s are included.[31]

By this standard, capital consumption appears to have been very rapid in Atlantic Canadian shipping: in Saint John, net capital formation was about 13 per cent of gross between the mid-1820s and the 1870s.[32] However, a large amount of tonnage was transferred from local registry, thereby deflating net investment. Most remarkable, where the transfer of tonnage was rare, capital consumption appears to have been remarkably low, even below the British levels of the 1820–49 period. Thus, in Yarmouth, net investment was 43 per cent of gross investment in the central decades of the "age of sail" (1844–79). In Windsor, the rate was 32 per cent (1854–79).[33] This suggests that by the third quarter of the century capital consumption in shipping, in Yarmouth and Windsor at least, was probably not much different from that in the economy as a whole.[34]

If this was so, then the evil reputation of colonial vessels must be reconsidered. If that reputation was sometimes well deserved in the early nineteenth century, it must not obscure the remarkable change in the durability and longevity of colonial vessels across the century. If capital consumption was lower in the third quarter of the century, the immediate reason for this was the increased service life of vessels, as shown in Table 3.5.

We should expect the average time on registry in the Maritimes to increase in the third quarter of the century, when fewer vessels were transferred quickly to British registries. But even if transferred vessels are excluded, vessel life increased significantly. Vessels "lost at sea" or wrecked gained an extra five years in service between the 1830s and the 1880s. The average vessel that survived into old age, then to be condemned or broken up, also gained five years in the same half-century.

In all categories there was extreme variation around mean service life, as is to be expected in an industry of high risk. But the general trend is beyond dispute. The increase of over 50 per cent in the life of wooden-hulled ships critically affected the viability of the industry. By itself the greater durability of vessels accounted in large part for the size of the industry in the third quarter of the century. If we recalculate the total tonnage on registry in Saint John in 1875, for instance, assuming that average vessel life had remained as it was in the 1820s, then the fleet in 1875 would have been 30 per cent smaller than it actually was.

What explains this change in the longevity of ships? The trend might not have surprised many shipowners of the 1820s and 1830s, for it was merely the realization of a potential that already existed. Although many vessels lacked durability in the early nineteenth century, we must not assume that all vessels were alike merely because of their softwood planking. And it is wrong to assume that a large proportion were built as "packing cases," to be quickly dismantled after their first voyage.

British experts in fact disagreed about the quality of colonial vessels, and unfavourable opinions were more often heard from London than from centres such as Liverpool, where more colonial tonnage was purchased. Parliamentary committees heard that colonial ships were inferior but that a third of the timber ships were "fit for any trade." In 1821 one shipbroker stated that "the ships that I have seen built of red pine at New Brunswick, have been superior to almost any

Table 3.5
Average Vessel Life by Reason for Disposal and Decade Built (New
Brunswick and Nova Scotia Fleets), 1820s–1914

Decade	Broken up/ Condemned	Marine Disaster	Transfers	Other	Total (Excluding Transfers)
1820s	15.4	8.1	4.4	6.7	9.1
1830s	16.0	7.8	4.7	13.1	9.5
1840s	18.3	8.6	3.8	9.0	10.3
1850s	18.0	11.0	4.1	10.7	12.1
1860s	19.8	10.0	6.6	8.8	11.5
1870s	20.8	11.2	10.3	13.1	12.9
1880s	21.0	12.8	11.7	13.0	14.9
1890s	19.3	12.3	11.1	14.0	14.9
1900–14	19.5	12.9	13.9	12.3	15.9

Source: Board of Trade 107/108 vessel registries.
Note: Average life is calculated as difference between date of disposal and date built.
Where date of actual disposal is not stated on the registry (as, for instance, in the entry
"registry closed 1856") the vessel is not included. The averages are for vessels registered
in Halifax, Miramichi, Pictou, Saint John, Windsor, and Yarmouth. "Other" includes
vessels sold to foreigners, vessels "supposed lost," vessels said to "no longer exist," and
the like (these categories account for only 6.4 per cent of the total). "Transfers" include
vessels transferred to other ports in British North America. The total excludes transfers
and vessels sold to foreigners.

ships except oak ships; indeed for myself, I would as soon have a red
pine ship as many that are built in this country, at Sunderland for
instance."[35]
    Much depended on the type of vessel to which observers referred.
Many vessels were built on speculation, but many were also built on
contract for local or British owners, often to very high standards. If
the purchaser resided in the United Kingdom he often sent a trusted
shipmaster or agent to supervise the work. Mindful of the reputation
of New Brunswick timber for speedy rotting if green wood were
used, purchasers insisted that "there must be no bad unsound timber
allowed to go in on any account nor yellow pine unless in the decks."[36]
Contract building allowed such close supervision, and although there
is no way to estimate the proportion of all tonnage built to contract,
existing shipbuilders' papers suggest that the practice was very common in the first half of the century. In the third quarter of the century,
when more tonnage was built for local owners, contract-building
certainly increased.[37]
    Colonial vessels were not built entirely of pine or spruce. Harder

woods were required and used for the keelson, beams, and treenails. Oak and pitch pine were often imported for this purpose, and, where oak was not used, hackmatack, the hardest of local woods, was preferred.[38]

Merchants and shipbuilders were often torn between the desire to keep costs low and the desire for durability. In the fastening, caulking, and sheathing of one vessel, the Wards of Saint John insisted on "the necessity of not spending a shilling more than is absolutely necessary for the safety of the ship," but when the same vessel (the *Avon*) was being built in 1840 the priority was durability: "the scantling of this Ship is large, compact, and as amply fastened as any vessel of her dimensions in every part can be. She has the best American oak for bolting streaks, Stem, Apron, & s post, first deck plank &c ... the cost of iron knees &c will considerably advance her cost / tons, but we will now consider her the best fastened & the strongest Ship out of this Port, and if we are so fortunate as to run her a number of years, will in time, we hope, fully save us so heavy an outlay."[39] Records surviving from the 1820s and 1830s make it clear that care was taken over the coppering of hulls, the fitting of iron knees (often done in England), and the use of adequate fastenings.[40]

Although there were no Lloyds surveyors stationed permanently in the Maritimes until the 1850s, the firm's classification standards did have an influence. In the mid-1830s, Lloyds insisted that if colonial vessels were to receive A ratings, they must "be secured in their bilges by the application of iron riders" to cover joints in the floors, there must be additional bolts, and "all such ships shall also be secured by iron-hanging knees to the hold-beams."[41] Iron knees became standard in New Brunswick vessels, and the 1830s also saw the beginnings of diagonal iron strapping in hulls for additional strength.

By 1850 New Brunswick vessels commonly received a Lloyds A rating for four years, but many vessels were also earning the A rating for six or seven years.[42] In 1852 a Lloyds surveyor arrived in Saint John: his duties included frequent inspections of vessels prior to their completion and classification by Lloyds. A decade later the chief Customs officer and registrar of shipping for New Brunswick believed that the Lloyds surveyors had had a considerable effect: "This system of inspecting the vessels while building has tended greatly to raise the quality and character of our ships, and make them more valuable either for owning in the Colony or selling in England."[43] By the mid-1850s, if not before, the majority of New Brunswick tonnage was earning the A rating at Lloyds for seven years.[44] In 1857, 71 per cent of tonnage constructed in New Brunswick was being built to class A7 by Lloyds standards.[45] By the 1870s the classifications A9 and A10 were very common.[46]

These ratings reflected further changes in building techniques. Pitch pine from the United States was still used for keelsons, and imported hardwood might account for 25 per cent of the cost of all timber used in the vessel.[47] The fastenings between keel and floors were strengthened.[48] In his recent examination of the hull of the *Egeria*, built in New Brunswick in 1859, Eric Lawson has discovered unusual methods of frame fastening that may be unique, New Brunswick responses to the search for durability.[49] Large quantities of mineral salt were used to preserve the ship's timbers.[50]

And by the third quarter of the century large quantities of iron were used – as much as sixty tons in a 1,000-ton vessel, according to Frank Killam of Yarmouth.[51] This included chain, windlasses, and pumps, but also the iron used in knees, strapping, and other parts of the hull. Recaulking and recoppering were much more common, partly because vessels from the Maritimes were now often carrying "dry" cargoes – which would be ruined if exposed to damp.[52] These and other changes in construction made the vessel of the 1870s much different from her predecessor of the 1820s.

The bad reputation of colonial vessels did not endure. Even when it was current in the 1830s and 1840s, shipowners in the United Kingdom continued to purchase these vessels: the advantage of cheapness was sufficient to compensate for their short lives. And colonial deep-sea vessels were initially designed for particular trades – for bulky cargoes of low unit value and high freight costs, where the cost of transport must be kept as low as possible. Timber and cotton were such cargoes. Neither required first-class ships, because timber could be carried in a "wet" hull, and cotton, because it was light, did not require exceptionally strong hulls.[53]

Whatever the trade, the low price was a critical advantage to the purchaser. Prices of colonial tonnage sold in Britain varied considerably from year to year. Other factors affecting the price included finishing and outfitting, the Lloyds classification, the number of decks, the builder's reputation, and the type of wood used. Perhaps most remarkable, the price of colonial tonnage rose little in the long run, despite the manifest increase in quality and durability. Graph 3.1 suggests the ranges of British prices in years for which data are available.

Detailed comparisons with tonnage built in Britain or the United States would merely confirm the considerable price advantage of the vessel built in the Maritimes. In the late 1830s, for instance, vessels built in the United Kingdom usually cost between £10 and £25 ster-

Graph 3.1
United Kingdom Selling Prices for New Brunswick and Prince Edward
Island Vessels, 1822–66

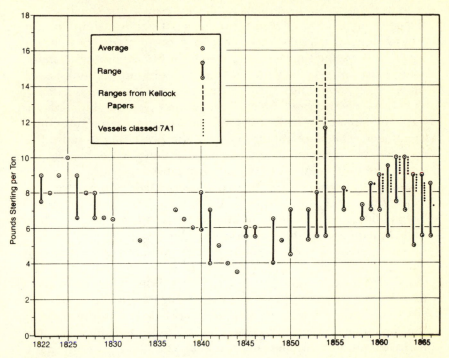

Sources: *Parliamentary Papers*, 1844, VIII, 179 (Select Committee on British Shipping);
Journals of the House of Assembly, Prince Edward Island, New Brunswick; Colonial Office
Blue Books; C.W. Kellock & Co. Papers; Rice, "The Rise of Shipbuilding"; and notes
from the files of the late Keith Matthews. Obviously the data are very incomplete, and
the ranges were probably more extreme than suggested here. Prices were usually in
pounds sterling per ton old measurement, the measure used when vessels were sold.

ling per ton. The cheapest were the Sunderland vessels, built to class
for seven to ten years and priced between £10 and £12 sterling per
ton.[54] In the same period, the best American vessels cost $55 per ton,
and the range for New England vessels was $46 to $57.[55]

Relatively cheap local timber facilitated the price advantage of
colonial ships, but the continuing advantage of colonial ships, even
after the repeal of the Navigation Acts, cannot be separated from
favourable state policies. The combination of British demand and
British protection in the first half of the century left the Maritime
colonies with a substantial shipbuilding expertise and infrastructure
designed for the building of large ocean-going vessels. The great New

Brunswick square-rigger was built not on a beach but in a shipyard. The shipyard was different from a factory because it was not a single enclosed space, its work was highly seasonal, and its labour was that of artisans rather than an unskilled proletariat. In the third quarter of the century, shipyards varied from small artisan workshops to large proto-industrial manufactories. The larger shipyards built several vessels at the same time and employed one hundred men or more. A large yard included a blacksmith's shop, bunk-house, cook-house, joiner's shop, mouldingloft, salt store, saw-pits, steam-engine, timber booms, warehouse, and wharf.[56] While the average shipyard was small and labour-intensive, the large yard represented a substantial investment. The shipbuilding boom of the preceding decades had left a substantial accumulation of capital and expertise that was the heritage of dependence on the British market.

Protection did not end with the Navigation Acts. Colonial tonnage retained duty-free access to the British market. Most of the imported shipbuilding materials entered duty-free. Imported woods, which might be a quarter of the value of all wood in a ship, entered without duty. Wire rigging, anchors, chains, salt, and other building materials entered duty-free or at very low rates. In New Brunswick in the early 1860s imports accounted for about a third of the value of materials used in building a deep-sea ship; the average duty on these imports was about 4 per cent.[57] The Canadian duty on cordage was 5 per cent for much of the 1870s. Pig iron was imported duty-free, but increasing amounts came from local sources.[58]

This complex of advantages led to a continuing supply of tonnage at remarkably stable prices through the 1860s and 1870s. In the late 1860s, vessels built in Nova Scotia and New Brunswick, with an A classification at Lloyds or Bureau Veritas for five to seven years, ranged from $30 to $40 per ton (fitted for sea), and there were vessels built in the outports that cost even less.[59] Prices increased in the early 1870s but fell again late in the decade.[60] In the 1880s, prices of between $30 and $35 per ton for large vessels fully outfitted were not unusual, although the range still depended very much on the vessel's classification.[61]

The merchant-shipowner was benefiting from more than a plentiful supply of building materials. He also gained from an inherited shipbuilding infrastructure which included an established network of relationships between builders and those who supplied timber, labour, iron, rope, canvas, food, and many other inputs. The shipbuilder by mid-century was more often an independent businessman; the integrated merchant shipowning-shipbuilding firm was giving way to greater specialization. But the shipbuilder's network also included his personal contacts with shipowners, and very often the builder held a few shares in the vessel he built and so remained in partnership with the new owners. Specialization and the scale of the larger shipbuilding operation suggested some movement toward industrial capitalism, but shipbuilding remained within the small and local networks of pre-industrial family firms.

Shipowners did not purchase much tonnage from distant sources: they bought tonnage from building yards located near their residences and near their ports of registry. Proximity to one's builders afforded several advantages: knowledge of the men and their reputations, the ability to supervise the work in progress, and the opportunity to take part in the supply of materials. Shipowning centres tended to appear, therefore, within shipbuilding centres. Almost 54 per cent of tonnage newly registered in Saint John came from Saint John County; 77 per cent of tonnage registered in Yarmouth came from Yarmouth County or Digby County; 50 per cent of the new tonnage on the Windsor registry came from Hants County.

The only exceptions among major ports were Halifax and St John's – neither port was located within a major shipbuilding area. But Halifax merchants had close connections with builders on the Fundy shore and purchased most of their large vessels from those builders (see Maps 3.2–3.5). Although the incentives and advantages that gave rise to shipbuilding were not merely local, the supply of tonnage remained within the personal and local framework of family-based merchant capitalism.

Shipbuilding was more concentrated, however, than the data in Maps 3.2–3.5 might suggest. It is a mistake to assume that any beach could become a shipbuilding yard or that "square-rigged vessels were turned out by the hundreds in nearly every Nova Scotia hamlet and town that had access to water."[62] Although 203 building locations in New Brunswick supplied vessels for the Saint John registry, a much smaller number provided the ocean-going square-riggers, and a mere fifteen accounted for over 61 per cent of all tonnage registered in the port. In Yarmouth, Windsor, Pictou, and Miramichi, the concentration of tonnage in a few building locations was even greater.[63]

This concentration of shipbuilding was limited, however, by the tendency of shipyards to locate near good timber supplies and by the exhaustion of timber resources in particular locations. Thus we see somewhat contradictory tendencies in the industry as vessel size increased. Shipyards tended to specialize in types and sizes of vessel;

Map 3.2
Building Locations of Tonnage Newly Registered in Saint John, 1820–1914

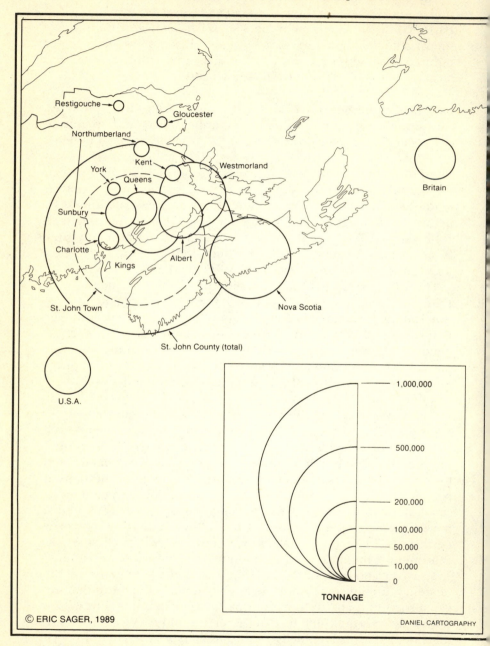

© ERIC SAGER, 1989

DANIEL CARTOGRAPHY

Map 3.3
Building Locations of Tonnage Newly Registered in Halifax, 1820–1914

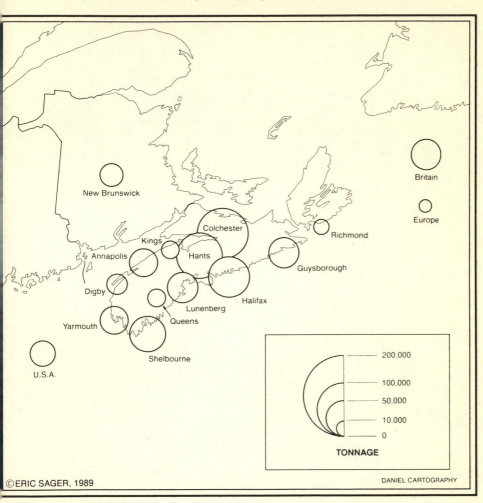

New Brunswick

Britain

Europe

Colchester

Richmond

Kings

Hants

Annapolis

Guysborough

Digby

Halifax

Lunenberg

Queens

Yarmouth

Shelbourne

U.S.A.

200.000
100.000
50.000
10.000
0

TONNAGE

©ERIC SAGER, 1989

DANIEL CARTOGRAPHY

Map 3.4
Building Locations of Tonnage Newly Registered in Yarmouth, 1840–1914

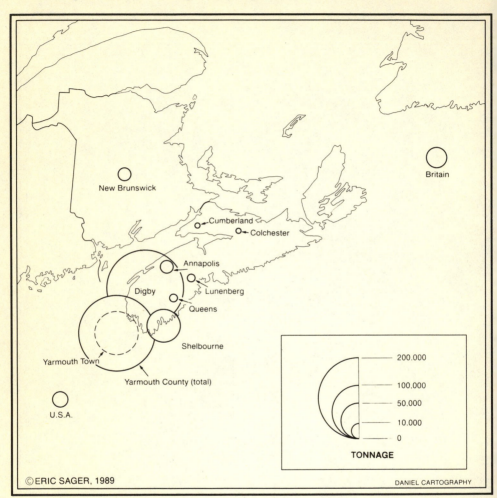

Map 3.5
Building Locations of Tonnage Newly Registered in Windsor, 1849–1914

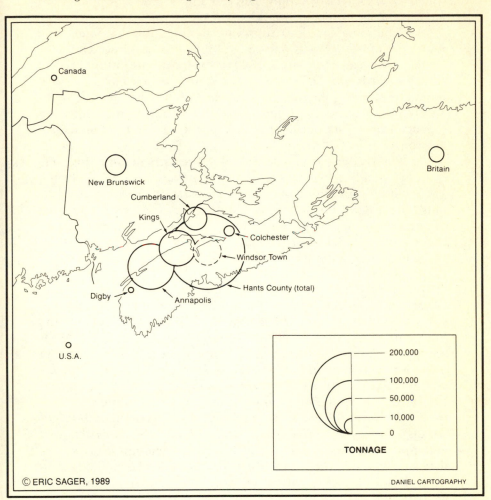

© ERIC SAGER, 1989

DANIEL CARTOGRAPHY

but shipbuilding tended to be spatially more dispersed as builders sought new sources of supply. Few building locations supplied tonnage in every decade.

Of all building locations supplying tonnage for the Saint John registry, for instance, only one – Saint John itself – produced tonnage in every five-year period from 1820 to 1914. And the output of Saint John shipyards was itself concentrated in time: almost half of the total output from Saint John shipyards appeared in two decades (the 1840s and 1850s); thereafter a larger proportion of Saint John – registered tonnage came from outside the port of registry and its immediate environs.

The vessels appearing on the Saint John registry in the 1840s came from 115 building locations (68 of them in New Brunswick); by the 1860s, although the number of new registrations had increased by only 29 (to 845), the number of building locations had increased to 169 (90 in New Brunswick). By the 1870s the number of new registrations had fallen to 625, but the number of building locations was still greater than it had been in the 1840s (145, of which 77 were in New Brunswick).

The Saint John pattern was repeated elsewhere. The boom in demand for tonnage in the 1860s and 1870s meant a wider distribution of building centres. Thus 26 places provided vessels for the Yarmouth registry in the 1850s; the number rose to 40 in the 1860s and 36 in the 1870s. But building centres tended to specialize: in Yarmouth the relationship between building location and tonnage class was twice as strong in the 1880s as in the 1840s.[64]   Shipyards, even when they represented an accumulation of capital and expertise, were still moveable assets. But specialization increased with larger vessels because only certain places had both suitable stands of timber and immediate access to a body of water deep enough to accommodate a large vessel when launched.[65] The dispersion of building locations does not suggest, however, that diminishing supplies were contributing to the decline of either shipbuilding or shipowning. A supply problem would have been reflected in higher prices, and as we have seen prices remained remarkably flat and may even have declined somewhat as more tonnage was produced in smaller outports.

In about half a century, shipbuilding had been transformed from a transplanted British enclave to an extensive indigenous industry controlled by local merchant capital. Early in the century the building of ocean-going vessels depended largely on technology, capital, and even skilled labour imported from the mother country.[66] The ships produced were part of the production function of colonial staples and part of Britain's supply of raw materials for her industrial revolution. Thus the colonial shipbuilding industry grew within the old mercantile system.

In the third quarter of the nineteenth century, shipbuilding survived the ending of that system, and some elements of a transition to industrial capitalism emerged. A new division between shipbuilders and shipowners appeared; a few shipyards became larger, proto-industrial operations; a degree of specialization appeared; more products of the industrial revolution appeared in wooden-hulled vessels; artisan labour was sometimes displaced by new technology.

But the great barques and ships of the 1880s still bore the imprint of their colonial heritage. They were producer goods themselves, inputs in the staple trades of North America. They were designed to carry bulky raw materials from North America and from Britain's colonial possessions to industrial Britain and Europe and to do so at the lowest possible cost to shippers. They were designed to give merchants control of staple production, through control of the distribution of colonial output and of imported manufactures and other consumer products. The great three-masted barque was a product of large craft workshops, a product that the colonists learned to make for themselves. It was also a water-borne packing case, the oceanic extension of the merchant's warehouse. Merchant capital was gradually transforming its sources of value from circulation to production, and the sailing ship was part of this process. It was a type of merchant capital on a colonial frontier.

CHAPTER FOUR

Maritime Merchants in the Old Colonial System

In the first half of the 19th century, shipping tonnage was deployed by people of many occupations, living in a few large commercial centres and many small outports. To analyse these shipowners, we focus on those who are listed as owners on the registries of eight major ports of registry in the region. In the British registration system, shares in ships were measured in 64ths, and a single share-holding might consist of only one or two shares, or as many as 64 shares in a vessel. The dispersal of ownership is indicated by the fact that there were some 40,000 shareholdings in all vessels registered in these eight ports between 1820 and 1914.

Only a third of these shareholdings belonged to people who gave their occupation as "merchant." Clearly shareholding went far beyond the merchant class: particularly to small owner-operators, especially those identified as "mariners," who accounted for 35 per cent of all shareholdings. Although the idea that most fishing families built or owned their own schooners is incorrect, nevertheless having a share in a decked vessel was not uncommon in the outports of the Maritimes and Newfoundland. Thus the registries of Halifax between 1820 and 1914 report some 8,966 separate individuals or firms to be shareholders in new or re-registered tonnage. There were over 6,200 unique shareholders on the registries of Saint John and over 5,000 on the registries of Newfoundland.[1] Most of these individuals were not merchants.

Shareholding might be extensive, but it was also concentrated, and the tonnage held by each occupational group much better indicates the structure of ownership. Graph 4.1 suggests the extent to which shipping tonnage became merchants' capital between 1820 and 1849.[2] In this period two-thirds of all newly registered tonnage in the major ports of the Maritimes was owned by merchants. In

Graph 4.1
Newly Registered Tonnage by Occupation Group in Seven Major Fleets,
to 1849

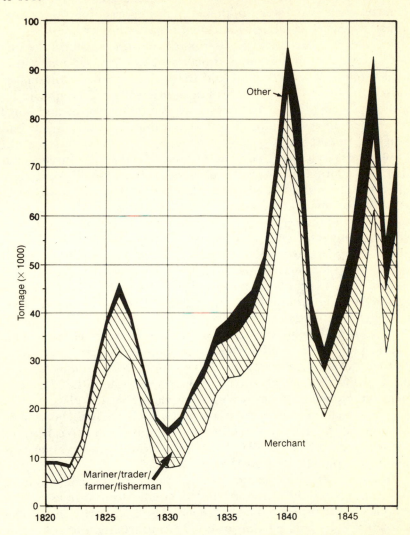

Sources: Board of Trade series 107/108 colonial vessel registries. The seven ports
are Charlottetown (1820–49), Halifax (1820–49), Saint John (1820–49), Miramichi
(1828–49), Yarmouth (1840–9), Pictou (1840–9), and Windsor (1849).

Newfoundland, merchants held an equally large share of new tonnage.

The first half of the century was an era of merchants and of independent owner-operators. In the seven main ports of the Maritimes, almost a quarter of all new tonnage was owned by mariners, fishermen, traders, or farmers. In Newfoundland these small proprietors were even more important, and planters alone held 24 per cent of all new tonnage between 1820 and 1849. They specialized in smaller vessels and owned a large share of those of less than 250 tons. Gradually shipowning would become more capital-intensive, and small owner-operators would be displaced, but this trend was only beginning before mid-century.[3]

Most vessels changed hands at least once during their careers, and there was a substantial market in used tonnage. The small proprietors often bought second-hand vessels. Before 1854 the laws on vessel registration usually required re-registry on change of ownership, and so it is possible to see the growing importance of smaller owners as vessels changed hands, at least before mid-century. About 38 per cent of all tonnage was owned by small owner-operators at the time of re-registry, and for small vessels their proportion was even higher.[4]

Many shipowners were independent producers or traders who engaged in fishing, farming, trading, and schooner-building. A visitor to Prince Edward Island described the local schooner fleet in 1818 and noted, with some exaggeration, the extent of vessel ownership: "These vessels are noted for their ugliness, but they are also famed for their durability; every farmer has one of his own, built by himself, the plan and execution being done by the eye without the help of an architect. No wonder they are ugly but who in such a place prefers not use to beauty? Canvas, rope and iron work come high, but timber being got at the door is a set off to that expense, and two cargoes of potatoes sent to Newfoundland leaves the farmer a clear vessel. This mode of shipbuilding astonished me at first."[5]

The schooner in this context was a type of rural smallholding: it was not capital, but a property independent of mercantile control and part of the diversified family economies of outport villages. The schooner was a vital part of production in farming and fishing: it could be used in catching fish and in carrying produce to local if not international markets, for the mariner and his neighbours. By allowing the surplus of village production to enter local and even distant markets, the coastal vessel also helped to preserve the outport family and the small farm in their self-sufficient independence and self-proprietorship.

Naval Office records for Nova Scotia in the early nineteenth century indicate how common was the owner-operator: at the port of Sydney in 1804, for instance, more than two-thirds of all vessels clearing had a master who was also reported to be an owner. Even in a larger port the owner-operator was common: in Halifax, in 1820, 36 per cent of clearances were by vessels whose master was listed as an owner.[6]

For the major investors in shipping, however, tonnage was a form of capital – a means of production controlled by its owners, in this case merchants, hiring wage-paid labour in a process of production. The three-masted barque or ship was a cautious and incomplete step toward industrial capital, because the ship remained subordinate to commercial exchange, which remained the primary focus of the shipowners' activity. The merchant realized profits in a process of exchange – advancing money in exchange for certain goods, for instance, and then selling those goods for more money. Ships were a vital but subordinate part of such commercial exchanges. Although sailing ships employed wage labour, they had not incorporated the complete subordination of labour characteristic of the industrial factory, and workers retained a degree of control over the ship and its machinery.[7] Furthermore, these ships were used to add value to commodities whose production also remained largely outside the direct control of merchant capitalists. To summarize a complex point: the great shipowners of Atlantic Canada were merchants first and shipowners second.

Our "major owner" sample consists of those who acquired more than 1,000 gross tons of newly registered shipping between 1820 and 1914. From the Saint John file this produced a sample of 358 individuals. A small minority of all shareholders, they nevertheless accounted for about 73 per cent of all new tonnage registered in the port. Most of these people were merchants, although many were shipbuilders. In the decades after the 1840s it was increasingly common for shipbuilders to hold several shares in the vessels that they built, while merchants retained most shares and also the role of managing owner.

In Halifax the small owner-operators were more important than in Saint John. But merchants held over half of all new tonnage, and the 106 "major owners," most of whom were merchants, held 33 per cent of all tonnage. In Pictou, which did not become a port of registry until 1840, forty-four of the fifty-four major owners were merchants, and merchant-shipowners sustained the industry so long as it lasted. In Yarmouth, whose registry also opened in 1840, there were seventy-seven major owners; of these, thirty-four are normally described on the registries as merchants, while forty-one are given the occupation "shipowner." Only in this port did ships become so important a part of mercantile investments that "shipowner" took precedence over "merchant" in defining a man's principal occupation. In Windsor, whose registry did not open until 1849, there were sixty-seven major owners; once again, the majority were merchants or shipbuilders.

There was a concentration of ownership here: in Saint John and Windsor, major owners held three of every five tons of new shipping; in Yarmouth and Pictou, two of every three tons. But this is not the concentration that occurs with industrial capital; it is instead a modest accretion of capital in the hands of widely dispersed mercantile élites in two major entrepôts, Halifax and Saint John, and in several smaller towns. A few individuals owned large fleets, of course – Samuel Cunard put 18,050 new tons on the Halifax registry between the 1820s and the 1850s, in addition to the tonnage that he registered elsewhere.

Nevertheless, the fleets of most major owners were not large, compared with contemporary British fleets or later Canadian ones. In Saint John, for instance, the total tonnage added to the local industry by each major owner was only 4,679 tons on average. Over the course of a "shipowning" career, this was hardly a large fleet, even if the average owner also invested in used tonnage as well. This was a pattern of mercantile ownership, in which ships were part of a diversified commercial enterprise, its risk spread among many ventures.

It is impossible to measure precisely the size of shipping capital in the overall mercantile portfolio of a port town. Analysis of the major shipowners confirms, however, that shipowning was one of many ventures, and often part of the process of production or distribution in those other ventures. In Saint John, the lumber merchant John Robertson acquired tonnage for the timber trade, often in partnership with his fellow Scots, James Kirk and John Wishart. Robertson's investment in landward properties, including city lots, was always far greater than his investment in ships. He had interests in sawmilling, a hotel, banking, and insurance, and he participated in planning the first railways in New Brunswick.[8]

In Saint John, the major shipowners also included shipbuilders, who were not always among the merchant élite of the town. The shipbuilders employed a specialized type of artisan labour. The sample of "great merchants" identified by T.W. Acheson does not include many substantial shipbuilders.[9] There were, however, close ties and the occasional overlap between the two groups: the shipbuilders "were essentially clients of the merchant."[10]

The shipbuilder John Duncan, also a major shipowner, illustrates the overlap, as well as the interconnections among shipbuilders themselves. Duncan was born in Scotland, emigrated to New Brunswick in 1821, and soon found work in the shipyard of John Owens of Saint John, a descendant of Loyalists. Eventually Duncan became Owens's partner; a business associate of John Robertson and other merchants; a director of the Commercial Bank, of insurance companies, and of the Mechanics' Whale Fishing Co.; and a founder of the gas and water companies.[11] Owens and Duncan sold ships to local merchants, held tonnage in partnership with them, and undertook merchandising on their own account.

No individual registered more tonnage in the Maritimes in the nineteenth century than did Thomas E. Millidge. The son of a Loyalist shipowner, Millidge was a shipbuilder, a timber merchant, president of the Bank of New Brunswick in the 1850s, an investor in railways, and a relative or partner of many other merchant-shipowners.[12] The overlap between merchant and shipbuilder occurs also with Robert Rankin, William and Richard Wright, and the Moran family of St Martin's. Most shipbuilders, however, were specialist manufacturers who sold ships to merchants and entered occasionally into commerce and shipowning themselves.[13] Whether merchant or shipbuilder, the "shipowner" was clearly not a discrete entity.

In Halifax, shipowning was even more clearly subordinated to trading, particularly to the business of the "commission merchant," who accepted and executed orders for specific goods, for buyers and sellers located abroad and around Nova Scotia. He might never have title to the goods that he conveyed from seller to buyer and made his profit from a commission agent's fee. Although many merchants also bought and sold goods on their own account, in the first half of the century commission transactions were very common, and at least one source suggests that every Halifax merchant was engaged to some degree in commissioning.[14] Of the twenty-nine major shipowners registering tonnage in Halifax between 1820 and 1854, almost all were commission merchants.[15]

The major Halifax shipowners were also the town's major merchants. They included Samuel and Edward Cunard and their brother-in-law John Duffus. The Allison-Fairbanks shipowning partnership included Jonathan C. Allison, his cousin David Allison and the latter's brother-in-law William Fairbanks. Other prominent merchant-shipowners were J.W. Barss and Co., Black and Brothers, George P. Oxley, and Stephen Binney. This was a mercantile élite with interlocking family and business connections. Of the twenty-nine major owners before mid-century, fifteen were members of six families. Although West Indies trading and the import/export business was the primary focus of family firms, nineteen were involved in the formation of public companies, and seventeen held insurance company directorships. Many were involved with steam shipping, harbour facilities, and utilities companies. Some helped to found a Commercial Society in 1822 to promote trade, and some helped to create the Chamber of Commerce. Samuel Cunard represented at its extreme the local trend toward diversified merchandising: he was a West Indies merchant who bought and sold sugar, molasses, tea, coal, timber, steamships, fish, whales, land, insurance, and credit.

In Halifax, as elsewhere in Nova Scotia, the major shipowners illustrate the role of merchant capital in developing the infrastructure of port towns. Merchant-shipowners were prominent among those who invested in the "social overhead capital" of an export-based economy: gas lighting, schools, transportation and communications networks, water supplies, wharfs, and other public services. In Pictou County the shipowning partners James Carmichael, George McKenzie, and Thomas Graham were prominent founders of New Glasgow and its industries and utilities. In the little town of Yarmouth, family connections and partnerships linked Elisha Moody to Thomas Killam, the Killams to Lyman Cann and Amasa Durkee, and the Lovitt brothers to the Burrells. From these families and partnerships came the town's public companies, its wharfs, its fishing supplies, its telegraph, its shipchandleries, the Bank of Yarmouth, the Yarmouth Steam Navigation Co., and the Acadian Insurance Co.[16] A similar pattern emerged in Windsor, where the major merchant-shipowners included the major shipbuilders and the providers of banking, insurance, gas lighting, and the temperance hall.[17]

Despite the presence of those who invested in mining and those who by mid-century were interested in railways, most major shipowners specialized in commerce, finance, and social infrastructure rather than in manufacturing. Their most conspicuous contribution to manufacturing was shipbuilding. Diversification occurred within the limits set by merchant capital, the activity of which was based in the processes of commodity circulation.

Most of the major shipowners of the first half of the century were "maritime merchants," as J.G.B. Hutchins called them.[18] These were men who specialized in moving goods by sea, trading on their own account or carrying goods on commission, and making a profit from the margin between buying and selling prices. The craft they used were "trading vessels" – owned by the merchant, carrying a cargo owned in whole or in part by the same merchant. Such vessels may be distinguished from the "general cargo carrier," which carried goods owned by the shipper, not the shipowner, the latter earning a profit from the freight rate established in a charter agreement. There was never a perfect distinction between these types, because many trading vessels also carried some cargo for freight money. Nevertheless, the "trading vessel" was more common in the first half of the century than it was later.

It is not self-evident that a merchant operating in international markets should have to own ships, since the alternative of chartering tonnage always exists. By observing the maritime merchant of the 1830s, however, we come to understand why vessel ownership was essential. Profits from staple trading depended on many things: specialized knowledge of many commodities and their prices in distant markets, a network of trusted agents in the markets, speedy communication with those agents, and successful management of subordinates, including the "supercargo" who went with the goods being shipped and acted as the merchant's agent in the market. Profits required, above all, successful timing of purchase and sale, to maximize the difference between buying and selling prices. To achieve this last condition, the merchant was prepared to own and manage ships and to hire wage labour to run them.

William Roche of Halifax was a minor shipowner and merchant whose letter-books tell us a great deal about the operations of the maritime merchant in his generation. Roche spent much of his time accumulating information about prices of commodities in the West Indies, South America, Europe, Quebec, Newfoundland, and Nova Scotia. He also kept a wary eye on his competitors: "correct information of the number of vessels which have sailed to Porto Rico" was necessary, for instance, because too many vessels would affect prices.[19] Possession and control of one's own vessel meant avoiding or beating other vessels: "I cannot too much impress on you the importance of getting your offer the first day if possible, as the signal for another vessel coming in will induce them to delay."[20]

Control of one's own vessel gave the supercargo a range of choices, which chartering from another owner might never have allowed: "If you find it impossible to make a saving sale of the Cargo you had better direct Capt Pengilly to proceed on for a market in the Islands but we leave to your judgment from the advices you may have to do what you consider most for our interest ... As we have before mentioned, our great object is a quick return."[21]

"Quick dispatch" in the exchanges of fish, lumber, sugar, and molasses required control of ships, and this in turn impelled the merchant capitalist into hiring wage labour. Although the sailing ship was unlike the industrial factory on land, the merchant-shipowner was acquiring extensive experience with wage labour, beginning with the labour of his shipmasters, who were usually paid a wage. Often the merchant had his own experience with ships – many had begun as mariners themselves, and others had served in vessels owned by their fathers. It is no surprise to find William Roche writing detailed instructions to his masters about their choice of course, where and when to bend new sails, when to replace spars, and how to navigate distant harbours.

Profits from buying cheap and selling dear depended critically on minimizing variable costs in the ship itself, and for this the wage-paid employee was responsible, however the merchant might resent the fact: "I have now to inform you that you must study the strictest economy in your disbursements if you wish to continue with us, and you must know how necessary it is to the profitable conducting a voyage that it be performed in as short a time and with as little expense as possible."[22] The next step was to use the wage relationship to compel "quick dispatch": "If the voyage be performed in two and a half months, without damage to the sails or spars of the vessel &c you will receive an addition of one pound p month to your pay for the voyage."[23]

A similar discipline could be applied to the crew: "You have heard and know my sentiments about advances to Seamen abroad – the more money due them from the ship, the more attatched [sic] they will become to her."[24] In the timber trade, the wage bonus was used to increase the number of winter passages, despite the increased danger. The timber merchant Allan Gilmour explained how this was done: "When I first commenced, twenty years ago, they made only one [voyage], but when we became more pressed we made a second trip; and when we came to be still more pressed I said to the captains, 'I will give you a present of 100 pounds if you will try and make a third trip' and we have accomplished lately three trips with those large vessels."[25] The merchant sought to extend a managerial influence, but effective control still lay with his employees.

Merchants became shipowners but in doing so shared control with many others in their pre-industrial society. Dominating the process of commodity exchange and the price mechanisms, merchant capital did not dominate production relations. Merchants were not yet industrial capitalists: they neither produced nor consumed the commodities that they handled but sought only value from exchange.[26] The mercantile attitude toward the fishery illustrates the point: the fishery was not a processed food industry but the source of a commodity to be exchanged in international markets. As Newman, Hunt and Co. told its agents in Newfoundland: "We wish you to understand that our business in Newfoundland is not to buy Fish, but to sell Goods, and that we only take Fish in payment because the planters have no money to give us."[27] Furthermore, there was no need for planters or fishermen to have cash or money wages, so long as they would exchange fish for goods. In such conditions, petty commodity production and pre-capitalist social relations had remarkable stability.

The major shipowners shared adjacent shipping lanes with fishermen, coastal mariners, and other owner-operators. It was difficult to eliminate these smallholders, and in any case the great merchants had many alternatives to pursue in the development of an entrepôt infrastructure. The great staple trades were risky and subject to extraordinary short-term fluctuations. The search for stability and profit encouraged merchants to defend vigorously the tariff structure of British mercantilism. The same search encouraged them to diversify, to spread and so to minimize their risks, in the social infrastructure of the growing export-based economy. Ships were a central element in this mercantile structure.

CHAPTER FIVE

Rise and Decline
of the Ocean Fleets

The "golden age" of sail began in the mid-nineteenth century. For five decades thereafter sailing ships from eastern Canada held a prominent place in many of the world's carrying trades. Merchants sent their great barques and ships to compete in international shipping markets, and "Bluenose" masters and men were known in every major port in the world. The industry was impressive in its scale and its international dimensions. It has rightly become part of the folklore and memory of our Atlantic peoples.

Impressive as it was, however, the industry was remarkably short-lived. It lasted for little more than a generation: a young Nova Scotian who went to sea for the first time in 1850 might have worked in barques and ships from his province until he was an old man, but his son could not have done so, and if the man lived to the age of eighty, he lived longer than the industry in which he worked. In the long history of European colonization and settlement of the Atlantic sea-bord of Canada, the great age of sail was a brief episode.

Explanations for the growth and decline of the industry must begin by recognizing the remarkable rapidity of its rise and fall. It is tempting to conclude that so ephemeral an industry existed outside the basic economic structure or resource base of the region. But such a conclusion would be misleading, for by the 1850s this was no longer merely an enclave industry, inserted and then removed by British capital. And the industry was declining long before its necessary raw materials were exhausted. Deep-sea shipping was an integral part of the economy of Atlantic Canada in the era of merchant capital, but the demand that it met was not sustained. The history of the small fishing and coastal schooners is very different: these craft were part of the regional economy well into the twentieth century. The deep-sea shipping industry, however, was part of the region's economy for a half-century, and its rise was part of a specific historical conjuncture occurring in a few places in the region.

Analysis must begin with a description of patterns of investment. The annual data on tonnage registered in the colonies is a measure not simply of ships and their capacity – but also of investment behaviour by those who were purchasing substantial capital assets. Graph 5.1 tells us something about that behaviour. It also says something about the completeness of the data base available to us. The official figures represent the total tonnage on registry in all ports in the four Atlantic colonies, as estimated by the registrars of shipping in the ports of registry. The eight-port total is the estimate of tonnage on registry in eight major ports, from our computer files of vessel registries. For various reasons the estimates from the computer files are likely to be more accurate than the official figures.[1]

Until the peak in 1879, the estimated tonnage in eight major ports usually represented over 80 per cent of all tonnage on registry in the region. This suggests that the sample of registries used in our computer analysis captures a very large proportion of the industry and that the great age of sail was concentrated in space as well as time. Eight ports of registry accounted for almost all of the growth in tonnage, and in one of those ports (St John's) larger ocean-going vessels scarcely existed. Since our eight-port sample does not include several of the new registries that existed during the last half of the century, our sample if anything underestimates the growth of ocean-going tonnage up to the 1870s (we list Nova Scotia ports of registry in the endnote).[2] The pace of decline is slightly faster in the eight-port sample: the ports of registry not included saw larger amounts of small-vessel tonnage, which did not disappear so rapidly, and perhaps also the official figures may overestimate tonnage on registry.[3]

By disaggregating the totals in Graph 5.1, we can be more precise about sources of growth and decline. The pattern of growth and decline was similar in most ports of registry, and one port – Saint John – accounted for a large share of the regional total. Graph 5.2 shows the estimated tonnage on registry for the major ports – those that contributed most to shipping throughout the region in the three decades prior to the peak in 1879. The Saint John fleet accounted for 36 per cent of the annual average of tonnage on registry in the eight fleets analysed by computer and 31 per cent of official tonnage on registry. But other fleets contributed significantly to the overall growth in the industry up to 1879. Table 5.1 gives the estimated annual growth in the major fleets to 1879 and the contribution of each fleet to the overall growth rate of 3.85 per cent a year.

Graph 5.1
Estimated Tonnage on Registry in the Atlantic Colonies, 1830–1910

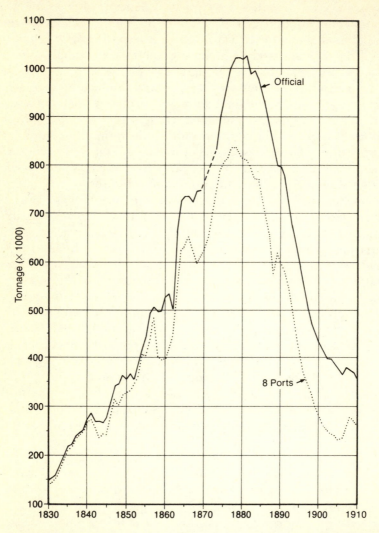

Sources: Board of Trade Annual Lists of Shipping; Great Britain, *Parliamentary Papers,* 1840–49, 1852–72; Canada, *Sessional Papers,* 1873–1910; Board of Trade series 107/ 108 vessel registries for Charlottetown, Halifax, Miramichi, Pictou, Saint John, St John's, Windsor, and Yarmouth. The change in tonnage measurement at 1854 may cause post-1854 growth to be underestimated; see chapter 3, note 10.

Graph 5.2
Estimated Tonnage on Registry by Port, 1849–79

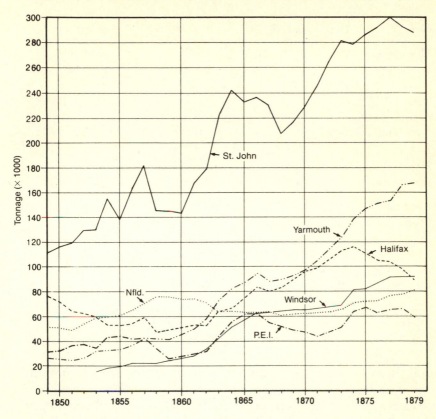

Source: Board of Trade series 107/108 vessel registries. On the 1854 change in tonnage measurement, see chapter 3, note 10.

Growth was most rapid in Saint John and in those ports that were not traditionally "transfer" ports (from which large volumes of tonnage were sold to owners in the United Kingdom or elsewhere). It is sometimes argued that growth in the industry was a reluctant response of short-term shipowners who were "trapped" into ship-owning by the collapse of prices in Britain for wooden sailing vessels. Builders and owners retained vessels that they could not sell, it is said, and so they became shipowners "by default."[4] This kind of explanation does not work for Yarmouth, Windsor, or Halifax: the transfer of tonnage from these ports to Britain had never been very substantial (see, above, Table 2.2). In these places, shipowning in the third quarter of the century was more likely to have been an expan-

Table 5.1
Annual Growth Rates and Port Contributions to Total Growth, 1849–79

Port	Annual Growth (%)	Weighted Growth (%)	% Contribution to Total Growth
All (official figures)	3.85	3.85	
Saint John	3.43	1.07	28
Yarmouth	7.27	0.88	23
Windsor	7.16	0.51	13
Halifax	2.49	0.29	7
Charlottetown	2.49	0.18	5
St John's	0.90	0.09	2
Pictou	1.65	0.06	2
Miramichi	− 0.42	− 0.01	0
Residual	7.00	1.00	26
Error		− 0.22	(− 6)

Sources: As for Graph 5.1.
Note: Total growth means growth as estimated in the official figures for the four provinces (New Brunswick, Nova Scotia, Prince Edward Island, and Newfoundland). The residual is the difference between official totals and the sum of tonnage on registry in the eight ports; it is accounted for by the registrars' overestimates of tonnage on registry, as well as by tonnage registered in ports of registry not included here. The growth rate of 7 per cent cannot, therefore, be taken as the growth rate for the sum of tonnage on registry in Digby, Liverpool, Maitland, St Martin's, Sydney, and so on.

sion of an existing shipowning industry. And in three important "transfer trade" ports – Charlottetown, Pictou, and Miramichi – growth rates to 1879 were relatively low. Clearly the discussion of growth must go well beyond the collapse of the export trade in ships.

In Table 5.1, annual growth rates are weighted by each port's share of all tonnage on registry, and this allows an estimate of each port's contribution to total growth in the industry as a whole. The residual is large because of new ports of registry not included here and because of registrars' overestimates of tonnage on registry. The percentage contributions to total growth are, if anything, underestimates.[5] The four major registries accounted for at least 71 per cent of all growth in the industry between 1849 and 1879. This means not that the age of sail bypassed smaller ports and outports in the region but that growth was concentrated in a few major ports and that analysis may focus on these few places.

Growth was concentrated in certain registries and in particular types of vessel. Graph 5.3 shows our estimate of small-vessel fleet size for eight ports. Dividing vessels into tonnage classes creates arbitrary

Graph 5.3
Tonnage on Registry: Vessels under 250 Tons and Vessels over
250 Tons, Excluding Early Transfers (Eight Fleets), 1849–79

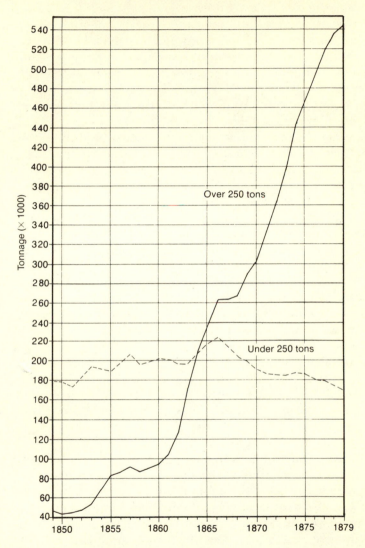

Source: Vessel registries.

distinctions. Obviously vessels under 250 tons served in many different trades, but most were used primarily in coasting, fishing, or long
coastal runs along the western side of the Atlantic Ocean. Most vessels
over 250 tons were used in longer ocean-going voyages. It is reasonable to conclude that coastal shipping and coastal trades had little to
do with overall growth in the shipping industry during the height
of the age of sail. The growth rate for small-vessel fleets – mainly
schooners and brigantines – was very close to zero between 1849 and
1879.[6] Overall growth was entirely the result of growth in the average
size of vessels and the concentration of investment in three-masted
vessels for use in transoceanic passages.

There is an even more important conclusion to be drawn from
Graph 5.3. Official estimates of fleet size mask the reality that many
vessels remained on local registry for a very short time. Vessels sold
to British owners were normally (although not always) re-registered
in their new home ports in the United Kingdom. Official estimates
of fleet size are inflated by tonnage that may have been owned and
registered very briefly in North America. Graph 5.3 offers a revised
fleet size estimate for eight ports, in which tonnage transferred from
local registry within three years has been removed.

Of course there is no way to estimate precisely the total tonnage
that was intended for long-term local use. But the revised estimate is
a much better measure of net capital formation in deep-sea shipping
within the region. It also allows us to time more precisely the rise of
long-term vessel ownership. Growth proceeded rapidly in the 1830s
and 1840s (at about 5 per cent a year), but there was a sudden
acceleration in the 1850s (to 9 per cent a year). Very rapid and
sustained growth followed in the next two decades, so that the growth
rate for retained tonnage was almost 10 per cent a year between 1849
and 1879.[7]

The sudden acceleration of net capital formation in the 1850s is very
important. It occurred despite the transfer of large amounts of tonnage to registry in the United Kingdom. Britain's market for sailing
tonnage had not dried up: total sailing tonnage on registry there grew
by 2.1 per cent a year between 1850 and 1865, and the proportion of
tonnage transferred there from New Brunswick and Prince Edward
Island in the 1850s was a high as in the 1840s (see, above, Table 2.2).[8]
Graph 5.3 tells us that long-term shipowning was increasing very
rapidly in the Maritimes, even before the collapse of the British
market. In the first six years of the 1850s, total ocean-going tonnage
(vessels over 250 tons) retained on local registry more than doubled.
The steep decline in investment in Britain following the Crimean

Graph 5.4

New Investment in Shipping (Gross Tonnage Added to Registries in Eight Major Ports) by Tonnage Class, 1849–1914

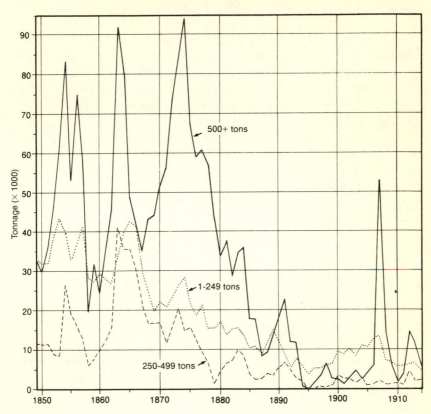

Source: Vessel registries.

War affected shipbuilding in the colonies, but net capital formation in shipping in the Maritimes faltered only slightly in 1858 and 1859 before resuming very rapid growth in the 1860s. In the 1860s, with rapid transfers excluded, the deep-sea fleet trebled in capacity.

The age of sail was essentially a shift from short-term to long-term shipowning. This fact simplifies the task of explaining the "age of sail": the shipowning boom resulted from the longer retention of local assets rather than the shift of capital into something new. The point is confirmed if we refer briefly to another measure of investment behaviour – gross investment, or total new tonnage added to colonial registries in each year (Graph 5.4). There was no acceleration in gross investment in the third quarter of the nineteenth century. In fact the great age of sail coincided with a slowing down in the rate of growth of new investment. Between 1849 and the investment peak in 1874, gross investment grew by slightly less than 1 per cent a year. This was much slower than growth in the first half of the century.[9]

The great shipping boom of the third quarter of the century was achieved not by a significant increase in shipbuilding production or new investment but by a shift toward larger and more durable vessels and longer retention of those vessels. The increasing average life of vessels by itself explains a large proportion – as much as 25 per cent – of the growth in the size of the shipping industry in the third quarter of the century.[10] The collapse of British demand for colonial ships helps to explain the slower growth of shipbuilding output in the third quarter of the century (2.2 per cent a year), but it cannot by itself explain the shift to long-term shipowning, which preceded the collapse of the British market for wooden sailing vessels. In any case, it is difficult to see why the growing disinclination of British owners to purchase colonial ships should have encouraged colonial investors to buy those same ships.

The growth of shipowning in the third quarter of the century seems all the more surprising because it immediately followed repeal of the Navigation Acts. The network of protection that had been part of the earlier rise of shipbuilding was partly dismantled. This does not mean, however, that the great age of sail occurred outside that earlier framework or that it resulted from the comparative advantages of Maritimers operating independent of state intervention. Without the shipbuilding industry created in the first half of the century, there would have been no "age of sail" to follow. Maritime merchants merely took the end products of an established shipbuilding industry and used them for longer periods of time.

In doing so, their decisions were influenced critically by state policies in the colonies, in Britain, and in the United States. Various events in these countries combined to affect international shipping markets in ways that encouraged long-term shipowning in the Maritimes. These included the Crimean War, the Reciprocity Treaty, the American Civil War, and the restructuring of colonial import duties. While external events were not designed to protect colonial shipping, war in Europe and the United States could have the same effect as a protective tariff, by weakening the ability of others to compete, or raising their costs, while stimulating demand for carrying capacity.

And both reciprocity and colonial duties worked deliberately to protect colonial shipping interests. Reciprocity, it was hoped, would increase trade with the United States and so encourage colonial shipowning. And import duties in the Maritime provinces remained low on all inputs to the shipbuilding and shipping industries. The battles between free traders and protectionists in New Brunswick in the 1840s ended with modest protection for artisans and manufacturers, but, as T.W. Acheson has shown, "virtually everything necessary to the lumber industry, the timber trade, the building of wooden ships, and the victualling of crews was admitted free to the New Brunswick market. The latter included mill engines, anchors, chain, canvas, cordage, tackle, felt, sails, spikes, cotton ways, and iron bolts, bars, plates, and sheathing, as well as rigging, tin and copper plate, sheathing paper, grain, flour, meal, bread, meats, fruit, and vegetables."[11] The merchant capitalist used the new tariff structure to limit capital and operating costs in shipping, even if this discouraged opportunities to develop backward linkages from shipbuilding and shipping.

The two decades that followed repeal of the Navigation Act in 1849 saw an unusual combination of circumstances in international shipping markets that gave colonial shipowners not only the advantages that T.W. Acheson has specified, but also certain forms of non-tariff protection. The volume of world trade grew very rapidly – by about 61 per cent in the 1850s and 60 per cent in the 1860s.[12] Tonnage entering British and US ports increased quickly in both decades.[13] At the same time total world carrying capacity – fleets available to transport this growing volume of trade – was expanding less rapidly.[14] Of course technological changes meant that total carrying capacity did not have to keep pace with total trade volumes. But steam power was still relatively unimportant, except in Britain, and the result was that the long-term decline in international freight rates was briefly arrested.[15]

Even more important were changes closer to the colonies themselves. While the European share of world trade remained constant in the 1850s and 1860s, the British and British colonial shares increased significantly. But so also did the US share in world trade.[16] While American trade volumes grew, along with demand for carrying capacity in American ports, the US merchant marine began its extraordinary long-term decline. The reasons are complex, and the impact of the Civil War is only a small part of the story.[17] For the shipowners of the Maritimes, this decline took place at an opportune time: it coincided with falling British demand for colonial sailing ships.

No less important was the nature of American protection of its coastal marine. Despite the colonies' wishes, the Americans did not grant British colonial vessels access to their large coastal trades. Furthermore, American vessel registration policies effectively excluded foreign craft from American registration. Successive US governments failed to protect their national deep-sea marine or to subsidize iron shipbuilding. By this combination of policies, American governments discouraged foreign vessels from entering their coastal trades and directed them instead into US foreign trades.

The effect was an incentive to foreign shipowners far greater than any form of protection that British colonists might have devised for themselves. In the 1840s, over 70 per cent of US imports and exports had been carried in American vessels. In the mid-1850s, there began a steep decline in American carriage of US goods: the proportion fell below 30 per cent in the mid-1860s and under 20 per cent by 1880.[18] In the 1860s and 1870s, the average annual increase in tonnage clearing American seaports was 500,000 tons. Since the American deep-sea fleet was in decline, this represented an enormous and sudden increase in demand for foreign tonnage (see Graph 5.5). Between 1860 and 1880, foreign tonnage clearing American ports grew by 10.3 per cent a year.[19] Not since the Napoleonic Wars had Maritime colonists witnessed such an increase in demand for shipping services in trades to which they had preferential access.

With passage of the Reciprocity Treaty in 1854, colonial vessels did have a specific type of preference in American import trades. The Americans remained protectionist in trade policy, but after 1854 natural products from the British colonies entered the United States duty-free. Most of the fish and timber entering the country went in colonial vessels. As British protection ended and as colonial politicians began to demand reciprocity with the United States, the expected benefits to shipowning became a major argument of colonial free traders and the advocates of reciprocity. "Let us have a free trade with that people [the Americans]," argued the Halifax shipowner Hugh Bell in 1839: "let us go to their ports buying as cheap and selling as dear as we could."[20]

By 1848 Samuel Cunard was writing to Joseph Howe supporting the reduction of tariffs with the United States in order to increase exports and shipping to that country.[21] Of course, what colonists wanted was what motions passed in Nova Scotia's assembly in 1850 proposed: reciprocity which included mutual elimination of restrictions on coastal shipping and admission of colonial-built vessels to American registry.[22] When neither concession was granted in the 1854 treaty, many still expected that the increase in trade would be a sufficient stimulus to shipowning.

Reciprocity was not the only reason for the growth of trade between the Maritimes and the United States, but there is no doubt that increasing numbers of colonial vessels were entering American ports

Graph 5.5
Tonnage Clearing US Seaports, 1857–1900

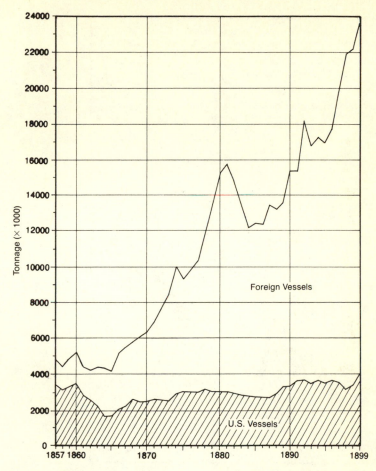

Source: Historical Statistics of the United States (1976), series Q506–17. Domestic trade is excluded; "seaports" means all ports except northern border ports.

in the 1850s (Graphs 5.6 and 5.7). In Prince Edward Island, for instance, there was a shift of locally owned tonnage from coastal to foreign destinations, principally the United States (although this shift clearly began even before Reciprocity).[23] Vessels from the Maritimes still dominated the passage to the West Indies, and the West Indies and US trades were often complementary, since many vessels returning from the West Indies carried cargoes to eastern US ports.

Even before the Reciprocity Treaty, Maritimers expected that

Graph 5.6
Destinations of Tonnage Clearing Nova Scotia Ports, 1840–66

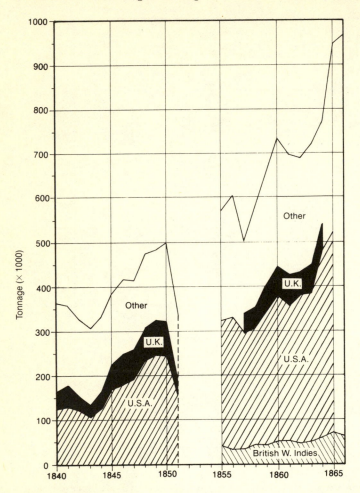

Sources: Colonial Office series 221 (Nova Scotia Blue Books); Nova Scotia, *Journals of the House of Assembly*. Data for 1852–4 are missing.

repeal of the Navigation Acts would help to open American ports to colonial vessels, and this is why so many Haligonians, for instance, supported free trade:

There can be no doubt that it will give an impetus to the carrying trade of the British Provinces ... Vessels can now take a cargo of fish to the West Indies, and instead of returning to this Province either in ballast or in cargo,

Graph 5.7
Destinations of Tonnage Clearing New Brunswick Ports, 1840–66

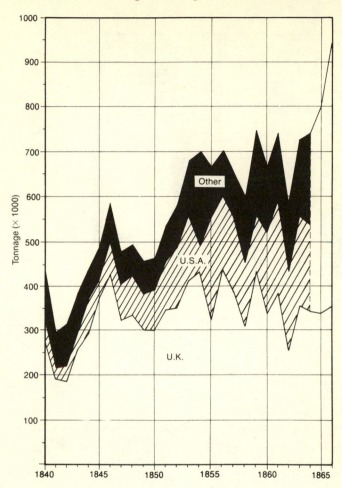

Sources: Colonial Office series 193 (New Brunswick Blue Books); New Brunswick, *Journals of the House of Assembly.*

can if profitable, take a freight for any port of the United States. Generally we think Colonial vessels can be built and sailed cheaper than United States vessels, which will give them an advantage ... The alteration will tend to relieve the commercial depression that prevails.[24]

Colonial vessels were entering eastern American ports in larger numbers than ever before. In the late 1850s and early 1860s many New

Graph 5.8
British and American Shares in Tonnage Entering and Clearing US Ports,
Selected Years, 1860–90

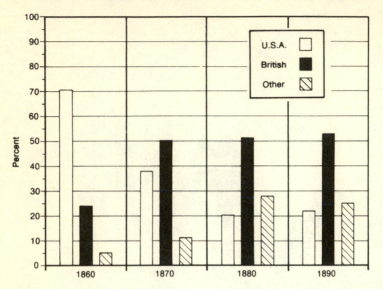

Source: Derek H. Aldcroft, *The Development of British Industry and Foreign Competition 1875–1914* (London, 1968). The US proportion here is slightly different from that in Graph 5.5 because in this graph all US ports are included. "British" includes British colonial tonnage.

Brunswick vessels acquired an unexpected familiarity with eastern American ports: by putting into an American port in autumn or winter, and clearing thence for Liverpool, they could evade the law prohibiting large deck-loads of timber in winter (official figures on New Brunswick exports to the United States are thus inflated in several post-Reciprocity years).[25] For these reasons, colonial shipowners and shipmasters were uniquely situated to learn about the enormous demand for tonnage in American export trades and to respond to that demand.

Between 1860 and 1880 British and British colonial vessels answered the demand for tonnage in the wake of the decline of the American merchant marine. While the American share of entrances and clearances in US ports fell, the share of British-registered vessels increase (Graph 5.8). It is not possible to separate Canadian vessels from British, but the Canadian share was high. By the early 1880s it is likely that almost 40 per cent of the entire Canadian merchant marine was to some extent involved in US export trades. In some eastern American ports 20 per cent of all sailing vessels were Canadian.[26]

Of course the decline of the American merchant marine had effects on shipping markets far beyond the United States itself. Among the trades to feel the effects of the Civil War, for instance, were those to and from both the East Indies and the West Indies. Shippers found themselves paying an insurance premium for "war risks" on goods carried in American hulls, and as a result British or colonial vessels had preference.[27] In the Civil War years the Moran family of St Martin's, New Brunswick, was among the shipowners who committed tonnage to the East Indies trades. And colonial participation in the West Indies carrying trade increased, despite repeal of the Navigation Acts: between 1855 and 1866 tonnage clearing Nova Scotia for the West Indies increased by 5 per cent a year.

The growth of the shipping industry in the "age of sail" was a function of the intersection of colonial supply with American demand and of the collapse in American supply. But this is only the beginning of the story. On both sides of the Atlantic, war and government policy influenced international trade and shipping markets. In the colonies, where tariff policies were calculated to assist shipbuilding and ship-owning, state policy was fully consistent with the interest of merchant capital as it had developed by mid-century. The colonial economies were heavily dependent on a narrow range of exports: in Nova Scotia, fish, agricultural products, and forest products (three-quarters of all exports at mid-century); in New Brunswick, forest products dominated the export statistics (80 per cent at mid-century). The most important manufactured export was ships.

In the 1840s or 1850s, however, the staple industries were reaching the limits to extensive growth, given existing technology. The long-term growth of timber and fish exports had been interrupted in the 1840s. Recovery in the 1850s should not conceal the underlying problems of low productivity, declining rates of return, and trade deficits. The "age of sail" occurred in this context: it was a search for increased mercantile profits and new opportunities in response to declining returns in the traditional export trades.

For a half-century the timber trade had generated sustained demand for shipping services in New Brunswick. Now the timber trade stagnated. Graph 5.9 shows the value of New Brunswick exports of timber, deals, and boards and the declining relative importance of these products after 1849. More telling perhaps was the decline in prices received for forest product exports after the brief recovery in 1853–4 (Graph 5.10). Combined with slow growth in

Graph 5.9
New Brunswick's Total Exports and Exports of Forest Products (Current Values), 1849–69

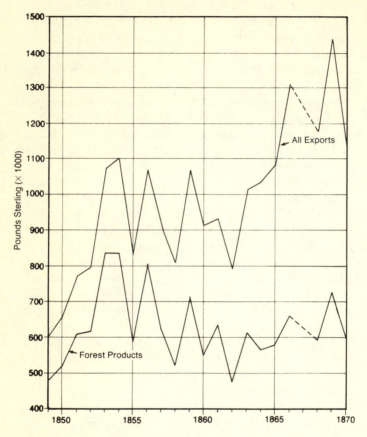

Sources: New Brunswick, *Journals of the House of Assembly,* Appendices; Canada *Sessional Papers,* Tables of Trade and Navigation. After 1860, data are reported in dollars, which are converted here at $4.86 per pound sterling. Exports to Canada before 1867 were insignificant.

volumes shipped, the decline in prices reduced rates of return on capital.

Timber merchants were left with a narrow set of choices: to restore productivity through major technological changes, to discover new markets, or to shift capital into other industries. Attempts at the first two alternatives met with limited success, and "the capacity of the New Brunswick lumber industry to fill adequately the role of leading sector within the regional economy was being progressively weak-

Graph 5.10
Index of New Brunswick Timber Prices, 1830–66

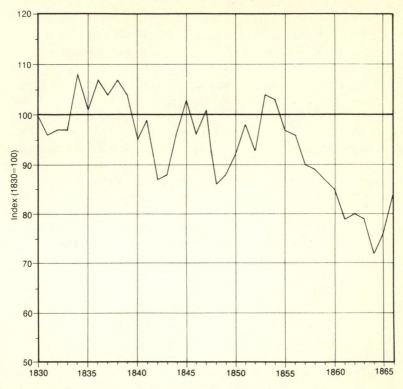

Sources: Colonial Office Series 193 (New Brunswick Blue Books); New Brunswick, *Journals of the House of Assembly,* Tables of Trade and Navigation. The index is based on stated export values of timber (pounds sterling per ton), deals (value per measured feet); and boards (value per measured feet). In the index, each commodity is weighted by its share of the total value of forest product exports.

ened."[28] In these circumstances merchants sought new uses for ships – manufactured commodities that were at once inputs in the timber trade and end products of timber production.

The pressure on timber prices constrained real incomes in a society so heavily dependent on timber exports. New Brunswickers continued to import manufactured goods and agricultural products, and the prices of these imports were rising. Thus the terms of trade moved sharply against New Brunswickers in the 1850s and 1860s. Peter McClelland compared export prices and import prices for New Brunswick and produced an index of net barter terms of trade (essentially the result of dividing export prices by import prices): the index stood at 1.3 for the years 1824–40 and 1.17 for 1840–50. Then export prices fell relative to import prices, and the index fell to 0.89 in the 1850s and 0.86 in the 1860s.[29]

New Brunswickers remained heavily dependent on imported manufactures and foodstuffs. Attempts to encourage import substitution met with limited success. Agricultural output (in constant dollars) grew by 2.8 per cent a year between 1851 and 1871, so that per capita output grew by less than 1 per cent a year.[30] Manufacturing output and employment grew between 1850 and 1870, but more slowly than in the Canadian provinces, for instance, and half of all imports consisted of manufactured goods.[31] All this suggests that New Brunswickers were dissipating an increasing proportion of savings and export earnings in the purchase of imports. Increasing prices for imports in the 1850s and 1860s severely constrained real incomes.

Information for Nova Scotia is less complete, and a terms-of-trade index does not exist. But the long-term trend in the real value of exports per capita was downward.[32] The West Indies trade grew in total value by about 3 per cent a year in the 1850s and 1860s, but, even before Reciprocity, exports to the United States had exceeded exports to the West Indies in value. Despite these apparently favourable trends, industrial employment grew slowly, and by 1870 per capita manufacturing output was much lower even than in New Brunswick.[33] The propensity to import was no less marked than in New Brunswick, and the trade figures indicate a growing trade deficit. Sales of ships (not entered in the export figures) helped to lower the deficit in the 1850s, but as British demand fell in the 1860s the visible trade deficit increased even more than Graph 5.11 indicates.

To the extent that a region's income flows out in the purchase of goods and services, it induces growth elsewhere and limits the opportunity for domestic development.[34] The propensity to import thus limited diversification of the regional economy. No less important, however, was the disposition of earnings from export trades. The relations of production in lumbering, fishing, and agriculture allowed efficient capture of economic surplus by merchants and resulted in highly inequitable distribution of incomes. Cash earnings in fishing and lumbering were meagre, and the truck system, where it existed, allowed a non-wage economy to persist in parts of the timber trade. Pre-capitalist production persisted in fishing and agriculture.

Occupational pluralism meant that cash wages earned in one trade, such as lumbering, merely supplemented the subsistence production of farmers and so allowed the small family farm to survive. A large proportion of agricultural production was for subsistence rather than

Graph 5.11
Nova Scotia's Imports and Exports, 1840–66

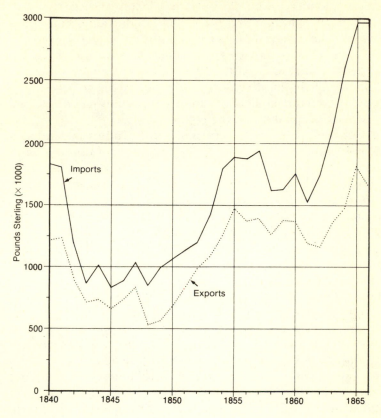

Sources: Colonial Office series 221 (Nova Scotia Blue Books); Nova Scotia, *Journals of the House of Assembly.*

for external markets. Agriculture tended to be labour-intensive; output per worker was low; and production was centred on low-value crops, such as hay, buckwheat, and potatoes, rather than wheat.[35] What little we know of agriculture suggests highly inequitable income distribution and failure of many farm households to gain even subsistence from farming.[36] Thus low per capita incomes in agriculture were combined with a highly inequitable income distribution, severely limiting domestic demand.

In this context the incentive to invest in industrial production existed, but was limited. The regional market was both small and loosely integrated; industrialization would remain small in scale, or it would require successful penetration of external markets. Growth-inducing linkages from staple production were limited: so long as merchants could increase output by adding labour rather than capital, they had little incentive to transform production. While merchants lacked the incentive, fishermen and lumbermen lacked the means to apply new technologies. As a result, the transition to industrial capitalism was slow. That transition was constrained not by the size or nature of the local resource base but by the structure and relations of production in the staple industries as they had developed under merchant capitalism on the colonial frontier.[37]

Faced with declining rates of return in staple production, and with limited opportunities or incentives for import substitution, merchants were not without other alternatives. Of course new industries did appear, and there is plenty of evidence that merchant investors in the third quarter of the century were finding opportunities in services, utilities, and finance as well as in industry. But within staple production and distribution lay another alternative: staple production had helped to create a massive transportation service which was highly mobile and easily diverted from local production into markets elsewhere.

At the same time as falling rates of return and limited domestic opportunities dictated a search for new investment opportunities, the demand for carrying capacity in American export trades grew. Even in local export trades the demand for carrying capacity was growing, disappointing as the returns in particular staple trades might be: the *volume* of trade to and from local ports was expanding rapidly in the 1850s and 1860s (Graphs 5.6 and 5.7). There was still a need and an opportunity to employ one's own vessels in transporting goods on one's own account.[38]

But now the same vessels might be used in carrying American staples, with the further advantage that cargoes were often available in American ports in autumn and winter months. Graph 5.12 presents Douglass North's index of US export freights, and Graph 5.13 shows an index of eastbound North American freights created by Keith Matthews. The decline of the American merchant marine and sustained growth in international trade briefly arrested the long nineteenth-century decline in ocean freight rates. The calculation of marginal utility in shipping changed: potential returns from North Atlantic carrying trades, either American or colonial, were increasing, relative to returns from the rapid sale of vessels in Britain. In these circumstances, Maritime merchant-shipowners retained more of their vessels for the profits to be had in the international carrying trades.

Graph 5.12

Index of US Export Freight Rates (1830 = 100), 1850–79

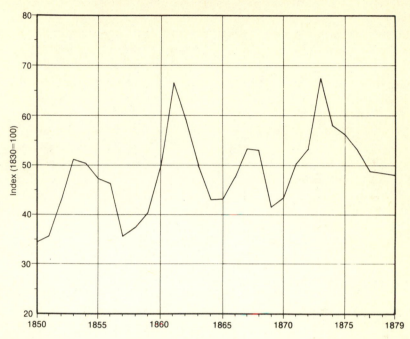

Source: Douglass C. North, "The Role of Transportation in the Economic Development of North America," in *Les Grandes Voies maritimes dans le monde XV–XIX siècles* (Paris, 1965).

In most years between 1850 and 1866 it was even possible to make money carrying timber to Britain. In 1867 the controller of customs for New Brunswick stated that "60s per standard is generally considered by shipowners the turning point below which freights are unremunerative."[39] As Graph 5.14 indicates, the rate for deals from Saint John to Liverpool was above sixty shillings in all but three or four years between 1850 and 1879.

As vessels were being used in distant and foreign carrying trades, a new specialization was emerging in the shipping sector. The vessel chartered to carry goods that were the property not of the vessel owner but of other merchants was a general cargo carrier, to be distinguished from the "trading vessel," in the cargo of which the vessel-owner had an interest. Of course the same vessel might serve both functions at different times, or even on the same voyage. But

Graph 5.13

Index of Eastbound North Atlantic Sailing Ship Freight Rates (1869 = 100), 1855–79

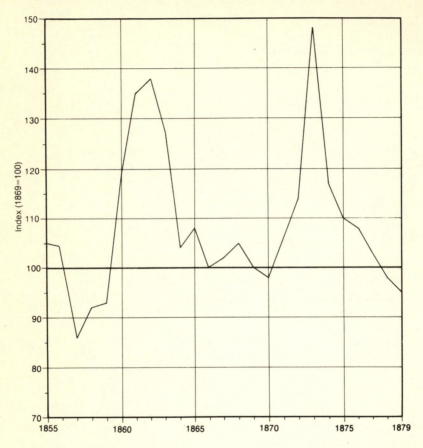

Sources: Keith Matthews compiled the freight rate data from *Mitchell's Maritime Register* and the *New York Maritime Register*, taking the average of the highest and lowest rates quoted in each month. The index is based on cotton (New York–Liverpool); grain (New York–Liverpool); cotton (New Orleans–Liverpool); petroleum (New York–London); grain (New York–Cork for orders); and deals (Saint John–Liverpool). Each commodity is given equal weight.

the deep-sea vessels from the Maritimes in the third quarter of the century were increasingly worked on charters, as general cargo carriers.

The interest of the shipowner changed accordingly: now there could be a difference between the shipowner and the shipper. The shipowner who had no interest in the cargo earned his profit from

Graph 5.14
Deal Freight Rates, Saint John to Liverpool, 1850–79

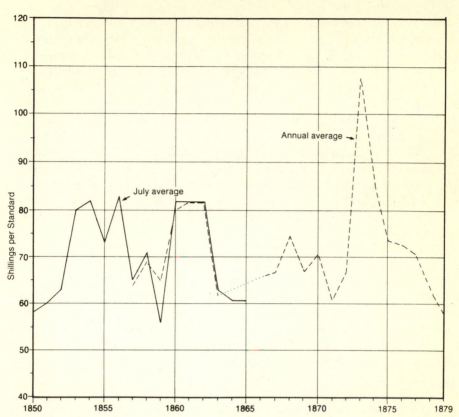

Sources: The July averages are by New Brunswick's controller of customs in his annual reports in New Brunswick, *Journals of the House of Assembly*; the annual averages are from Keith Matthews's collection of timber freights from Saint John to Liverpool. (Matthews took the average of monthly highs and lows and the average of the resulting monthly estimates.)

the freighting charges specified in the charter party; he had a vested interest in a high freight rate. The shipper earned his profit from the difference in price for a commodity from one place to another; he had a vested interest in low freight costs. The different functions implied a degree of specialization and a distinction between shipowners and shippers. This distinction scarcely existed in Atlantic Canada before 1850, because merchants usually combined both activities. But the separation of shipper and shipowner was basic to the fate of the shipping industry in the decades to follow.

Contemporary observers knew that such changes were taking place in their shipping industry, and some commented on them as early as 1850. Some also knew that the shift to long-term shipowning was related to "the emergencies of the times": "It is really gratifying to see our Shipbuilders and Shipowners ... adapting themselves to the emergencies of the times, by building Ships of a very superior description, for the purpose of enabling them to compete with those built in Britain, as well as those in other countries, in the Foreign Trade, which we trust, will prove equally remunerative to them as the North American Colonial Trade, in which they have been formerly engaged for the most part."[40]

In 1853 Lieutenant-Governor Le Marchant wrote that Nova Scotians "enter largely into the carrying trade of other countries" and now compete successfully "with the merchant marine of the neighbouring republic": "During the six years which have elapsed since 1846, the growth of this branch of industry has been most gratifying ... That Nova Scotia is destined, at no distant day, to be one of the largest ship-owning countries in the world, is apparent from the status already achieved."[41] Four years before, the previous governor, Sir John Harvey, had said much the same in arguing that free trade would help Nova Scotian shipowners: since they were already engaged in foreign carrying trades, free trade would help them by expanding the volume of international trade, thereby increasing available freights.[42] Behind these statements lay the assumption that ships were no longer simply inputs in local staple trades but also part of a service industry independent of local staples.

The more perceptive observers also realized that the failure to penetrate US vessel registration laws had, however inadvertently, encouraged shipowning in the Maritimes. William Smith, New Brunswick's controller of customs and registrar of shipping, was also a shipowner in his own right. In 1866 he commented on the increasing participation of New Brunswick vessels in trades between South America and the United States and between the West Indies and the United States:

This carrying trade, in which our medium sized shipping has been much employed of late, is more likely to increase than to diminish, as the Americans cannot compete with us in the production of shipping under present circumstances, and the Government of the United States has shewn as yet no disposition to relax their navigation laws, so as to allow their shipowners to purchase British Colonial built ships, with the privilege of registry in their own country, although many of them would be desirous to do so if their laws would allow it.[43]

Smith welcomed the trend toward long-term shipowning: "New Brunswick is gradually becoming more of a shipowning country than it has been formerly, and this is one of the best features in the prospects of the country." Smith knew that shipowning was serving the same purpose as shipbuilding in previous years – reducing the balance-of-trade deficit: it "has been the means of introducing into the Colony a large amount of gold or its equivalent in exchange, to pay for our heavy imports during the year."[44]

Smith also connected the expansion of shipbuilding and shipowning in the early 1860s with falling rates of return in the timber trade: "The Shipbuilders in New Brunswick, as a general rule, did a good business last year, and many of them are now beginning to own vessels ... In the very depressed state of the deal trade ... Shipbuilding operations have been the means of bringing money into the country and producing employment for a large portion of the population."[45] The barques and ships of the Atlantic colonies were as much a part of the local economy as ever before. But now they operated in wider freight markets and were no longer a water-borne extension of the local merchant's warehouse.

As the deep-sea vessels of the Maritimes moved beyond the local export and import trades, their movements in the international shipping markets became very complex. For one thing, the number of individual units of production in this industry was very large. Even if we were to study only barques and ships from four major ports (Saint John, Yarmouth, Halifax, and Windsor) in the last half of the century, we should be looking at 1,920 vessels. On average vessels made about two complete voyages in a year and survived for thirteen or fourteen years. Even for this sample of deep-sea ships, therefore, the total number of voyages is likely to be more than 50,000.

The problem of describing vessel utilization becomes even more complex if one wishes to describe seasonal choices of trade route or the movement of vessels between trade routes. There were about 720 ocean-going vessels from the four major ports in operation in 1875; within the North Atlantic alone, each vessel had a choice between a dozen major trade routes and about forty major destinations for its first passage in that year – and the same range of choices on its second passage. The total combination of passages that constitutes the market activity in this industry becomes a very large number indeed.

It is commonplace to emphasize the diminishing number of trade routes in which sailing ships competed with steamers by the 1870s. While in some trades, particularly in the North Atlantic, steam was rapidly displacing sail, the total range of ports and routes in which sailing vessels still operated was remarkably large. For Canadian vessels, which moved increasingly between the North Atlantic and ports in South America, Australia, and the Far East, the market range was actually expanding.

The geographic dispersal of trading activity was possible only because managing owners in the Maritimes enjoyed access to the necessary market information. This information was not universally accessible in the Maritimes. In the coastal trades and in the local staple trades, the information on available cargoes, freight rates, and market conditions was more readily available in local newspapers and by word of mouth.

Those who would operate successfully in more distant markets required access to the telegraph, that indispensable means of communication between managing owners and shipmasters in distant ports and between owners and distant ship brokers. The arrival of the electric telegraph at mid-century, connecting ports in the Maritimes with eastern US ports, was almost a prerequisite for the penetration of American export trades. Successful operation also required information on freight rates, current and anticipated, in ports around the world; information on port charges, demurrage rates, insurance rates, labour costs, and much else; and connections with distant brokers who arranged charters, acting as liaison between shipowners and shippers.

The cost of this information was small by comparison with the cost of capital invested in shipowning, but it was not insignificant, for it helped to concentrate business in the hands of merchants. These were the men who had access to the telegraph, to the foreign shipping press, and to distant brokers in American and British ports. These were the men who by virtue of past experience, and family and trade connections, inherited the necessary access to information and the training required to use it.

The data in Table 5.2 suggest how far the ocean-going fleets of the Maritimes moved beyond their home ports after 1860. Few voyages began in British North America, and few ended there. The overwhelming majority began in Britain, Europe, or the United States, and most vessels departed for ports on either side of the North Atlantic. Clearly the shipping industry had moved well beyond its original base in the staple trades of the North American colonies. Just as clearly, shipowners minimized the complexity of vessel operation by clinging to the familiar: their vessels remained very largely within the major shipping markets of the North Atlantic.

Though the knowledge required of managing owners was vast, most voyages commenced from a limited range of ports. The 8,728

Table 5.2
Starting Ports and Intended Destinations by
Region (Four Major Fleets), 1863–1914

Region	Starting Ports (% of Total)	Intended Destinations (% of Total)
British North America	11.2	16.6
Britain	55.5	14.4
Europe	20.5	4.1
United States	12.5	43.0
West Indies	0	5.3
South America	0.1	10.8
Africa	}	1.1
India		2.2
Far East		1.6
Australia/ New	} 0.1	
Zealand		0.8
Other		0.1

Sources: Crew Agreement sample for fleets of Saint John, Yarmouth, Windsor, and Halifax, from Crew Agreements, Maritime History Archive, Memorial University of Newfoundland. Steamers and auxiliary steamers are excluded. See notes 48 and 49.
Note: The total number of voyages for the four fleets was 18,265. Missing cases (excluded from the above) were 1,862 (intended destinations) and 19 (starting ports).

voyages in the Saint John sample, for instance, began in no less than 269 different ports around the world. But the fleet was not nearly so dispersed as this number suggests: three ports – Liverpool, Saint John, and New York – accounted for 42 per cent of all voyage starts, and ten ports accounted for 64 per cent.[46] The range of intended destinations was much broader – 446 ports. Once again there was concentration on a limited range of ports: twenty ports, most of them in Britain or the United States, accounted for the majority of intended destinations.[47] Many vessels cleared for a "port for orders" on the American seabord – a place where the master could receive instructions by telegraph about his destination or his next charter.

Information on voyage patterns confirms the importance of export trades from the eastern and southern United States. In the period of rapid growth in the industry, US ports were critical to the growth of chartering activity by Maritimes fleets.[48] There was a pattern to the dispersal of shipping activity, beginning with increased movement into US ports. The pattern was one of gradual movement from the British North America – United Kingdom nexus, into a broader North Atlantic specialization, based on British North America, the United States, and Britain.

Map 5.1 suggests the importance of passages between British North America, the eastern United States, and Britain in the period of rapid growth in the industry, up to 1878. When the industry began to decline in the years from 1879 to 1890, a more diversified trading pattern emerged, but the concentration on major North Atlantic routes remained (Map 5.2). To the older triangular nexus was added the increasingly important United States – northern European trades. Although relatively more tonnage was being deployed outside the North Atlantic, the proportion of all tonnage working the six major North Atlantic trade routes actually increased.[49] Not until the period after 1890 (Map 5.3) did a significant proportion of a much smaller industry move beyond these major North Atlantic trades.

Although historians have often stressed the dispersal of sailing ships into long-distance ocean trades in the last decades of the nineteenth century, the geographic concentration and specialization of shipping activity are equally striking. The specialization of Maritime shipowners was very different from that of their counterparts in the United Kingdom. Although British vessels entered the major North Atlantic trades, they remained more often on the other side of the Atlantic, relying on the huge British–European trades in which Canadian vessels rarely appeared. Canadian shipowners deployed their vessels in trades where there was still considerable demand for sailing tonnage. But they were being selective, after all, and choosing specific trades and cargoes from a plethora of global opportunities. Their choices were more like those of Norwegian than of British shipowners.

In entering the major North Atlantic trades, shipowners involved themselves in a paradox that was important to their industry: as shipping expanded in the 1860s and 1870s, its linkages with the economy of the Maritime provinces decreased. The vital link with shipbuilding remained, of course, and ship construction depended on local timber as its single most important input. But shipowners more than ever depended on freight markets rather than on returns from the sale of cargoes. Shipowners in the Maritimes were vulnerable, as never before, to fluctuations in demand for tonnage in the

Map 5.1
Passages by Four Major Fleets, 1863–78

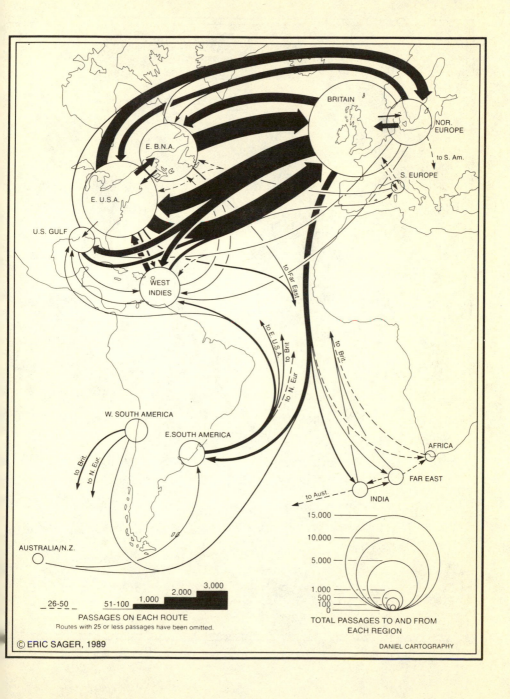

BRITAIN

NOR.
EUROPE

to S. Am.

S. EUROPE

E. B.N.A.

E. U.S.A.

U.S. GULF

WEST
INDIES

to Far East

to E.U.S.A.

to Brit.

to N. Eur.

to Brit.

W. SOUTH AMERICA

E.SOUTH AMERICA

AFRICA

to Brit.

to N. Eur.

FAR EAST

to Aust.

INDIA

AUSTRALIA/N.Z.

15.000
10.000
5.000
1.000
500
100
0

26-50   51-100   1,000   2,000   3,000

PASSAGES ON EACH ROUTE
Routes with 25 or less passages have been omitted.

TOTAL PASSAGES TO AND FROM
EACH REGION

© ERIC SAGER, 1989

DANIEL CARTOGRAPHY

Map 5.2
Passages by Four Major Fleets, 1879–90

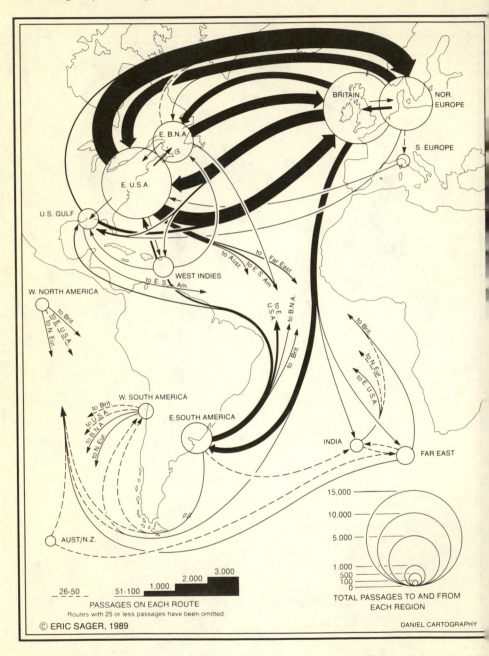

W. NORTH AMERICA

to Brit.
to E. U.S.A.
to N. Eur.

W. SOUTH AMERICA

to Brit.
to U.S.A.
to B.N.A.
to N. Eur.

E. SOUTH AMERICA

AUST/N.Z.

BRITAIN

NOR. EUROPE

S. EUROPE

E. B.N.A.

E. U.S.A.

U.S. GULF

WEST INDIES

to Aust.
to Far East
to E S Am
to E S. Am.
to E U.S.A.
to B.N.A.
to Brit.

INDIA

FAR EAST

to Brit.
to N. Eur.
to E. U.S.A.

15,000

10,000

5,000

1,000
500
100
0

TOTAL PASSAGES TO AND FROM
EACH REGION

3,000

2,000

1,000

_ 26-50   51-100

PASSAGES ON EACH ROUTE
Routes with 25 or less passages have been omitted.

© ERIC SAGER, 1989

DANIEL CARTOGRAPHY

Map 5.3
Passages by Four Major Fleets, 1891–1912

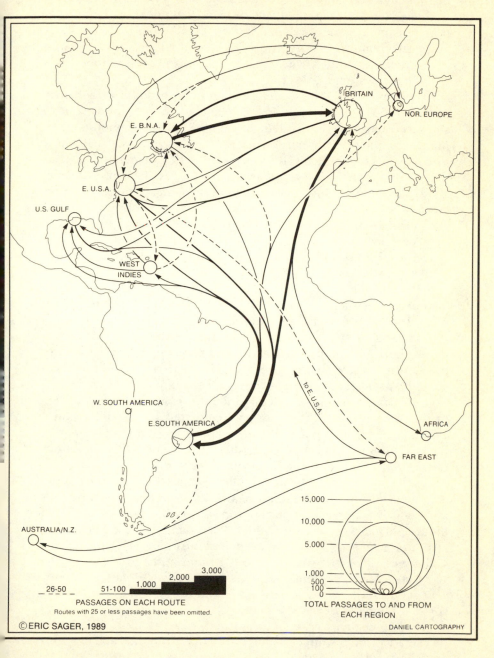

BRITAIN

NOR. EUROPE

E. B.N.A.

E. U.S.A.

U.S. GULF

WEST
INDIES

W. SOUTH AMERICA

E.SOUTH AMERICA

AFRICA

FAR EAST

to E.USA

AUSTRALIA/N.Z.

15,000

10,000

5,000

1,000
500
100
0

26-50   51-100   1,000   2,000   3,000

PASSAGES ON EACH ROUTE
Routes with 25 or less passages have been omitted.

TOTAL PASSAGES TO AND FROM
EACH REGION

©ERIC SAGER, 1989

DANIEL CARTOGRAPHY

international carrying trades. A collapse in demand in those markets did not by itself doom the Canadian industry to extinction. But declining demand would narrow the choices of investors: either they must remain in the international market with new types of technology and management, or they must reintegrate their industry with national export trades, where they might enjoy preferential access and other advantages.

Deep-sea sailing ships were no longer the product of a British enclave industry. Yet even at the height of the age of sail, these ships were not fully integrated with the rest of the economy of the Maritimes, and their connection to local export trades was weakening. The interests of merchant shipowners led to deployment of substantial portions of their capital far beyond the shores of Atlantic Canada. By deploying maritime capital in this way, merchant shipowners created the "golden age" of sail, when Maritimers ventured far into the international shipping markets of the world. And in so doing they loosened their industry's links with the colonial economy and conceived the first of the conditions in which the shipping industry would decline.

The decline in demand began in the 1870s. The best measure is offered by indices of freight rates, although the choice of index is difficult and there are striking inconsistencies between existing indices. There is no doubt that Isserlis underestimated the peak in rates in 1873 and missed the recovery in the late 1880s. The other indices are to be preferred, and that of Norwegian shipowners' rates is relevant, because Norwegians operated sailing vessels in large numbers in the same North Atlantic trades frequented by Canadian ships. Despite the differences between the three series, there is no resisting the conclusion that in most years after 1873 owners of sailing ships confronted a sharp decline in freight rates (Graph 5.15).

The decline in freight rates resulted in part from the increasing volume of steam-powered tonnage available for charter in the 1870s and 1880s. Steam propulsion and iron construction strongly affected the freight markets of the period.[50] The opening of the Suez Canal at the end of 1869 suddenly permitted steamers to compete with sailing vessels on the route between Britain and India. During the 1870s steamers were competing with sailing vessels in the same American export trades – particularly grain and cotton – in which so many colonial sailing vessels had entered.

These coincidences cannot be ignored, however much their effect on Canadian shipowning may have been oversimplified and exaggerated, both at the time and in much historical writing since then. The

Graph 5.15
Selected Freight Rate Indices, 1869–99

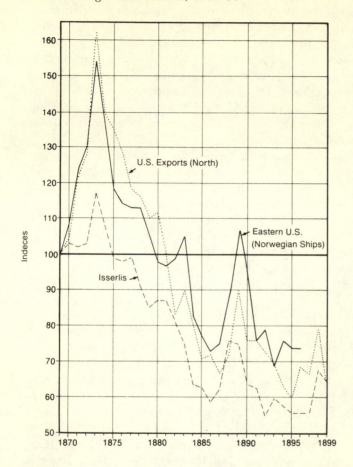

Sources: L. Isserlis, "Tramp Shipping Cargoes and Freights," *Journal of the Royal Statistical Society* (1938), reprinted in Mitchell and Deane, *Abstract of British Historical Statistics* (1962), 224; North, "The Role of Transportation," 236; Lewis R. Fischer and Helge W. Nordvik, "Maritime Transport and the Integration of the North Atlantic Economy, 1850–1914," in Wolfram Fischer, R. Marvin McInnis, and Jurgen Schneider, *The Emergence of a World Economy 1500–1914: Papers of the IX International Congress of Economic History* (Wiesbaden, 1986), 537. North's index includes all types of vessel; the index is converted to the base 1869 = 100 for ease of comparison. The Norwegian index is based on annual reports from Norwegian shipowners to the Norwegian Central Bureau of Statistics; the overwhelming majority of that country's vessels were sailing ships.

relationship between the advance of steam and the decline in demand for sailing ships was not simple; for many years sailing ships continued to find cargoes in many North Atlantic, European and American coastal, and long-distance trades.[51] But there was certainly a coincidence between the movement of freight rates and the pattern of investment in shipping in Maritime Canada. The long-term decline in new investment in shipping began in the mid-1870s, just as freight rates resumed their long-term decline (compare Graphs 5.15 and 5.18). The long-term decline in *net* investment in ocean-going shipping began in 1880 or 1881 – just as US export freight rates dipped back to the levels of the 1850s.

Which investments were most vulnerable to a decline in international demand? The larger vessels – those of 250 tons and more – had been deployed most often in the international carrying trades. The collapse of the shipping industry was essentially a decline of investment in these vessels, and again the coincidence seems to confirm the primary importance of a collapse in demand, as measured by declining freight rates. In the eight major fleets of the Atlantic region, ocean-going tonnage on registry (larger vessels) declined at an annual average of 6.1 per cent a year between 1879 and 1899 (graph 5.16). The coastal fleets (vessels under 250 tons) declined at a much slower rate – 1.9 per cent a year. Because of the steep and rapid decline of the ocean fleets, in the first decade of the twentieth century the shipping industry of the Atlantic region was smaller than it had been in the 1840s. By 1910 the three Maritime provinces possessed less than a third of all Canadian tonnage. Even if Canada still ranked 10th or 11th among the world's maritime nations, the deep-sea fleets of the Atlantic region of Canada had been reduced to insignificance.

The investment collapse was very steep in precisely those places where shipowners had committed themselves to freight markets outside their own region. Where four major registries had accounted for most of the growth of the industry up to 1879, the same four registries accounted for an even greater share of the decline (Table 5.3). All fleets except that of Newfoundland followed similar patterns of decline, although in Windsor the decline was delayed by a decade (Graph 5.17).

A glance at the pattern of gross investment seems to confirm the direct connection between shipping investments and international freight rates (Graph 5.18). Investment in larger vessels began to decline in 1875, and by the mid-1880s, when freight rates were 40 per cent below the average level of the 1860s, new investment in ocean shipping had almost disappeared. A slight recovery followed

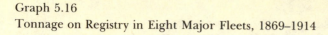

Graph 5.16
Tonnage on Registry in Eight Major Fleets, 1869–1914

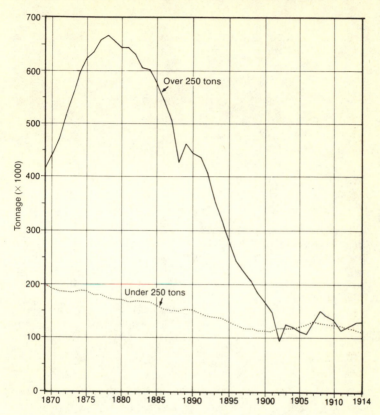

Sources: Vessel registries of Charlottetown, Halifax, Miramichi, Pictou, Saint John, St John's, Windsor, and Yarmouth. Since the transfer and rapid sale of vessels to the United Kingdom were not so important as in earlier decades, vessels transferred within three years are not excluded from the total for larger vessels, as they were in Graph 5.3.

closely on the rise in freight rates in 1889–90. Only in 1907, when a few large steamers were registered in Saint John mainly for the coasting trades, was there another small recovery in investment. Many of the new vessels of 500 tons and more registered after 1900 were not intended for regular use in deep-sea trades at all, and so the decline in ocean shipping was even more rapid than the graphs suggest.[52]

The coincidences are appealing – the rise of steam and the decline of sail; the decline in international demand and the collapse of Cana-

Table 5.3
Annual Growth Rates and Port Contributions to Total Decline, 1879–99

Port	Annual Growth (%)	Weighted Growth (%)	% Contribution to Total Decline
All (official figures)	−4.15	−4.15	
Saint John	−6.69	−1.65	40
Yarmouth	−7.38	−0.98	24
Halifax	−7.24	−0.46	11
Charlottetown	−6.15	−0.24	6
Windsor	−1.72	−0.21	5
Pictou	−6.79	−0.21	5
Miramichi	−5.49	−0.08	2
St John's	−0.21	−0.02	0
Residual	−1.67	−0.40	10
Error		+0.10	(−3)

Sources: Canada, Sessional Papers, 1880–1900; Newfoundland, Journals of the House of Assembly; Crew Agreement Sample. Official figures also appear in Keith Matthews, "The Shipping Industry of Atlantic Canada," in Keith Matthews and Gerald Panting, eds., Ships and Shipbuilding in the North Atlantic Region (St John's: Maritime History Group, 1978), Appendix 1.
Note: The growth rate of −4.15 per cent is based on official figures for tonnage on registry in the three Maritime provinces and in Newfoundland. Weighted growth means the growth rate weighted by each port's share of total tonnage from 1879 to 1899.

dian supply. In addition, they serve not only to explain but also to exonerate: the golden age of sail came to an end because of forces outside the region and beyond the control of anybody in the region. But this kind of explanation can serve us no longer.

Precisely because the patterns of investment in shipping are unravelled here in such detail, we may now test the coincidence between declining freight rates and declining investment in shipping. The coincidence, it turns out, is not very close. There is a correlation between freight rates and ocean-going tonnage on registry in the Maritimes in the last decades of the century, but it is weak,[53] mainly because investment in shipping collapsed, while freight rates merely declined. Even if we measure the decline in freight rates from the 1873 peak, the decline was between 2 and 3 per cent a year. This was serious enough – but it cannot by itself explain a 6 per cent annual decline in tonnage on registry. Still less can it explain the collapse of new investment in large vessels: new investment in vessels of 500 tons and more fell by an annual average of 15.5 per cent a year after

Graph 5.17
Estimated Tonnage on Registry by Port, 1869–1914

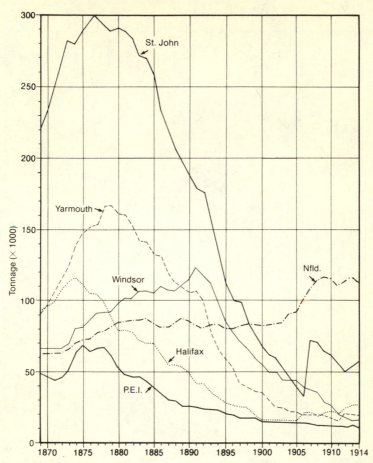

Source: Vessel registries.

1874.[54] Furthermore, if the industry were able to cut costs and so improve productivity, the decline in net returns need not have been so steep as the decline in gross revenues. We know that Canadian sailing ships were cutting operating costs in the last decades of the century: to the extent that this was occurring, further doubt is cast on the importance of declining freight rates.

More serious, however, industries may expand even where gross revenues are declining, particularly in transportation, where the benefit to other industries that transportation serves may outweigh

Graph 5.18
New Investment in Shipping (Gross Tonnage Added to Registries in Eight
Major Ports) by Tonnage Class, 1869–1914

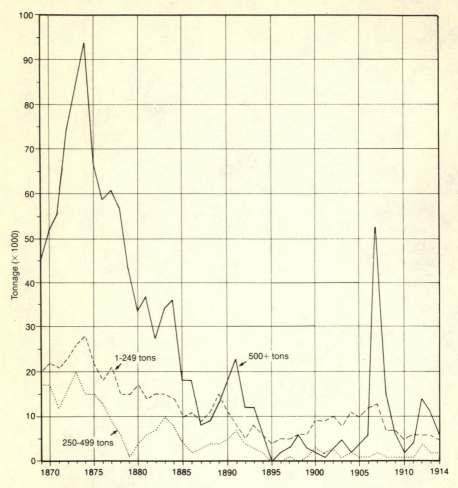

Source: Vessel registries.

losses in the industry itself. There is nothing particularly surprising
about the continuing expansion of world shipping capacity in the
last decades of the nineteenth century, even during the so-called
depression in world trade. Between 1870 and the end of the century
world tonnage increased by about 56 per cent.[55] The Maritime Canadian experience was out of step with that of all major maritime

countries, with the possible exception of the United States.[56] The decline in freight rates does not explain the Canadian anomaly.

The old argument – that falling demand for sailing ships doomed the Maritimes shipping industry – founders under the weight of evidence and logic. The fact is that world sailing ship capacity was greater in 1910 than it had been in 1850.[57] The transition from sail to steam and other forms of power was slow, and sailing ships operated in many international trades into the twentieth century. In the 1870s – when new investment in sailing ships began its steep decline in the Maritimes – the world's sailing fleets were still growing, and at the end of the decade over 70 per cent of world tonnage lay under the decks of sailing vessels. In the 1880s, when Maritimers were dismantling their industry, Norwegians expanded their sailing fleets, in part by purchasing used Canadian tonnage. In the last two decades of the century, sailing fleets in the Maritimes declined three times as quickly as did world sailing tonnage.

Falling demand for sailing ships merely begs the interesting question: if profits in international carrying trades did at some point require adoption of new technology, why did Maritime Canadians fail to make the transition? Falling rates of return normally prompt a search for new technology or new markets. Norwegian shipowners – whose industry was similar to that of Maritimers in composition and markets – made both responses, and their shift to steam vessels was particularly rapid after 1900. Elsewhere in Canada other shipowners took part in the transition to industrial capitalism. The Maritime Canadian anomaly remains unexplained.

International demand, particularly American, helped to explain the rise of shipping in the third quarter of the century. The age of sail was also a product of the opportunity structure within the domestic economy of the Maritimes. It was an outgrowth of the previous experience of merchant capitalists and their quest for profits within an export-based economy whose channels of distribution and exchange they owned or controlled. Just as the rise of the shipping industry occurred within this context, so did the decline of the industry. The golden age of sail in the Canadian Maritimes was doomed not by the inevitable advance of technology or by impersonal market forces but by Maritimers themselves.

CHAPTER SIX

Capital, Labour, and Profits

In the autumn of 1863 John B. Dickie and his brother James purchased eight shares each in a new brigantine, the *Sharon* of Halifax.[1] "She is a splendid ship – faithfully built – and has, I think, a first rate captain."[2] John Dickie's pleasure in his new vessel did not last. It took more than a sound hull and a good master to survive in so risky a business, and the *Sharon* was not a lucky ship. She made little money for her owners, and in 1870 she was lost at sea somewhere off the east coast of the United States.

But these were good times for the merchant-shipowners of Nova Scotia, and John Dickie knew that his other shipping investments would make up for the *Sharon's* losses: "Though not very fortunate or profitable, yet it is not so bad as might have been ... I feel thankful myself that it is no worse. It is hard to lose money, but sometimes we can't help it: and I suppose it's no use crying over spilt milk. Unlimited success would not be good for us."[3] From the merchant-shipowner operating softwood ships in international trades, this is a startling admission: it is hard to lose money, he says, and we can afford the occasional loss. Dickie, a dry-goods merchant in Truro, Nova Scotia, went on to state the simple and pragmatic optimism of merchant capital in the age of sail: "There is quite a stir now in ships and shipping – and prospects of good business in freights."[4]

What exactly did profit or "good business" mean? An answer to this question is essential, since profit, or the expectation of profit, was basic to the rise of the shipping industry and to its decline. But the measurement of profit is bedevilled by problems of definition and of evidence. Obviously profit cannot mean simply the amount of money that a business accumulates through its operations. In simple accounting terms, gross profit is total earnings minus payments for labour, raw materials, and other inputs. Net profit is total earnings minus all costs, including the cost of depreciation, the wear and tear incurred during production. With sailing ships this latter cost is particularly important. This does not exhaust the definition of profit, since still other costs may be incurred in production.

When John Dickie said that it was hard to lose money in ships, it is implicit throughout that he might have been doing something else with his money. In order to put money in a ship, Dickie lost an opportunity to put his money in another venture, and this forgone opportunity is also a type of cost (known as opportunity cost). Furthermore, if profit comes in the form of a sum of money, the value of that money may change over time: if Dickie's vessel earned a profit of one thousand dollars within her first year, this may be worth much more to him than the same sum earned in her third year. Thus the passing of time may itself incur a cost, and a "true" profit may be the one that includes a discount for time preference.

The historian's problem is not simply to decide which measure of profit should be applied. It goes much deeper: we do not know what Dickie meant by "good business," because he and his fellow merchants did not specify which costs they included in their own assessment of their investments. And it is entirely possible that among their earnings were non-pecuniary benefits that remain unspecified and defy measurement. When William D. Lawrence invested over $100,000 in the largest wooden ship built in the Maritimes in the nineteenth century, he expected a large money return on this investment, but he was also investing in the *William D. Lawrence,* an object of prestige and even of beauty. It is, after all, much easier to feel affection for a sailing ship than for a warehouse: "There was a time, *in my memory,* when merchants prided themselves in charming gallies they sent to sea; they saw and admired them with a lover's eye, and did not reckon on *much gain* on them, merely as a *ship-account.*"[5] Any measurement of profit in money terms must begin by admitting that it is only a partial measure of the rewards of possession.

This leads directly to another problem of particular concern to the historian. Can profits, however, measured, tell us anything at all about investment choices? It is, after all, the rise and the decline of investment in shipping that we wish to understand. But an industry may expand even when its nominal profits are declining: it may confer a return on another industry that it serves, or investors may expect future returns to be very different from present ones.

Despite these problems, neo-classical economics assumes a direct relationship between investment and returns: given pervasive scarcity and the desire to maximize utility, human beings will invest in whatever capital stock has the highest rate of return.[6] To predict investment behaviour – or to explain such behaviour in the past – it is necessary to define the investor's utility function and to discover which activities exhibited high returns. The risk of a circular argument is obvious enough: if people put their money into railway stock, then railways must have had high profits, and the conclusion follows from one's assumptions rather than from evidence.

But even if the evidence for high profits in railways is sound, consequential investment in railways assumes that the investors knew about those high profits. It is entirely possible that imperfect information prevents investors from perceiving high rates of return where they do exist or persuades them that returns are high where in fact they are low. Information and knowledge are differentially distributed between individuals, social classes, and regions. Thus, to assume a dependent relationship between profit and subsequent investment may beg the interesting questions: how was information transmitted, and how did non-economic factors condition the environment in which investors made their choices?

The discussion of profit in these terms may lead to yet deeper misunderstanding. To know the net profit of a firm in any given year is to know very little. By what measure is one to judge whether that sum is large or small? Perhaps the most sensible answer is to compare net profit with investment: what total profit came from what investment? The result is a ratio, or rate of return, which is simply net profit (after depreciation) as a percentage of capital employed in a business. This measure allows comparison between firms and industries.

In neo-classical economic analysis, however, the discussion may obscure as much as it reveals. The standard by which profit is measured is capital, narrowly defined as net assets used in production, and the purpose is to measure the relative efficiency of capital. The measure has a particular meaning, but to measure profit against capital is to pretend that those profits are returns to capital or returns to the stock of goods used in production. This obscures the fact that inanimate objects do not produce value by themselves. It obscures the historical reality that profits are also returns to the labour embedded in machines and to the labour power used in operating machines. To the historian who wishes to be sensitive to these issues, the "rate of return on capital" is at best a misnomer. At worst it is obfuscation, for it may obscure the fact that profit comes from a historically specific set of social relations, of which capital itself is part.

Marx's concept of surplus value avoids such obfuscation by incorporating labour power into the definition: surplus value is the difference between the new value produced by labour in the process of production and the value of labour power employed in production. For Marx, profit was "the same thing as surplus-value, save in a mystified form," and at the level of the firm profit was a subset of surplus value, or that part of social surplus-value that was appropriated by each capitalist firm.[7] Critical to Marx's analysis was a further concept, the rate of profit (the ratio of surplus value to the sum of constant and variable capital used in production). At the macro-economic level, the secular tendency of the rate of profit to fall is basic to his analysis of capital and its inherent tendency to crisis.[8]

Problems of definition and theory notwithstanding, there is a point to the analysis of profits in the shipping industry. Profit, after all, is the driving force of capitalist activity. It can be measured, within specified limits. The principal measurement used here is the estimate of rate of return, or the ratio of net profit after depreciation to capital employed. This measure is easily understood, but, more important, it allows comparison of profits between industries and sectors. In no sense do we understand this rate to measure the returns to capital alone; indeed, what we are measuring is a subset of surplus value.

This measure is also likely to approximate the merchant-shipowner's own understanding of his profits. As Marx himself noted, the individual capitalist was interested only in comparing "the excess value which he receives from selling his commodities, to the total capital advanced for the production of these commodities"; he was not interested in the more complex ratios of surplus value to the particular components of his capital, and "it is actually in his interest to disguise these particular ratios and inner connections."[9] Thus the simple ratio of net profit to capital is likely to approximate what the shipowner himself observed and at this level may help explain his investment choices.

Analysis may not end, however, with profit or with the conscious decisions of the shipowning investor. The profits that he observed were still part of an economic structure whose evolution was not contingent on conscious decisions of individual capitalists. Profit levels, defined in this way, were an integral part of the economic structure that constrained and limited the choices of investors. If, for instance, very high rates of return existed in shipping, then this does help to explain subsequent investment in the same industry, even if non-pecuniary rewards also existed. If the rate of return fell – or the rate of profit, in Marx's sense – then an industry (or an entire sector) was probably entering a crisis, experienced most acutely by those who observed the falling rates in their ledgers. Knowing that profits were declining, we should be better able to understand the responses of capital and its subsequent movement within the opportunity structure of the economy.

If, in contrast, rates of return remained high relative to other industries, and yet capital was withdrawn and placed elsewhere, then one hypothesis may be rejected and another must be tested: that the movement of capital had less to do with objective measurement of existing rates of return, and more with investors' expectations of future returns in different industries and that this assessment must have been contingent on the existing structure of information about present and future returns on investment.

It is unlikely that non-pecuniary considerations had much to do with mercantile investment in sailing ships in Atlantic Canada. Shipowners were interested in freight markets, and surviving records suggest that they were well informed about those markets. By the 1850s they knew about the current demand for shipping in eastern US ports and about the expansion of shipping volumes between their colonies and the US. In the late 1850s, when the rate of return on railway stocks was slightly under 10 per cent, and when New York short-term money rates were slightly over 8 per cent, American clipper ships were earning over 10 per cent of the value of their capital even in a poor year and over 50 per cent in good years.[10]

Of course, clippers were being paid a premium for their speed, but their rate of return is based on a much higher average unit of capital than British colonists deployed. Maritimers knew about the American clippers, and they were certainly aware of the potential for profit in deep-sea sailing ships: in the 1850s and 1860s, in the wake of repeal of the Navigation Acts, they saw many more foreign ships entering colonial ports than before. They believed that Norwegians, for instance, could make very good profits because of their low running costs and low wage costs, "owing to the frugal habits of their people."[11] In these circumstances, as New Brunswick's registrar of shipping pointed out, local shipowners saw well-built wooden vessels as "a profitable investment" and thought that they would be able "to compete in the carrying trade with the ships of any country." By 1863 the registrar was saying that shipowners in New Brunswick were "more numerous and wealthy" than ever before.[12]

The evidence that shipowners were becoming "more wealthy" comes partly from the testimony of contemporaries. It comes also from our estimates of shipping profits, using two methods. The first method is a reconstruction of profits for large numbers of vessels based on a range of sources. To estimate gross revenue, we take known quantities of specific cargoes carried by Canadian vessels, and we apply current freight rates.

Cargoes and quantities are taken from the United Kingdom's bills of entry: this indispensable source lists vessels by name and by port of registry as they entered United Kingdom ports and states cargo details for each vessel. We have taken all vessels registered in the major ports in the Maritimes (Saint John, Halifax, Yarmouth, and Windsor) that entered Liverpool and London in 1863, 1873, and 1883. The bills of entry give us cargoes for these vessels, but not the freight rates. From the shipping newspapers we take the freight rate for each cargo that was current at the time when the vessel was likely to have begun its passage to Liverpool or London. From these sources we derive estimates of gross revenues per passage for vessels in major trades to the United Kingdom.[13] Instead of reproducing all gross revenue calculations here, we include samples in Appendix A. Appendix B summarizes the gross revenue estimates for major cargoes in the three years selected.[14]

It is not possible to apply this technique to all passages by Maritime Canadian vessels, but the sample used here is a fair representation of the major freight-earning passages in the North Atlantic. In the 1860s and 1870s the following commodities accounted for about 65 per cent of all entrances into Liverpool and London by vessels of the four major ports: deals from New Brunswick; cotton from the United States; grain from Montreal or the eastern United States; petroleum from the eastern United States. Our estimates of profits are based mainly on the freights earned from these commodities. Most earnings came from eastbound cargoes, but there were occasional westbound cargoes, and vessels could earn something even by carrying ballast.

Furthermore, by shifting their vessels to trades outside the North Atlantic many shipowners tried to solve the problem of under-utilization in the North Atlantic. The *N.B. Lewis* of Yarmouth, for instance, was deployed in trades to South America and the Far East: she carried ballast on only seven out of twenty-one long distance passages between 1886 and 1893.[15] Our estimates of profits must be adjusted to allow for occasional earnings on westbound passages from the United Kingdom or continental Europe.

What about costs? In order to estimate net profits, we must deduct such operating costs as wages, victualling, port charges, insurance on the hull and cargo, brokerage charges, repairs, remetalling, and depreciation. Costs could be very high, and they varied enormously, depending on time at sea, trade route, and luck. Fortunately it is possible to estimate average annual operating costs for sailing vessels in major trade routes, from the testimony of shipowners before government inquiries and from shipowners' account books. In 1876, for instance, Frank Killam of Yarmouth reported that the annual costs of wages, supplies, repairs, and insurance for a 1,000-ton vessel would total about $12,500. We know from other sources the average port charges in Canadian and US ports.[16] If we add this to Killam's estimates, the average annual cost would be between $14.50 and $15.50 per ton, not including depreciation.[17]

Killam's estimates were high, and costs could be lower for vessels remaining within the North Atlantic and hiring crew in Britain or continental Europe. Port charges were also lower in Saint John and Halifax than in the major US ports. The records of actual disbursements by individual vessels in the 1870s and 1880s suggest annual operating and repair costs of $12 to $14 per ton, although vessels carrying little insurance or enjoying small repair costs could operate for less.[18]

Depreciation costs are difficult to estimate because owners rarely tell us what value they placed on their tonnage. The insured value of tonnage is an unreliable guide, because vessels were often underinsured. The resale values of shares in tonnage are known in many instances, but these varied a great deal, depending on the earnings record of the vessel and the current market for vessel shares, both in the Maritimes and in Europe. Depreciation rates of 7 per cent a year up to 1880, and 9 per cent after 1880, remain our best estimates.[19]

We cannot estimate rates of return for entire fleets with any precision. It is possible only to estimate potential returns, within very broad ranges, for vessels that operated exclusively in major trades terminating in the United Kingdom. Graph 6.1 presents the ranges for vessels of differing ages in 1863. The estimates are based on returns for vessels carrying timber, petroleum, grain, molasses, and guano, and we assume that most passages (55 per cent) were with timber, a freight offering relatively low gross returns. An average annual gross revenue was estimated, and from this was deducted annual operating and repair costs ranging from $12 per ton per year (yielding the maximum potential rate of return) to $15 per ton per year (yielding the minimum rate of return).

We assume, very cautiously, that most vessels earned nothing on westbound passages but that by carrying ballast and occasional cargoes on the westbound passage the average vessel covered 10 per cent of annual costs (or, alternatively, increased its annual gross earnings by a mere 6 to 8 per cent). Depreciation is deducted, and the resulting net return is expressed as a percentage of the depreciated value of capital employed.[20] Obviously the rate of return is

Graph 6.1
Estimated Rates of Return for Vessels in Major North Atlantic
Trades, 1863

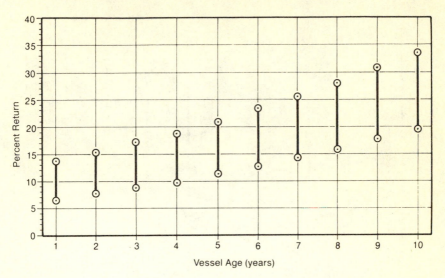

Sources: United Kingdom bills of entry, and sources listed in notes 14–20; Appendix
A; Appendix B.

higher in an older vessel, where the value of capital employed was
lower.

Although one cannot compare profits in shipping with profits in
other industries in the Maritime provinces in the 1860s, it is clear
that most shipowners must have been doing very well. Even if one
could earn an 8 per cent return on railway stock, it is likely that
shipping was a preferable investment. Another way to express the
results in Graph 6.1 is as follows: one could reasonably expect net
profits to pay for the initial purchase price of a vessel in five or six
years; everything earned thereafter would be clear profit; at this time
vessels survived for twelve years on average, and many operated for
twenty years and more.

Graph 6.2 presents similar estimates for 1873, when freight rates
were very high. Costs were higher than in 1863: it is assumed that
average annual costs were between $14 and $17 a ton.[21] We assume
no increase in vessel use and minimal earnings on westbound passages. The estimates are, if anything, underestimates of the rate of
return. We may reasonably conclude that most ships were earning
20 per cent or more of the value of capital employed. Even if the

Graph 6.2
Estimated Rates of Return for Vessels in Major North Atlantic
Trades, 1873

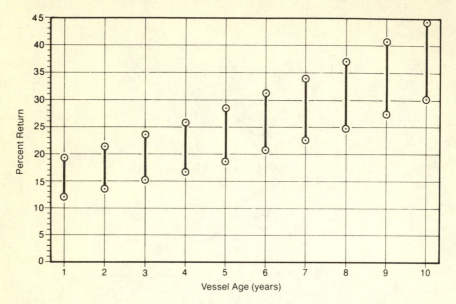

Sources: United Kingdom bills of entry; Appendix B; see notes 14–21.

shipowners of 1873 did not quantify their profits so exactly as this, such profits would be sufficient to attract investment and to explain the continuing interest of Maritimers in wooden sailing ships. Shipping investments would remain attractive, even if we allow an extra premium for the degree of risk that shipowning entailed.[22]

Estimating returns to shipping capital in the 1880s and 1890s is much more difficult, because the bills of entry do not allow analysis of outward cargoes to markets outside the North Atlantic. We can, however, make inferences about rates of return in the 1880s from the estimates for 1873. If rates of return declined at the same pace as did freight rates, then shipowners were still making profits in the mid-1880s. If most vessels were making returns of between 15 and 30 per cent in 1873, then the decline in freight rates (about 4 per cent a year) suggests that most were making between 10 and 20 per cent in 1883. By this time the decline in investment in shipping was well under way.

By 1886 – the low point in freight rates for the decade – rates of return might still have been between 9 and 18 per cent. For vessels

Graph 6.3
Estimated Rates of Return for Vessels in Major North Atlantic
Trades, 1883

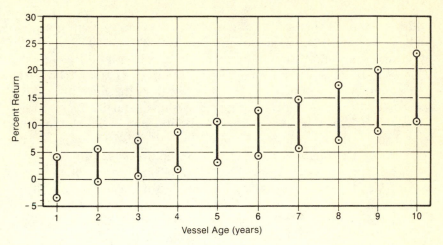

Sources: United Kingdom bills of entry; sources listed in notes 14–20; Appendix A;
Appendix B.

that remained within the traditional North Atlantic staple trades,
however, returns were unlikely to have remained so high in the
1880s. Graph 6.3 indicates the range of potential returns for vessels
carrying cotton, grain, petroleum and timber in 1883.[23] Although
operating costs had fallen since 1873, the chances of amortizing the
initial investment within five or six years were poor. By the mid-
1880s shipowners were probably receiving two conflicting messages
from shipping markets: it was possible to make a profit with sailing
ships; but the rate of profit had fallen steeply from the levels of the
1860s and early 1870s.

The experience of particular vessels and their owners tends to
confirm these conclusions. To estimate profits exactly, we require a
record of dividends received by a shareholder, after the managing
owner had deducted all costs.[24] Such dividends must appear continuously for several years and for more than one vessel. Fortunately such
records do exist. In Appendix C appear the actual returns on six
vessels that continued in Nova Scotian ownership as the shipping
industry declined.[25] The average annual return for the six vessels up
to 1880 was 25.9 per cent (the number of vessel-years was 22). The
average return after 1880 was 14 per cent (*n* = 44), but of course the

variation around the mean was very great.[26] This average should not conceal negligible or non-existent returns for several years in the 1880s.

Shipowners and others in the Maritime provinces knew that substantial profits were made in shipowning in the 1860s and 1870s. They were aware also that rates of return fell very sharply in the 1880s. The contrast between the earnings of the early 1870s and those of the mid-1880s was much more important than the fact that some profit could still be made with sailing ships. Martin Dickie, for instance, was discouraged by the mid-1880s, but he knew that he could still make a profit with ships. When the *Linden* completed a passage to Rotterdam with oil and returned a small profit for that year he commented: "These bits, though small, are nonetheless acceptable."[27] Two years later Dickie was commissioning another sailing ship from his favourite builder.[28]

But the optimism of 1873 had long since gone by 1887: "Discouraging times, these, to make money with vessels. I am almost sick of it."[29] Some shipowners, such as the Moran family of St Martin's, New Brunswick, were thoroughly discouraged by the late 1870s.[30] But by the mid-1880s, Dickie's despair was commonplace. "Sailing vessels are such uncertain properties that we cannot reckon the profit arising from them ... We cannot make our vessels pay, and I sometimes think it would be better to lay them up for a while."[31]

Only ten years earlier Peter Mitchell of New Brunswick, a former federal minister of marine and fisheries, had urged businessmen in Quebec and the Maritimes to own locally built ships rather than to sell them abroad. Canadian-built vessels, he said, "sailed on every sea and were frequently absent from the ports where they were owned for three or four years, during which they were earning large sums. There was no doubt that the Yarmouth ships, for example, made a better return for the money and labour invested in them than almost any industry in the province."[32]

This view is confirmed by other contemporary estimates of profits in shipping.[33] A few years later, preparing his report on manufacturing in the Dominion, Edward Willis stated that shipping and shipbuilding "had made for many citizens of this place [Saint John] comfortable competencies, if not colossal fortunes." Willis also reflected the growing pessimism of the 1880s: "the competition of iron steamers and iron ships" had "destroyed" a "magnificent business."[34]

This situation helps to explain the response of many shipowners in the 1880s. First, they tended to retain vessels until close to their maximum life expectancy, since it was only after several years that a vessel could be expected to earn a profit. Hence it was older vessels that were sold to Norwegians and others. Second, shipowners had to be flexible in their deployment of vessels and willing to put them into trades outside the North Atlantic. Third, profits were possible, but they could be guaranteed only if operating, insurance, and repair costs were reduced wherever possible. The result was that the shipowner's normal concern to minimize costs became an obsession. Shipowners struggled to wrest productivity gains from ships and labour, by applying modest changes to the old sailing-ship technology, by shifting vessels into new trades, by exercising closer managerial control over the operation of vessels, and by reducing labour costs wherever possible.

The obsession with speedy turn-around times and quick passages is reflected in the correspondence of managing owners. There is no typical managing owner, but the irascible Robert Quirk of Charlottetown represents the sailing ship owner in extremis, his determination to exploit vessels and men brooking no compromise. "My feelings at the present time are none of the pleasantest," he warned a broker in Galveston in 1881. "Shipowning nowadays is such a poor business that every attention must be given to the minutest details."[35] A flurry of letters and telegrams followed to the same broker, complaining about the arranged freight rate, the size of the broker's commission, and the length of loading time.[36]

These letters coincided with detailed instructions to the master in Galveston: "The one thing I must urge upon you the absolute necessity of is to get the utmost possible dispatch – *time is money*."[37] A year later the same master had died, and we find Quirk quarrelling with his widow and demanding that she pay for the cost of furnishings in the master's cabin: "I think any extras which Capt. Dunn ordered for your comfort and his, should not be charged to the ship, and what is more I will not allow it."[38] Like other managing owners, Quirk was underinsuring his vessels: "I take considerable risk in each of my vessels myself and therefore I cannot afford to send vessels to ports which are dangerous."[39]

At the same time Quirk argued for increased deck-loads and urged his partner to ignore the objections of their masters: "It will be as well not to listen to the advice of a captain, as I have found out that they begin crying out long before they are hurt."[40] Embedded in this shipowner's exploitation of ships and men was his awareness of falling rates of return: "Shipowning is not what it was in 1870, and things must be worked on a different basis altogether," he wrote in 1881.[41]

Faced with falling rates of return, shipowners wrested productivity

Table 6.1

Average Turn-around Times in Days (Four Major Fleets), 1860s–1890s

Decade	Saint John		Yarmouth		Halifax		Windsor	
	X	n	X	n	X	n	X	n
1860s	31.4	809	29.5	252	30.3	107	31.5	288
1870s	27.1	2705	24.0	1,341	26.7	575	25.9	772
1880s	26.7	2011	25.6	1,022	25.8	277	22.6	882
1890s	29.1	524	29.3	161	29.7	39	30.0	378

Source: Crew Agreements.
Note: X is the average; n is the number of cases.

gains from sailing ships and from labour. There is convincing evidence that they succeeded. "Quick dispatch" meant speeding up the labour of loading and unloading and the labour applied to sailhandling and navigation. Between the 1860s and the 1880s turn-around times (spent in port at the end of a voyage) shortened. This was achieved by entering ports that still had ready accommodation and cargoes for sailing ships and by quicker loading, unloading, taking on of supplies, hiring of new crew members where necessary, and completion of other ship's business.

The average saving, of six days, between the 1860s and the 1880s was a remarkable achievement (Table 6.1). Many of the gains won by the 1880s were lost in the 1890s, as sailing ships had to wait for cargoes and as steamers were increasingly given priority in major ports. Nevertheless, average turn-around times in the 1890s were still slightly below those of the 1860s.

Vessels also spent time in port during voyages. A voyage was simply the series of vessel movements occurring between the opening and closing of the labour contract, the crew agreement. Vessels often carried cargoes between several ports in the course of a single voyage. Time spent in ports of call also shortened between the 1860s and the 1880s, before lengthening again in the 1890s (Table 6.2). More impressive evidence of speed-up appears when we examine sailing times between ports. Table 6.3 shows the average sailing days on the major passages frequented by Canadian sailing ships between the 1860s and the 1890s. In almost every passage sailing times shortened. Between Liverpool and New York, for instance, six days were saved between the 1860s and the 1880s. The average passage from the United Kingdom to Rio de Janeiro was eleven days shorter in the 1880s than in the 1860s. Six days were cut from the passage between Liverpool and Philadelphia, and six days from the Liverpool–

Table 6.2
Port-of-Call Times in Days
(Averages for Four Major
Fleets), 1860s–1890s

Decade	Average	No. of cases
1860s	32.3	2,947
1870s	31.1	8,363
1880s	31.5	7,111
1890s	37.2	2,524

Source: Crew Agreements.

Baltimore run. The average change in passage times between the 1860s and the 1880s (weighted by the number of cases for each route) was 8.4 per cent; the average saving between the 1860s and the 1890s was 12.7 per cent.

By itself the saving of a few days in a passage may not seem significant. But over the lifetime of a vessel the cumulative effect of savings in sailing times and port times could be large. In the 1860s it was unlikely that many vessels could make three complete voyages in a year between New York and Liverpool (where each voyage included eastward and westward passages and port stops on both sides of the Atlantic). By the 1880s the *average* vessel could make three such voyages in a year, assuming no delays for repairs.

Even if we allow considerable extra time in port for repairs and recoppering, the vessel built in the 1880s, and remaining within the North Atlantic, was likely to make three or four more transatlantic voyages during a ten-year career than was her predecessor built in the 1850s or 1860s. If freight rates had remained constant, the lifetime gross earnings of the average vessel could have increased by 10 to 15 per cent. Taken together with the increasing longevity of vessels, these savings compensated for the steep decline in sailing-ship freight rates in the 1880s.

Further savings were achieved by moving vessels out of the North Atlantic and into South American trades and various trades to and from Asia and Australia. This movement increased time spent at sea, during which revenues were being earned, relative to time in port. The ratio of sea-time to port-time for Saint John vessels was 1.16 in the 1860s and 1.26 in the 1880s. For Yarmouth vessels there was an even more impressive increase in this ratio, from 1.03 in the 1860s to 1.27 in the 1880s.[42] Shipowners were certainly aware of the costs

Table 6.3
Average Passage Times between Ports in Days (Four Major Fleets),
1860s–1890s

Passage	1806s		1870s		1880s		1890s	
	X	n	X	n	X	n	X	n
New York– Liverpool	30.5	24	31.9	63	28.7	76	24.1	8
New York– London	35.4	7	30.7	97	31.9	184	31.0	30
New York– Antwerp	36.4	9	33.6	133	32.9	212	31.7	5
Saint John– Liverpool	32.9	28	31.9	92	31.4	100	29.3	31
Quebec– Liverpool	33.2	38	31.9	89	32.0	47	26.7	7
Philadelphia– Antwerp	37.1	9	37.8	134	35.1	79	–	–
Baltimore– Antwerp	–	–	40.9	39	36.7	21	–	–
Liverpool– New York	48.2	61	47.9	172	42.4	127	40.9	14
Liverpool– Philadelphia	55.0	34	52.3	101	48.7	41	47.1	7
Liverpool– Baltimore	55.7	29	53.6	51	50.0	25	–	–
Liverpool– Saint John	43.5	40	45.2	112	42.6	102	41.8	30
Liverpool– Quebec	41.7	30	42.1	91	41.5	44	–	–
Antwerp– New York	–	–	48.4	126	44.5	239	–	–
Antwerp– Philadelphia	–	–	53.8	72	48.9	74	–	–
United Kingdom– New Orleans	62.5	54	60.5	151	58.6	78	59.6	5
United Kingdom– Rio de Janeiro	64.3	16	55.9	85	53.3	158	53.2	101

Table 6.3 – *continued*

Passage	1806s		1870s		1880s		1890s	
	X	n	X	n	X	n	X	n
United Kingdom– Montevideo	70.6	19	68.3	16	64.1	95	66.2	36
United Kingdom– Callao	108.4	9	114.5	32	114.9	11	–	–
United Kingdom– Bombay	131.8	32	123.5	95	121.9	29	–	–

Source: Crew Agreements.
Note: X is the average; n is the number of cases.

of port-time, and some chose long voyages over short ones for this reason.[43]

Shipowners in the Maritime provinces clearly approached the limits of attainable output in wooden sailing ships. They increased the ratio of capital to labour to its maximum in wooden vessels of 500 to 2,000 tons.[44] The ratio of men to tonnage fell by 2 per cent a year between 1863 and the end of the century.[45] Much of the change in capital-labour ratios was caused by the increase in average tonnages of ocean-going vessels: as hull size expanded, the number of masts and sails did not increase, and so the labour requirement did not increase proportionately.

But more than a quarter of the change in capital-labour ratios occurred for other reasons. Whatever the tonnage and the rig of a vessel, shipowners and masters required that fewer men work the same tonnage across oceans and work it faster. All classes of sailing ships owned in the Maritimes sailed with fewer men than did sailing ships registered in the United Kingdom (see Table 6.4).

At the same time as labour was shed, the pressure on wages intensified, as managing owners insisted that all "disbursements" be minimized. Average wages in the Saint John fleet fell by 20 per cent between 1874 and 1886 (Graph 6.4), and in other fleets, such as that of Windsor, the decline was even greater.[46] The average wage for "All Crew" is weighted by the numbers at each rank, and so the average follows closely the average for able seamen, who were most numerous. Pressure was greatest on wages of able seamen and other deckhands.

Table 6.4

Man-Ton Ratios (Men per 100 Tons) in Sailing Vessels of Yarmouth and of Britain, 1860s and 1890s

	250–499 tons		500–999 tons		1,000–1,400 tons	
	Yarmouth	Britain	Yarmouth	Britain	Yarmouth	Britain
1860s	2.95	3.98	2.16	3.04	1.73	2.52
1890s	2.30	2.78	1.49	2.16	1.30	2.00

Sources: Yarmouth crew agreements; sample of non-Canadian crew agreements, Maritime History Archive, Memorial University of Newfoundland.

These pressures increased the share of returns to capital compared to the returns to labour. A crude measure of output in shipping is vessel-days at sea, or tonnage at sea, which we may then adjust by a freight rate index. Labour requirements and wages paid increased much less than did the movement of carrying capacity up to the industry's peak in 1881. Thereafter the decline in labour and wages was faster than the decline in "gross output" (Table 6.5). In other fleets, particularly Yarmouth's, savings in labour were probably even greater.[47]

Pressure on wages, reduction of the labour force, speed-up, and pressure on masters intensified the conflict between employers and wage-earners. Rising desertion rates between the 1860s and 1880s, especially in larger vessels, are the clearest indication of a class struggle which took many forms, including resistance at sea and criminal prosecutions on land. In this intensifying conflict, shipowners depended on a wage-paid subordinate – the ship's master – who was beyond immediate supervision and control. In this industry, merchants confronted a nascent proletariat, and their correspondence reflects the anger and frustration that followed.[48]

Merchant shipowners sent into ocean trades a type of capital that shared many characteristics with industrial capital on land: they deployed concentrations of wage labour and a technology of iron as well as wood, and shipowners made a profit from such capital as it was used in production. Yet there was little more that Canadian shipowners could do with a technology that they had already altered and pushed to its limits.

In the logic of industrial capital, the next step was clear, and it was well known to the shipowners of the Maritimes. They must further extend the longevity of each capital asset, speed up the work of men and machines, accelerate the growth of capital relative to labour, and reduce significantly the risks of investment in shipping, by reducing

Graph 6.4
Average Monthly Wages of Crew by Rank, Saint John Fleet, 1863–1902

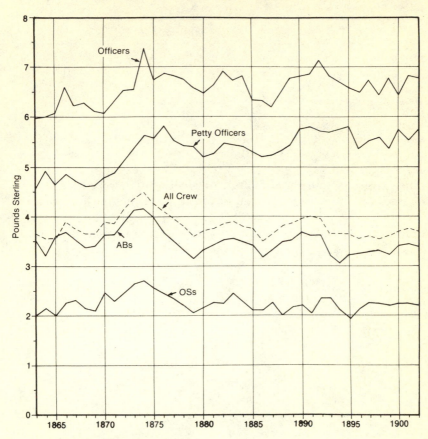

Source: Saint John Crew Agreements.

their dependence on labour and its skills and the extreme vulnerability of ships to total loss at sea. Such were the lessons of falling rates of return, of the struggle to maintain returns from wooden sailing ships, and of the ensuing class conflict.

The decline in freight rates and the competition of iron and steam did not put an end to the shipping industry of the Maritimes. These were necessary but not sufficient conditions for the decline of investment in shipping; for the sufficient conditions of decline, we must look elsewhere. What the international conditions did, however, was to narrow the choices available to investors in the Maritimes. One alternative followed precisely from the lessons just listed: shipowners

Table 6.5
Annual Growth Rates (%) of Tonnage at Sea and Labour Inputs, Saint
John Fleet, 1863–99

	1863–81	1881–99
Ton-months	+6.5	−12.6
Ton-months adjusted by freight rates	+4.9	−14.1
Man-months	+3.5	−13.9
Total wages paid	+3.5	−14.7

Source: Saint John Crew Agreements.
Note: All growth rates are estimated from regression equations. The Matthews sailing
ship freight rate index is used to 1881; thereafter the Isserlis index is used.

must invest in hulls built of iron or steel and powered by steam-
engines. When possessors of capital in the Maritimes declined to take
this further step into the age of industrial capital in shipping, they
did so in full knowledge of those lessons and for reasons firmly rooted
in the history and experience of merchant capital in their region.

CHAPTER SEVEN

Merchant Shipowners in the Industrial Era

The age of sail was also the final stage of merchant hegemony. As the sailing fleets grew, ownership was increasingly concentrated in fewer hands. Independent smallholders were undercut and displaced. Technological change allowed larger units of production, operated increasingly by a "free" and highly mobile labour force hired in international labour markets. In shipping, as in other industries, there was a more clear distinction than ever before between those who owned means of production and those who owned none. More commonly than ever before, ships were capital, and those who responded to falling rates of return were a diminishing number of powerful capitalists. In their responses we must locate the conditions for the decline of the shipping and shipbuilding industries.

In shipping, the transition to industrial capitalism was begun but not completed by 1900. The incomplete transition is reflected in the pattern of ownership of capital in shipping. Had industrialization proceeded in Atlantic Canadian shipping as it did in other industries and other regions, the majority of shipping by the First World War would have been concentrated in a small number of incorporated companies. Instead, the merchant family remained the dominant form of ownership in the major ports of the Maritimes until the end of the nineteenth century. Not until 1907 was the incorporated shipping company responsible for most capital formation in a declining industry.[1] We have not been able to trace all ownership for all vessels beyond the time of first registry, and so a complete profile of the owners of all new and old tonnage at one point in time is not possible, but there can be little doubt that up to 1914 a minority of tonnage was held by incorporated companies.

Two important trends distinguish shipowning between 1850 and

Graph 7.1

Newly Registered Tonnage by Occupation Group in Seven Major Ports, 1850–99

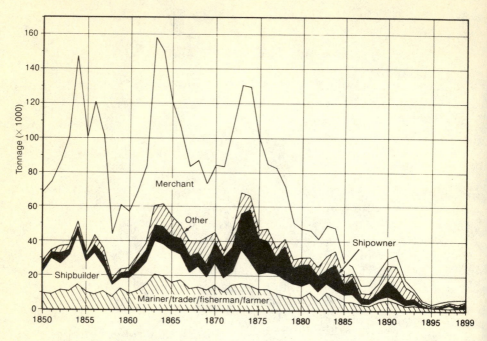

Sources: Vessel registries of Charlottetown, Halifax, Miramichi, Pictou, Saint John, Windsor, and Yarmouth.

1900 from shipowning before 1850. First, small owner-operators held a much smaller share of tonnage after 1850 than before, and only after the industry collapsed did they recover their share of new investment (see Graph 7.1).[2] Even in the coasting trades, and in the ownership of small sailing vessels, smallholders were being displaced. Table 7.1 shows the proportion of new schooner tonnage held by various occupations. Merchant domination of the schooner fleet was particularly clear in Newfoundland, but all ports saw a decline in the share owned by smallholders (farmers, fishermen, mariners, planters, and traders). Of course, small owner-operators owned a larger share of all schooners on registry than these figures suggest, since we have analysed ownership at the time of first registry only, and in subsequent transactions non-merchant shares increased. Nevertheless, the trend toward both mercantile and corporate ownership is clear. In coastal trading as a whole this trend was accelerated when

Table 7.1
Newly Registered Schooner Tonnage by Occupation Group (%),
1820–1936

Occupation	1820–49		1850–79		1880–1914		1915–36
	7 ports	Nfld	7 ports	Nfld	7 ports	Nfld	Nfld
Merchant	29	58	37	57	33	64	63
Smallholder	64	38	45	40	38	30	23
Shipowner/ship company	0	1	2	2	12	1	8
Shipbuilder	4	0	8	0	4	1	2
Other	3	3	8	1	13	4	4

Source: Vessel registries.
Note: "Smallholder" means trader, mariner, planter, farmer, or fisherman. The seven ports are Charlottetown, Halifax, Miramichi, Pictou, Saint John, Windsor, and Yarmouth.

steamships began to displace schooners and other sailing vessels toward the end of the nineteenth century.

A second trend reflected in Graph 7.1 was the rise in investment by shipbuilders and "shipowners." This trend did not end merchant control, however: in the 1880s and 1890s merchants held about 30 per cent of all newly registered tonnage in the seven major ports of the Maritimes (in Newfoundland merchants remained dominant into the twentieth century).[3] To the merchant share of tonnage we may add the tonnage owned by people who gave their occupations as "shipowner."

Only in one port – Yarmouth – did the "shipowner" emerge as a major force, a specialist owner of ocean-going shipping for whom shipowning was so important that it justified the term *shipowner* rather than *merchant*.[4] But even in Yarmouth most of these shipowners came from mercantile families, long since involved in trading on their own account to and from the West Indies, the United States, and Britain. The vessel registries for the major ports, newspapers, business directories, and other sources suggest that our major "shipowners" were more likely to be referred to as merchants, commission merchants, West India traders, and the like, and there seems little doubt that this is how they saw themselves.[5] If we treat merchants and shipowners as a single category, they still owned a majority of new tonnage in our seven ports in the 1880s and 1890s (see Graph 7.1).

The incorporated company and joint stock ownership existed in the shipping industry but was dominant only among investors in steam-powered vessels. In the Maritimes, shipping companies held 54 per cent of newly registered tonnage in steamships or auxiliary steamers.[6] One owner, William Thomson of Saint John, held a considerable proportion of this tonnage, but the degree of concentration was not very marked.[7] Even with the new industrial technology of steam and iron, mercantile ownership remained significant.

The fate of the shipping industry lay in the decisions of a diminishing number of major merchant-shipowners. Like their fathers before 1850, merchants of the last half of the century were much more than shipowners. They had extensive interests in the social and financial infrastructure of their port towns. The evidence on major shipowners suggests that these interests expanded even in the "golden age of sail."[8] Even before freight rates and profits in shipping fell, merchant-shipowners were increasing their landward investments. The evidence that follows leads to a single conclusion: capital was not simply pushed out of shipping (whether wood or iron) by falling returns; capital was also pulled out of the maritime sector by conditions in the landward environment.

It is difficult to argue that shipowners, finding themselves trapped in an unprofitable shipping industry, suddenly shifted capital into landward industries after 1879. Instead merchant-shipowners were among those who initiated the gradual movement of capital from maritime to landward enterprise. The provincial statutes that incorporated new companies help to confirm this. We cannot infer the size of investments from this source, but since an incorporator of a company was almost always an investor, we can use the source to say something about investment and its timing.[9] There were 467 company incorporations in Nova Scotia between 1850 and 1889: about a third were in the primary sector or primary manufacturing; slightly over a third were in the tertiary sector (including merchandising, services, and supplying); a quarter were in secondary manufacturing; only 8 per cent were in the financial sector.[10]

There were 2,047 individuals named as incorporators in these statutes. Only 7 per cent were major shipowners in the ports of Halifax, Windsor, Yarmouth, or Pictou. But major shipowners appeared more frequently than did others, and no less than 41 per cent of all incorporations involved at least one shipowner. More often than non-shipowners, shipowners tended to be involved in several companies, and most of the individuals who incorporated six or more companies were major shipowners. Two individuals – Edward W. Dimock of Windsor and Thomas E. Kenny of Halifax – were involved with fifteen incorporations, and both were major shipowners.

Merchants appear to have welcomed the joint stock company as a vehicle for investment in landward ventures. At least 63 per cent of major shipowners in these four Nova Scotian ports of registry were involved with at least one newly incorporated company. Furthermore, it appears that before 1870, at least, shipowners were critical to such company formation in the province: two-thirds of all incorporations involved major shipowners in the 1850s and 1860s. Shipowners did not follow a path of economic diversification created by others; they cut that path themselves, and they did so at the height of the age of sail.

Even outside shipping, the activity of shipowners was primarily mercantile or financial. Although many invested in manufacturing, more were involved in merchandising and finance, and almost every financial venture involved shipowners.[11] Equally important to our argument is the timing of this activity: in all major ports, non-shipping activity coincided with, or preceded, the peaks in investment in shipping.[12] In Yarmouth, for instance, a small group of merchant-shipowners founded the major public companies in the town, including the Bank of Yarmouth (1859), the Exchange Bank (1867), the Western Counties Railway (1870), and the Burrell Johnson Iron Co. (1878).[13]

The interest in tertiary and financial sectors is even more obvious in Windsor, where thirty-two of the forty major shipowners took part in the incorporation of financial companies. Bennett Smith's shipping investments continued into the 1880s; before then he helped to create the Commercial Bank of Windsor, two marine insurance companies, two fire insurance companies, and the Windsor Cotton Mill. Edward W. Dimock's shipping investments continued into the 1890s; before then he had interests in banking, the cotton mill, fire insurance, gypsum, hardware merchandising, marine insurance, the plaster company, and the tanning company. Despite Dimock's example, manufacturing was still a minority interest. Major shipowners were more often interested in local utilities, such as electric lighting, gas lighting, the street railway, and telephones.[14]

In Halifax, the merchant-shipowners' interest in finance, merchandising, and utilities far exceeded their interest in manufacturing. Although shipowners were involved in the Sugar Refinery and the Nova Scotia Cotton Manufacturing Co., three-quarters of the shipowners' incorporating activity was outside secondary manufacturing. Businesses formed by merchant-shipowners included – apart from the inevitable banks and insurance companies – building societies, electrical utilities, the gas lighting firm, and coal, mining, publishing, railway, and wholesale grocery companies.[15] For such shipowners as

Table 7.2

Incorporators of Public Companies Who Registered New Tonnage in
Saint John before and after 1860

	Pre-1860		Post-1860	
Sector	No.	%	No.	%
Manufacturing	159	18.7	100	9.6
Mining	54	6.3	50	4.8
Timber, boom, and related	37	4.4	40	3.8
Railways	117	13.8	203	19.5
Finance	172	20.2	133	12.8
Public service/utilities	132	15.5	329	31.5
Steam ferries and other marine	85	10.0	105	10.1
Landward transport	52	6.1	27	2.6
Agriculture/emigration/land	38	4.5	32	3.1
Trading company	4	0.5	24	2.3
Total	850		1,043	

Sources: New Brunswick Statutes; Saint John vessel registries.
Notes: "Pre-1860" means owners with all but four or five first registries dating 1859 or
earlier. "Post-1860" means all other registrants of new tonnage.

   "Timber, boom, and related" includes mainly timber sluice or boom companies,
and also some lumber or wood patent companies. "Public service/utilities" includes
mechanics' institutes, halls, schools, libraries, law societies, telegraph companies, har-
monic and music societies, parks, gas lighting companies, electricity companies, telephone companies, water companies, skating rinks, hotels, and cemeteries. "Steam
ferries and marine" includes mainly steam-boats but also whaling companies, canal
companies, and dock or harbour improvement companies. "Landward transport"
means road, bridge, and stage-coach companies.

Robert Boak Jr, Alfred G. Jones, Thomas E. Kenny, John Stairs, and
William J. Stairs, many of these landward investments preceded the
peak of their new investment in sailing ships.

   What is perhaps most striking about the merchants of the Maritimes is the range of the investment portfolios. The diversity is perhaps best revealed in Saint John – always the major shipowning
centre in these colonies. From the New Brunswick statutes we have
compiled a list of all incorporators; from this list, those who registered
new tonnage in Saint John (including those who registered small
amounts) have been identified, where identification is certain.[16] Both
major and minor shipowners were interested in a wide range of
activities (Table 7.2). There was considerable interest in manufacturing, and shipowners were prominent among the creators of railway
companies, even before mid-century.

But more noticeable is the interest in the range of public services and utilities, which increased proportionately after 1860, while interest in railways and manufacturing became relatively less important! Shipowning was merely one part of the creation of social infrastructure. It was one of the many activities of those merchants who sought profits and prestige in the building of towns and the provision of banks, cemeteries, electricity, gas lighting, hotels, insurance, schools, skating rinks, and water.

We cannot measure precisely the contribution that merchant capital made to the growth of manufacturing industry. But this evidence suggests that merchant-shipowners were less likely than others to initiate new manufacturing enterprises. The major shipowners of Saint John include 358 individuals who put no less than 73 per cent of all new tonnage on the registry books of the port. Most of these individuals were involved in the incorporation of companies, at one time or another, but only 10 per cent of their incorporating activity involved manufacturing. Even if we add railways to the manufacturing total, the industrial activity of major shipowners was significantly less than that of minor shipowners. These merchant capitalists made a greater direct contribution to financial, transportation, and other social overhead capital than they did to secondary manufacturing.[17] The pattern of directorships in public companies tends to confirm this point.[18]

There are many examples of the diversified merchant portfolio in New Brunswick in the third quarter of the century. Frederick A. Wiggins is one of several whose roots lay in the decades before the great age of sail. Wiggins was in partnership with his father and registered new tonnage between the 1830s and the 1860s. By 1864 R.G. Dun's reporter in Saint John wrote that Wiggins was worth over a million dollars, and by 1866 he was perhaps the richest and "meanest" man in town.

Wiggin's wealth was very broadly based. Even if Wiggins had registered all of his new tonnage in the early 1860s, instead of over four decades, his shipping would still have been worth less than a third of all his assets. Wiggins was in the import and export business, but he also invested in property, and at his death 17 per cent of his estate consisted of real estate. Indeed, by 1866 it appears that most of his business was done in England, and according to Dun's credit record he kept an office in Saint John merely in order to collect rents. In the course of his career he had been more than a rent-collector, however: he was an incorporator of an ice company, mining companies, a railway company, a stage-coach company, and a timber-boom company. For such a man, and especially for those who inherited his business, the sale of shipping shares was relatively easy, and in the context of his overall business interests it was a relatively minor series of decisions.

The Troop family was perhaps untypical of Saint John shipowners, because its shipping investments were an unusually large share of its assets. But even the Troops secured themselves with real estate and a number of landward ventures.[19] More typical was William A. Robertson, a merchant who registered new tonnage in the 1860s and 1870s. The Robertson family imported and sold anchors, chain, and cordage. By 1871 William was worth $160,000, with his assets spread among sailmaking, ship brokerage, shipowning, and real estate.[20] He was an incorporator of two insurance companies and a bank. By the 1880s he was moving capital from shipping into his existing commission merchant and grocery wholesale business.

Another example is a smaller shipowner – Archibald F. Randolph of Fredericton – who registered 1,239 new tons in the late 1860s and early 1870s. Randolph represents the investor who scarcely merits the name shipowner at all, since his shipping property was so small a part of his capital. He was a major Fredericton grocer and banker, and incorporator and the manager of the People's Bank of New Brunswick. By 1869 he was worth between $40,000 and $50,000, and 10 per cent of this was in real estate. By 1875 he had sunk no less than $80,000 in a flour mill, but the mill was not profitable. He was also interested in the timber trade, deal exports, and a bank and a railway in Rivière du Loup. His assets, according to Dun's reporter, were "too widespread."[21] By 1875 he was selling his vessels in order to secure his other investments. Here is a good example of a "shipowner" for whom shipping tonnage was a kind of rentier investment, to be easily liquidated when other ventures appeared more attractive.

In general, diversification of the merchant portfolio began long before the decline in shipowning and continued as interest in shipping waned. Probate records suggest also that major shipowners made substantial investments in land, mostly in their own towns, and speculated in stocks and bonds of companies outside their home province. Among the major shipowners of Halifax, about 20 per cent of assets listed in probate records were in real estate. Most of the assets on death were in stocks and bonds, and interest in government debentures was very common.[22] Probate records for the largest shipowners in Saint John suggest a similar pattern: while real estate holdings were usually substantial, about two-thirds of all assets were in cash, stocks, or bonds.[23]

The liquidity of capital in shipping is very striking. By the time of their deaths, major shipowners held few ships, or none at all. The shift in investments took place within a single generation, and by the 1880s and 1890s ships were merely one item, along with municipal bonds and bank stock, in the portfolio of the merchant investor. The merchant portfolio was also a cautious one, seeking to avoid the risks and conflicts that shipowning entailed: "Hence the necessity of turning our special attention to those pursuits, which no amount of competition can take away from us."[24]

No longer did the merchant watch his ships go to and from his own home port. No longer did he send his sons to sea as masters and mates, to learn the business of trade at first hand. No longer did the merchant carry his own goods in his own ships. More ships than ever before had multiple shareholders, and except for people who were managing owners, ships were a type of rentier capital, yielding a dividend, but nothing more. Such capital was easily exchanged for the variety of stocks and bonds that circulated in the Maritimes in the 1880s and 1890s. The age of sail came to an end in a large number of relatively minor decisions by merchant investors.

CHAPTER EIGHT

A Culture of
Entrepôt Growth

Why were so many shipowners and their sons shifting capital into landward sectors? It is tempting to say that sailing ships were inefficient, profits were higher in other industries, and that capital was thereby pulled out of shipping and into the expanding landward economy. Disinvestment in shipping would then be a simple consequence of the wealth-maximizing tendencies of capital, allowing for some delays caused by imperfections in the market or in the flow of information. "A powerful insight of neoclassical theory, with fundamental implications for economic history, is that under conditions of uncertainty it is impossible for individual profit, or wealth, maximization to exist (since no one knows with certainty the outcome of a decision), but that the wealth-maximizing result nevertheless occurs. It occurs simply because competition in the face of ubiquitous scarcity dictates that the more efficient institution, policy, or individual action will survive and the inefficient ones perish."[1]

Economic historians recognize, however, that conditions of uncertainty were pervasive in the past, and information was never perfect. Even if the evidence for high returns in railway stock is sound, for instance, consequential investment in railways assumes that the investors knew about those high returns. It is entirely possible that imperfect information prevented investors from perceiving high rates of return where they existed or persuaded them that returns were high where in fact they were low. Despite the logic of neoclassical theory, it is possible for investors to withdraw from an industry in which rates of return are high. This leaves us with a troubling thought: even if the profits to be made from sailing ships had been much higher in the 1880s than they actually were, the shipping industry might have declined anyway.[2]

We might easily dismiss such speculation were it not for the fact that this very phenomenon did occur in a shipping industry located very near to the Maritimes. In the 1860s and 1870s the deep-sea merchant marine of the eastern United States declined, even though demand for tonnage in US ports was growing rapidly, and despite the increase in freight rates in the early 1860s and early 1870s. There are differing interpretations of the decline of the US merchant marine, but one view is that capital was shifted into landward industries regardless of the profits to be made in shipping.[3] This means not that our earlier discussion of profits was irrelevant but that we must look further if our explanation for the decline of shipowning is to be complete.

A further problem with the neo-classical formulation is the risk of circular argument. The sentence quoted above comes close to the tautology inherent in Darwinian "survival of the fittest" evolutionary theory: those institutions or firms best adapted for survival have a better chance of surviving than those not so well adapted.[4] The proposition cannot be tested against evidence, since it is a truism. The historian sets out to "prove" that industries of low productivity collapsed, while those experiencing productivity gains survived, but the conclusions follow from assumptions rather than from evidence. This does not mean that economic historians have ignored these problems. For Douglass C. North, whom I have quoted above, such problems are central to economic history. Precisely because knowledge is imperfect, and because information and expectations intrude on market mechanisms, neo-classical economists have grappled with "the economics of information and knowledge."[5]

The choices made by businesspeople, therefore, cannot be understood simply as the outcome of a maximizing calculus and opportunity costs. The merchant capitalists of Atlantic Canada operated in conditions of pervasive uncertainty. Very often they were investing in industries with which they had no prior experience. Their prediction of future returns on capital was based not on personal or local experience but on information transmitted from elsewhere. They knew that the same information might be available to others and that others might respond to the same predictions of high returns in particular industries, thereby encouraging overproduction and reducing or eliminating anticipated profits.

Control of information was critical, and there is no better testimony to this fact than the action by the directors of the Truro Condensed Milk and Canning Co. – among whom there were shipowners – after paying a 15 per cent dividend in January 1887: "We have had such a good year that we are not having any statements printed and it was the wish of all the stockholders that were at the annual meeting yesterday that nothing be said about it in order to prevent, as far as possible, competition."[6]

Discussion of investment choices became a debate over the lessons of experience outside the Maritimes – a debate in which the equation of information with economic power was fully understood: "We have been for the last year or two urging, by all the means in our power, the capitalists of Yarmouth to invest some of their surplus funds in the erection of a Cotton Mill. We have pointed out to them that if cotton cloth can be manufactured in Massachusetts at a fair profit, it can be made here at a heavy profit, the large import duties on the foreign article being taken into account ... Something must be done and that in short order."[7]

At this point the subject of profits in shipowning acquires more than merely antiquarian or regional interest. What did the merchant capitalist know, and how did he know it? The question takes us beyond neo-classical economics, to the point where the history of culture and communications must intersect with economic history. The subject is an old one, of course – it is a long time since Max Weber grappled with the paradoxical effects of theology and morality on economic behaviour. And today, when recent theorists have so forcefully reminded us of the domains of "power / knowledge," discourse and language, and the ability of these to define and limit fields of perceived truth, the economic historian can no longer be content with truisms about opportunity costs and profit maximization as determinants of investment behaviour.

None of this recent theoretical work offers clear guidance to the economic historian, but it does bear on the shipping industry: if information is treated, at least initially, as an independent variable in the arena of investment choices, then the decline of a regional industry may be connected not only with differential rates of return between industries but also with transmission of information and its receipt by a specific social class at the point of transition from merchant to industrial capitalism.[8]

What the merchant-shipowner appears to have known in the third quarter of the nineteenth century was that the shipping industry was doomed to decline or extinction. This knowledge did not come from reading of ledgers, since the knowledge in so many quarters preceded the steep decline in profits in the 1880s. "The shipping business is a comparatively profitable one generally," said Frank Killam of Yarmouth in 1876. Moments later, asked if there was a depression in his industry, Killam's answer was unequivocal: depression was "universal."[9] Depression, it seems, was "universal" – though average returns on capital were above 15 per cent and, as another expert put it, "Yarmouth ships ... made a better return for the money and labour invested in them than almost any industry in the Province."[10]

In 1876 Killam's pessimism followed not from past experience but from a specific prediction – which Edward Willis heard and repeated in his report a few years later: the competition of iron and steam had "destroyed a magnificent business."[11] Not only was the industry doomed, but nothing could be done to save it, said Willis: "Government edicts could not be made to shackle the wheels of progress." Willis's analysis tells us more about contemporary thinking than about economic reality. For one thing, he was treating shipbuilding and shipowning as a single industry and begging an obvious question: if iron steamers were more productive, then why did local shipowners not purchase them?

Even shipowners used the same flawed analysis, with all its revealing pessimism. "I regret to say that this great shipping industry of the lower Provinces has almost virtually ceased," said Thomas Kenny in 1888 – despite Canada's having the fifth largest merchant marine in the world. "That has been caused by the improvement in steam ... and also by the iron sailing ships. We, who wish to continue in the shipping business, have discovered that the iron sailing ship is a more profitable investment than our wooden ships."[12]

But Kenny and his fellows were rarely if ever investing in iron ships, whatever their proved advantages. His decision to pull his capital out of shipping flew in the face of his own economic analysis. In the 1890s Kenny's pessimism led him to even odder conclusions: "The depression in shipping is owing to the fact that we cannot build iron ships in this Dominion, not at least on the Atlantic coast."[13] Kenny did not stop to ask how it was that iron ships were then being built elsewhere in Canada; nor did he explain why he did not purchase iron ships. Little wonder that one of his listeners said: "I do not understand why a maritime people ... cannot keep pace with the times, in shipping."[14]

What was the source of this pervasive pessimism about the shipping industry? The speaker who followed Thomas Kenny, A.H. Gillmor, had a perceptive answer: "It has occurred to me during this debate that we are looking now with our mind's eye towards the great Atlantic; whereas all the time in the past we have been looking to the west, as though the whole Dominion and all its interests were settled in the great prairie."[15] Of course there were Maritimers in the confederation era who looked both west and east and saw railroads to the west as part of a seaborne and landward transportation system linking Canada and Britain and thereby encouraging the local shipping and shipbuilding industries.[16] An interest in western development was certainly not incompatible with an interest in shipping.

Nevertheless, Gillmor had a point: Confederation and railway development had put the west in "our mind's eye." Even for Joseph Howe the critical thing about railways was their capacity to expand commercial activity and population growth in landward directions. All railways in the United States are made to pay, he said, "by directing latent resources and by growth of internal commerce and manufacturing."[17] And as Rosemary Langhout has noted, the development strategy behind railways was often that of "entrepôt growth," whereby trade was concentrated in specific locations.[18] The benefits would come from expansion of commerce and port development – the expansion of shipowning was a corollary, or an ancillary benefit, not a primary stimulant of development in its own right.

In the decades following Confederation, in Halifax and Saint John, attention focused increasingly on port development. Politicians and civic boosters often lost sight of shipowning altogether. Shipping and entrepôt development were equated, and the word "shipping" acquired a new and profoundly ambiguous meaning: it refers both to the export and import of goods – the work of the shipper – and to the business of carrying goods in ships, the work of the shipowner.

These two activities were not the same, and after mid-century they were less often combined in the operations of merchant-shipowning firms. Very often the word "shipping" refers not to shipowning at all, still less to shipbuilding, but to entrepôt growth and commodity exchange.[19] Confederation turned the "mind's eye" and revived the economic discourse of mercantile exchange. "Something has come to fill the gap" left in the wake of shipping and shipbuilding, said one optimist in 1885: "We send more to the Upper Provinces and Manitoba than they send to us."[20]

We are not able to define with statistical precision the flow of information available to merchant capital and politicians in the Maritimes. But newspapers were transmitters or receptacles of much of that information, and it is reasonable to ask what views they expressed about shipbuilding and shipowning, as these industries expanded and declined. The answer one finds is sometimes astonishing, and it bears directly on the pervasive pessimism that preceded and accompanied the decline of these industries.

The press of Yarmouth, Halifax, and Saint John reflected very little about the fourth largest merchant marine in the world. Of course newspapers in the nineteenth century were different from those a century later, and one must not expect regular "feature articles" on local industries. Nevertheless, in the late 1860s and the 1870s newspapers did discuss local businesses and their fate in Confederation. One knows that the shipping industry existed from the "Shipping Intelligence" columns which reported the movement of vessels. Otherwise one might wonder if the industry existed at all.

A content analysis of the *Yarmouth Herald* in 1867 suggests that the fate of the US merchant marine was of more interest than the fate of local shipowning and shipbuilding after Confederation. There was no discussion of the anticipated impact of Confederation on shipowning. The local shipowning and shipbuilding industries were the principal topics of only 2 per cent of all articles in the paper in 1867.[21] Shipbuilding in the United States "is all but completely destroyed," and a "high tariff operates severely against the shipping interest," but even in this anti-Confederation newspaper the fate of local shipowning appears to be irrelevant to the discussion of Confederation.[22]

A random sample of 10 per cent of issues of the Saint John *Globe* (a daily) produced a similar result – more articles on shipbuilding outside the Maritimes than in New Brunswick – but in either case the message was almost uniformly pessimistic.[23] "Many of the [ship] yards are now closed with ships half unfinished upon the docks" because of "the ruinously low prices" for wooden ships in Britain.[24]

Insofar as there was a lesson from this experience, it was not that local shipowners could now benefit from the lower initial capital cost of ships. It was rather that iron ships and steamships were now in demand and that there should be a "handsome subsidy" from the new Dominion government to attract these new steamships into local ports.[25] The steamships would be owned by Cunard or Allan or British firms – that they would then compete with local ships, drive down freight rates in Saint John, and contribute ultimately to the collapse of shipowners' profits appears to have excited no concern. The decline of wooden shipbuilding in the 1860s must certainly have encouraged many to turn their eyes westward and to assume that shipowning would soon meet the same fate as shipbuilding.

All of this is testimony to the commonplace equation of economic development with commodity exchange in continental markets. The equation follows not only from local experience but from the massive borrowing of information about economic development from elsewhere. That information carried the message that commodities would henceforth be transported by rail, and some people even concluded that all waterborne transportation was becoming obsolete:

Trade will continue to grow, but it will not be carried on through the instrumentality of wooden ships, under sail. In fact, a large and continually increasing proportion will not use ships at all. Not many years ago, the trade between New Brunswick and Nova Scotia, as well as between this province and the upper provinces, was carried on by water ... The Intercolonial and other railways have changed all this, and the coasting trade has suffered accordingly; but the same thing, on a large scale, has happened the world over! ... Commerce may easily increase without increase in water carriage.[26]

This analysis was, of course, entirely incorrect, even with respect to Canadian coastal traffic, where the demand for carrying capacity and even for sailing ships was still increasing. It is not necessary to show that this analysis was typical or even widely shared. The fact that such an argument could be heard at all, in one of the major shipowning ports in the British Empire, is testimony to the massive impact of landward development on economic discourse in the Maritimes.

Given such pessimistic analysis, and given the accumulation of vested interests in the Intercolonial Railway, it is no surprise to find even shipowners arguing that coastal shipping between the Maritimes and Montreal was dead. The railway was now "the great national highway," and "without a perfect railway system we would almost fall back on our old Provincial prejudices and isolated condition."[27] Pessimism about shipowning became a self-fulfilling prophecy. Only a few years later Norwegian vessels were carrying coal from Cape Breton to Montreal.

Railways, cotton, iron, and sugar – these were the bedrock of economic development. Such were the lessons of external experience, as a Yarmouth newspaper, for instance, sought to impress on local capital: "we have warned those who 'go down to the sea in (wooden) ships' that 'the day of their destiny' is about over – that steam tonnage is fast driving the old wood-built sailing ship off the ocean ... But they, with an absolutely sublime heroism, prefer to stand by their posts and await the slow crumbling of the ground beneath them."[28] Of course Yarmouth shipowners did not await the slow crumbling of their shipping industry. They dismantled it themselves.

These lessons were also filtered through the experience of merchant capitalists long since engaged in exchange rather than production. They were interested in industrial manufacturing, and many invested in it.[29] One cannot use the story of merchant-shipowners to prove that a dominant commercial sector led, in R.T. Naylor's words, to "stultification of industrial entrepreneurship."[30] But industrialization and Confederation reinforced the powerful mercantile interest in commercial exchange, transportation, and port development.

Often manufacturing was the servant of commerce: it was another means of "buying cheap and selling dear."

The mercantile interest in trade goods guided much of the lobbying by merchants and politicians after Confederation. They would not unite to demand protection for shipowning or shipbuilding; instead they demanded readjustment of the sugar tariffs, extension of the Intercolonial Railway, creation of a "winter port," and the building of grain elevators. These were the causes for which even the erstwhile shipowner now fought, and the concessions that Dominion governments slowly gave. All these causes were intended to benefit "shipping" in its new sense – the work not of the shipowner, but of the shipper of goods.

The shipowners of Halifax and Saint John were merchants first and shipowners second. After Confederation the interests of the shipper collided with those of the shipowner as they never had before – and the interests of the shipper took precedence. The division came to a head over government subsidies to steamships. In the 1870s we find Maritimers blaming the decline of the West Indies trade on the absence of regular steam communications and linking this to the sugar tariffs.[31] Members of Parliament from the Maritimes were quite capable of pointing out that if subsidies could be given to a Canadian Pacific Railway, then they could be given to steamships to serve the vital West Indies trade: "I would like to know what difference there is between granting a subsidy to a steamship line like this, and a line of railway?"[32]

But there was a problem with steamship subsidies: the steamships would compete with vessels owned by Maritimers themselves. William Welsh of Prince Edward Island and A.G. Jones of Halifax led the charge: "Do hon. gentlemen want to destroy the marine interests of this country? ... I shall, in all cases, oppose any subsidy for any steamboat service for commercial purposes. I want to see steamers and sailing vessels try and compete with each other on a free trade basis. I do not want to subsidise one man and leave another out."[33]

The shipowners lost this debate – to other shipowners from the Maritimes, such as Thomas Kenny of Halifax:

As a ship-owner I can say that the great depression which now exists in the Lower Provinces is mainly due to the fact that our shipping is so unremunerative; but I think our duty here is to facilitate in every way our export trade, and we cannot accomplish this unless by means of steam. I regret to have to say that sail as a competitor with steam has now no chance on the ocean; I regret it because I am a sailing-ship-owner myself. But we must do all we possibly can to cultivate our export trade ... We cannot develop a large export without regularity of shipment, and that can only be attained by the use of steam.[34]

Embedded in this bitter exchange lie the reasons for the decline of the local shipping industry. On one side a shipowner argued for subsidies to encourage his competitors, the British and central Canadian firms who owned steamships. On the other side shipowners argued against subsidies which were essential if Canadians were to make the transition to the new industrial technology. Maritimers would not unite, either to invest in new shipping technologies or to demand policies that would encourage such investment.

Both sides argued from the same premises. The premise was that of merchant capital – "buying cheap and selling dear" – and vessels were always a means to that end, even for shipowners who argued against subsidies. They were not trying to maintain artificially high freight rates by keeping steamships from their ports. They were trying to keep steamships out of the West Indies fish trade, because steamships threatened to glut the markets and so lower the prices received: "In a market like Porto Rico, where we ship 150,000 to 160,000 quintals of fish a year, a steamer would require to take about 8,000 to 9,000 quintals of fish every trip, of two trips per month ... The arrival of such a quantity of fish ... in the West Indies, would cause the price to go down at least $1 a quintal."[35] By threatening the winter employment of schooners and fishermen, steamers might also discourage fishermen and reduce the local labour force in fishing, to the further disadvantage of the merchant. The shipowner was a trader first and a shipowner second.

This, then, is why even shipowners, including those who had at first opposed Confederation, were receptive to a landward development strategy. Even as shipowners they were primarily interested in commodity exchange, and Confederation afforded new opportunities for commercial activity because of the promise of railroads and entrepôt growth. Shipowners have a vested interest in high freight rates; commodity traders have a vested interest in low freight rates.

Even when ocean freight rates reached a peak in the early 1870s, shipowners were losing interest in those freight returns. It dissolved under the influence of external models of industrial development and the merchant capitalists' reception of them. A merchant marine would require protection: cargo reservation policies, preferential port charges for Canadian vessels, or reservation of steamship and mail subsidies for Canadian-flag ships. Maritimers did not unite in support of such policies because such policies would raise, not lower, the cost of freight. Furthermore, a merchant marine meant continuing conflict with wage labour in conditions disadvantageous to capital and entirely new managerial strategies to subdue and control labour over long distances.

Protectionist policies were therefore outside the merchant capitalists' perception of his self-interest. Many merchants and politicians in the Maritimes argued for precisely the opposite of protection: "My strong opinion is that it is the bounden duty of the Government of Canada in the interests of the trade of Canada to make the great ports of Canada absolutely free to the shipping of the Dominion, aye, open to the shipping of the world."[36]

The mercantilist obsession could easily liquidate even the memory of shipowning. This is precisely what happened in 1904, when Maritimers entertained the Royal Commission on Transportation. Canadians never had a royal commission on the decline of their shipping and shipbuilding industries; the Royal Commission on Transportation came closest to the issue. In hearing testimony, the commissioners made clear to their hosts that they were studying the entire transportation sector, both landward and seaward. As they moved from Saint John to St Andrews, and from Halifax to Sydney, they heard almost nothing about the local shipping industry. Apart from a parenthetical remark by George Robertson in Saint John, and a brief reference to shipbuilding by James Fraser of New Glasgow, there is no mention of the fate of the merchant marine of Canada, in an entire volume of testimony.[37] Maritimers instead urged the merits of their harbours as the future winter port of the Dominion and urged the commissioners to ignore the claims of other harbours, until the commission became largely an investigation of harbour facilities. Some argued for elimination of harbour dues; others insisted on better communications with the West Indies; others wanted a fast line of steamers to Britain (it was apparently of no consequence whose flag these steamers flew).

Haligonians wanted a new lightship, new grain terminals, and further extension of the railways along the harbour. "Halifax is the front door of Canada and the great outlet for Canadian commerce."[38] Entrepôt growth was a matter of national pride and even of manhood: "In 15 years we are likely to grow in Canada 300 million bushels of grain. Are we going to be true to ourselves and have that shipped through Canadian ports, or are we going to sacrifice our manhood as we have been doing, and ship 90 per cent of that grain through American ports? That is a question that touches our manhood."[39]

More important than local shipowning or shipbuilding was the problem of how to persuade American firms to ship 800,000 bunches of bananas to Canada through Saint John or Halifax, rather than through US ports.[40] Finally, at the end of the commission's first visit to the Maritimes, the issue of shipbuilding was raised: a speaker said that he was prepared to recommend a bounty for the building of steamships in Nova Scotia. The speaker was not a Maritimer. He was chairman of the commission – John Bertram of Toronto.[41]

Despite their remarkable lack of interest before the royal commission, in the early years of the century some Maritimers did launch appeals for protection for domestic shipping and shipbuilding. These requests were encouraged by several factors: belated recognition that local coal, iron, and steel production had made feasible the building of iron ships in the region; the increasing share of local coastal trading taken by foreign vessels; government purchases of steamships for the various marine services of the Dominion; and recognition that shipbuilding was an expanding industry elsewhere in Canada, particularly in Ontario and British Columbia.

Maritime MPs and civic politicians found new allies and new reasons to argue for protection. But the lobbying of the period was too little and too late. Maritimers interested in shipbuilding could no longer argue for maintenance of an existing industry and count on the support of capital and labour in that industry. Shipbuilding was collapsing, and even though a steel-hulled vessel had been built in Nova Scotia in 1893, Maritimers were compelled to argue for creation of a new industry.[42] And if they did win concessions, benefits would accrue to other regions, since the new industrial shipbuilding capacity was already located elsewhere in Canada. The ineffectual lobbying of these years was more symptom than cause of the decline of shipbuilding in the region. The lobbyists never overcame the reluctance of governments in a British Dominion to provide effective protection against competition from the mother country.

Much of the lobbying for bounties for shipbuilding came from politicians rather than from the steel industry, although at various times J.F. Stairs and Thomas Cantley of Scotia Steel took part.[43] The lobbying was sporadic and localized, coming at various times from different towns in the Maritimes. The Maritime Board of Trade supported shipbuilding bounties and a subsidy for Canadian ocean-going tonnage, but there was no regional consensus and no coherent regional bourgeoisie to create one.[44] Lobbying was often a response to specific actions by government and was therefore an occasional reaction rather than a sustained campaign.

In Parliament, for instance, the purchase of steamers for the various marine services of government provoked frequent debates over the tendering process and gave Maritimers an opportunity to lament the decline of their marine industries. The government purchased most of its steamers from shipyards in the United Kingdom, because they were usually much cheaper than Canadian-built steamers.[45]

And why were domestic-built vessels expensive? Some referred to the cost of labour, but most MPs agreed that the tariff structure was a more serious problem. Vessels built in the United Kingdom could be owned by Canadians and obtain Canadian registry without paying duty.[46] But many shipbuilding materials were subject to duty on entry to Canada, the "drawbacks" on duties paid were limited, and the government was not about to change this arrangement.

The interests arrayed against tariff protection for shipbuilding were formidable – and they existed in the Maritimes no less than in central Canada. The minister of finance, W.S. Fielding, explained one obstacle to his fellow Maritimers in 1907:

We are in this curious position. The British ship goes free the world over where the British flag flies. She is admitted free into Canada, while many of the materials out of which that ship is built, if brought into Canada separately, would be subject to duty. The conditions are therefore such as to discourage, if not to prevent the building of iron and steel ships in Canada, in competition with the shipyards of the mother country. Unless we are prepared to adopt the principle of taxing British ships coming into Canada – there might be some difficulties in the way of doing that, and honourable gentlemen on both sides might see grave objections to it – there is no way in which we can aid our shipbuilding enterprise other than by the direct way of granting a bounty ... We have not power to tax British ships.[47]

Among the "difficulties" in the way of tariff protection was Canadian acceptance of British maritime law and the British vessel registration system. It was virtually impossible to distinguish between British and Canadian ships, and hence a customs duty on British-built ships would be impossible to enforce: Canadian owners would simply keep their vessels on the United Kingdom's registers, as some did already. Domestic protection required much more than a mere tariff: it required independence from British jurisdiction in shipping. But Maritimers would not unite to demand independence of an imperial system to which they were committed by trade and tradition. They would continue to accept what one MP called "the inconveniences of the colonial regime."[48]

There were other "difficulties." Duties on imported iron and other ships' materials protected domestic iron and steel industries. While some would forfeit this protection to support shipbuilding, many others would not, especially if they represented iron-producing towns and industries. Furthermore, it was not clear that Canadian shipowners would benefit from protection given to domestic shipbuilders. Why should William Thomson and Co. of Saint John, which operated steamships in the Caribbean and elsewhere after the turn of the century, insist on bounties for domestic shipbuilding, when it could purchase tonnage from British shipyards? For shipowners, a new British enclave industry in shipbuilding was of little interest.

Would the coal and steel companies operating in Nova Scotia enter the steel shipbuilding business and join a campaign for bounties? Without their support, a campaign would never get off the ground. But the Dominion Iron and Steel Co., founded in 1899, had no mill for rolling the steel plate that might be used in ships.[49] The local iron and steel companies were much more concerned with meeting the demand from Canadian railways and other landward industries.[50] A single shipyard, itself facing uncertain markets, offered at best marginal demand for steel. Nova Scotian capital would not venture into this highly risky area without a guarantee of direct assistance from the state.

The obstacles were revealed most clearly in 1901 and 1902, when Harry Judson Crowe mounted a campaign to set up a shipyard in Halifax, won the apparent support of Swan and Hunter, the British shipbuilders, and won the promise of a bonus from the Halifax municipal government. Halifax investors and civic boosters were still obsessed with the idea of Halifax as "one of the world's main channels of commerce." The opportunities for commercial investment in "gathering and distributing" seem to have discouraged the longer time horizons required for investment in steel shipbuilding. As the initial capital requirement failed to be met, the need for duty-free entry of imported materials increased, and so did the size of the federal bounty that G.B. Hunter required.[51] Capital would not move without government support; Dominion politicians would not move without the firm commitment of capital. The project collapsed.

A century earlier no such obstacles had confronted the creation of an enclave industry in shipbuilding. Then the producers of shipbuilding materials made common cause with those who used ships and those who exported staples. Then the shipowner and the shipper were often the same merchant firm, and the builder was their client. Imperial protection, applied as it was to both goods and ships, encouraged sustained, albeit fluctuating demand for the products of the shipbuilder and the services of the shipowner. Now, a century later, no such integration of state policy and capital existed. The same imperial framework that once protected shipbuilding in the colonies now discouraged shipbuilding in the Canadian provinces. The raw materials for shipbuilding existed in the Maritimes, just as they had before, and now the manufactured inputs could be supplied locally too. Skilled labour could be imported, as it had been a century before, and Canadians elsewhere were proving that this was possible by building iron ships, even with minimal protection.

The difference now was that capital in the Maritimes was fragmented by the conditions of disarticulated development and an incomplete transition from merchant to industrial capital. Iron manufacturers, shipowners, and shippers were not part of a coherent regional or national bourgeoisie. They were urban élites of remarkable diversity, and many lived in towns that were still in the first stage of industrialization; they were rivals as often as they were political or class collaborators.

Furthermore, in the maritime sector, capital lacked any such integrated program of protection as had existed a century before. No national policy integrated the interests of capital in shipping with capital in trade so as to sustain a local shipbuilding industry. Divided among themselves and obsessed by landward development, merchant and industrial élites in the Maritimes united only briefly to demand such policy. Only a few years later, Maritimers would be among the more vigorous opponents of the Canadian Government Merchant Marine and the government shipbuilding program.[52]

The conditions of fragmented development are nowhere better revealed than in the debate over Canadian coastal trades. How far would the Canadian state protect capital invested in coastal shipping, and how far would Maritimers demand such protection? The United States offered a model: American coastal shipping was protected by navigation laws that simply excluded foreign-flag vessels from the carriage of goods between US ports. Canada failed to follow the precedent, and Maritimers participated in this failure. Without agreement over protection for coastal shipping, protection for ocean-going shipping was even more unlikely.

In the first decade of the century many Maritimers discovered to their surprise that Canadian coastal shipping was largely unprotected. A growing proportion of tonnage clearing Atlantic ports, in coasting and in ocean-going trades, was neither Canadian nor British. Why not simply bar Norwegians and other foreigners from our coastal trades, asked MP's? In 1906 W.S. Fielding replied that "you could not do so because of an existing imperial treaty."[53] Fielding was wrong. It was not imperial treaties but rather Canadian orders in council that granted foreigners entry to Canadian coasting. Such was the ignorance of parliamentarians that they failed to point out his error but went on to discuss the possibility of exemption from imperial treaties.

In fact, orders in council dating from the 1870s allowed several countries entry to Canadian coastal trades, those countries having agreed to allow Canadians to enter their coastal trades. The United States was not included, because that country would not grant reciprocal right of entry to its coastal trades.[54] It required only a Canadian order in council to revoke the right of foreign entry to Canadian coastal trades. At one level, this debate revealed not only "the inconveniences of the colonial regime" but also the accumulation of ignorance and uninterest, even among politicians from the Maritimes, in coastal shipping and its protection.

But would a Canadian government revoke the rights of foreign vessels in Canadian coastal trades? Some politicians and boards of trade had no doubt that it should. "Along the coast of Nova Scotia the Norwegians have driven our vessels from the sea. They have almost a monopoly of the coasting trade of Nova Scotia," said one MP, angered into exaggeration.[55] In 1908 foreign steamers provoked even more fury when owners and masters of schooners found themselves taking second place to Norwegian steamships loading coal in Cape Breton. In response, the Dominion government agreed to place some restrictions on foreign steamers.[56]

Norwegian ships would not be banned from Canadian coasting trades, however.[57] Just as the earlier debate over steamship subsidies became a debate between Maritimers, so too this was a debate between fractions of capital in the region. To the owners of ships, E.M. Macdonald of Pictou and Alexander Johnston of Cape Breton replied on behalf of shippers: "Until we have in Canada a sufficient supply of vessels for the purpose, it will be imperilling the coal industry of Nova Scotia to take too drastic measures with regard to the vessels at present engaged in that trade."[58]

The debate continued up to and even after the First World War, as governments restricted the coasting privilege to vessels of specific tonnages but declined to ban all foreign vessels. The Ship Masters Association and the National Association of Marine Engineers demanded that "our great shipping industry be placed on an equal footing" with coal and steel. In reply, the Nova Scotia Steel and Coal Corp. insisted that "it is a matter of supreme importance to them that no change should be made whereby the cost of freighting their product should be increased, which would be the immediate result if foreign vessels are debarred from coastal trading."[59] Norwegians remained in the coal trade, and the interest of shippers took precedence.

These episodes occurred at the end, not the beginning, of the decline of the shipping industries. They reveal the weakness, not the strength, of the marine industries and their defenders in the Maritimes. Nova Scotia Steel, with only modest exaggeration, made the point very clearly: it used foreign ships because similar Canadian ships did not exist. We are in favour of fostering the Canadian merchant marine "if this can be done," but "the fact remains that not a single dollar of Canadian money has gone into the type of vessels required for the coal trade since the agitation against foreign vessels started." Referring to the large Norwegian colliers hired on multi-year contracts, Thomas Cantley argued that there was no "Canadian-owned collier that would take the place of the boats now trading between Cape Breton and Montreal. The Companies themselves have not the necessary finances to build these steamers."[60] All of this was the end of the process by which the interests of shippers departed from those of shipowners.

If Maritimers could not protect their coastal trades, still less could they protect ocean trades. Foreign tonnage was, in any case, a small fraction of all tonnage in Canadian coasting.[61] The real losses to Canadian-flag shipping took place in external trades, where participation of Canadian tonnage fell to a mere 12 per cent by 1904, while foreign (meaning non-British) ships continued to account for over 30 per cent of tonnage. The more substantial competitors were British ships, and W.S. Fielding pointed out to his fellow Maritimers that if foreign vessels were excluded from Canadian trades, the beneficiaries would be British rather than Canadian ships.[62] Restrictions on British ships were scarcely thinkable.

The development of coal, iron, and steel led away from, not toward, the survival of shipbuilding and shipowning in the Maritimes. To a few civic boosters these new industries seemed to offer an opportunity to save the region's shipping industries. But these industries also emerged in a region whose development was shaped by merchant capitalists who were interested in trade goods and entrepôt growth and thoroughly predisposed to landward development. At the end of the age of sail, Maritimers were still a great trading people. More accurately, they were not a single people at all, but members of fragmented and diverse communities, moving at varying paces from the age of commerce to the age of industry and from the old Atlantic world to a new continental destiny.

CHAPTER NINE

Maritime Capital and Economic Development

Did it matter that the shipping and shipbuilding industries collapsed? In the depression of the 1920s and 1930s many Maritimers had no doubt, and Harold Innis, writing about New Brunswick, echoed their nostalgia:

Nothing that has occurred in this Province for the last half century has done more to create difficulty, has been a more serious blow to the development of that section of the Dominion than the decay of the industry of shipbuilding ... The competition of iron and steel destroyed a magnificent achievement, an integration of capital and labour, of lumbering, fishing and agriculture, on which rested a progressive community life. The linchpin was broken.[1]

Four decades later the lament for a golden age had faded, and a new generation had applied itself to the question of regional economic weakness. Far from being the linchpin of progressive development, shipbuilding and shipping "provided a mere ripple upon the existing economy."[2] So argued Peter McClelland, applying the new tools of export-base theory: shipbuilding was too unimportant, and too meagre in its linkage effects, to have been a central contributor to growth, and the decline of the industry had little to do with subsequent retardation. It was even possible that shipowning diverted capital and energies from more productive sectors: "To the extent that more attractive opportunities were available elsewhere, the growth of shipowning in the province was regrettable."[3]

Between these extreme positions lies the balanced conclusion of T.W. Acheson: although McClelland's argument may have merit in the context of New Brunswick as a whole, the sale of ships and of shipping services "played a vital role" in enabling Saint John merchants to settle their London and Liverpool accounts, and "the importance of shipbuilding to the economy of the city is inestimable."[4] The word "inestimable" is appropriate: the contribution of shipbuilding and shipping ultimately lies beyond precise measurement. And Acheson avoids the troublesome questions that Innis and McClelland raised.

The logical problem in Innis's formulation of the issue is obvious enough: if shipbuilding was obsolete anyway, how could it deal such a fatal blow to the economy, and how could it do so in the half-century after its disappearance? McClelland's rebuttal raised another question: if shipbuilding and shipowning were unproductive and unattractive, why should Maritimers have invested in such industries for so long as they did?

Like so many others who have written about Canada's Atlantic provinces, Innis and McClelland were deeply aware of the subsequent economic fate of these provinces. McClelland was seeking the sources of regional economic retardation: he found these in nineteenth-century economic sectors characterized by relatively slow productivity growth. Implicit in all of this is a comparison with other industries and other regions. Such comparisons may enlighten, but they may also mislead, for they may cause us to ask certain questions of the past but not others.

It is perfectly appropriate to ask why subsequent industrial growth was slower in the Maritimes than in central Canada. But it is necessary to ask also what form industrialization *did* take in the Maritimes and in what conditions the transition from mercantile to industrial capitalism occurred. Shipbuilding and shipowning had only a small place in the industrial economy of the Maritimes of the twentieth century. Both were part of the mercantile economy of the nineteenth century, and the decline of these industries was part of the transition that followed.

The economic history of the Maritime colonies in the two centuries after the founding of Halifax is the story of integration into an expanding international capitalism emanating from Britain, followed by integration into the economy of industrializing Canada. The pattern of this integration was directed by the ways in which merchants exploited resources and labour in these colonies. Very often merchant's capital acted as a solvent of pre-capitalist modes of production, particularly of independent commodity production. Even in shipping, merchants expanded both ownership and control, hiring wage labour to work larger sailing ships. Merchant ownership and wage labour appeared in shipbuilding, mining, iron, and other industries.

Parts of the region, especially the major urban centres, were well advanced toward industrial capitalism at the time of Confederation, and the emergence of trade unions is merely one indication of the appearance of an embryonic proletariat.[5] In some trades, the costs of labour, combined with difficulty of access to a resource, impelled merchants to replace labour with a more capital-intensive technology. In shipping his took place most clearly in Newfoundland's seal hunt, where falling rates of return encouraged a few merchants to invest in steamships in the 1860s and 1870s.

Merchant capital did not always have such a role, however. In many colonial frontiers, given a plentiful supply of land or resources, growth may occur through continued increase in the number of independent smallholdings and petty producers. Sometimes merchants could not undercut these small producers, and sometimes it was not in their interest to do so. The truck system in fishing and in lumbering allowed merchants to capture economic surplus through exchange relationships, without revolutionizing production or hiring wage labour.[6]

Although timber licensing led to high degrees of merchant control of timber output, small producers could still operate and farmers moved between agriculture and lumbering. In agriculture and fishing, small units of production persisted, and production was highly labour-intensive. So long as merchants could make profits from their domination of exchange relationships, and to the extent that immigration helped to lower labour costs, the incentive to transform production was weak. Pre-capitalist production could persist in many areas, and, as the history of Newfoundland's fishery most clearly attests, merchant capital was able to encourage such persistence, even to discourage the appearance of wage labour.[7]

Shipping and shipbuilding were part of the ambiguous heritage of merchant capital. Both industries were essential to the integration of the region with British and other overseas markets. Both industries facilitated accumulation of savings in the region, and both contributed to the rise of large family firms and a merchant class bent on economic diversification. At the same time, these industries placed specific limits on capitalist development and diversification.

Shipbuilding in the early nineteenth century had the character of an enclave industry. It was, in other words, established largely by external investors, with a large portion of both inputs and output exchanged in markets outside the colony or region. Every spring in the 1810s and 1820, small ships arrived in Prince Edward Island, laden with cordage, tar, pitch, resin, salt, lead, nails, anchors, and canvas – virtually all the materials required for building a vessel, except the timber. In 1826, imports into the island for shipbuilding were valued at over £25,000 sterling, or more than a quarter of the value of all imports.[8] English merchants also sent skilled labour, often on a seasonal basis.

The island's settlers cut and hauled timber, both for building the ship and for its cargo, and in return the merchants supplied the settlers with most of the necessities of survival – rope, cloth, powder and shot, oil, soap, salt, fishing gear, pots and pans, iron stoves, and many other producer and consumer goods. From the ships that brought such goods there quickly extended long lines of debt and credit: ships brought both the settlers and their supplies, merchants provisioned them for farming and timber-felling, and settlers repaid their debts in timber and agricultural produce. So began "the inevitable process by which the settlers passed into the thrall of the storekeeper," the process that allowed James Yeo to begin "driving his debtors to bring timber down to the creeks" whenever he wanted.[9] The wooden ship was an essential link in this process.

Even when those who financed much of the shipbuilding were colonial merchants, many of the inputs and much of the capital still came from Britain. In the 1840s we find the Wards of Saint John ordering building supplies from Gibbs, Bright and Co. of Liverpool: cordage, lead, nails, spikes, paint, oakum, compasses, and an array of other manufactured products.[10] Much of the final outfit of a new vessel was provided after the first passage to Liverpool. Even if the vessel were to remain in colonial hands, chains and anchors were often purchased and fitted in Liverpool, and in the 1860s this practice continued in order that colonial import duties might be avoided.[11]

Long after the 1820s, much of the capital for shipbuilding came from across the Atlantic in the form of credit extended by a Liverpool partner. In 1841 the Wards stated that "it had been our intention to build one ship every year" but admitted that "our own available capital is not sufficient for us to do so"; much of their building depended on the "continued assistance" of Gibbs, Bright and Co.[12] James Duncan of Charlottetown depended heavily on his partner in Liverpool and by 1878 owed him over $119,000.[13] Sometimes credit was extended in kind, in the form of chains, anchors, cordage, and other equipment.[14] Family connections as well as lines of credit often extended across the Atlantic, as they did with the Moran family and the Wrights of Saint John.[15]

The connections between such an enclave industry and the host society are necessarily very complex. The interaction was dynamic, not static, since both shipbuilding and the host economy were growing, and the links between shipbuilding and the surrounding population tightened with growth. Among theorists of economic development, an older view holds that dynamic linkages between such an enclave industry and the peripheral economy will be limited. Furthermore, intrusion of an imperialist "centre" into a dependent "periphery" is likely to involve the transfer of economic surplus from the latter to the former.

This simple "dependency" approach can no longer be sustained. In the present context, many of the more sophisticated inputs in shipbuilding were produced in Britain, and some portion of the profits from timber and ships went to capital in the mother country. But this was counterbalanced by a continuing flow of investment into the colonies (the deficit in the visible trade balance for New Brunswick, for instance, must have been covered from such investment, from the savings brought by immigrants, and from other "invisibles"). And even if many producer goods were imported, many small-scale processes of accumulation resulted from exchanges between shipbuilding and surrounding people.

This population did not consist of peasants engaged only in subsistence production: it was already involved in labour and commodity markets, if only at local levels. In the 1800s and 1810s a manufacturing industry was transplanted into many small communities that depended on fishing, farming, and timber-felling. A series of exchanges between the manufacturing industry and the primary sector followed, which served to sustain both. Shipbuilding brought some diversification, expansion of local markets, and increased employment opportunities for settlers.[16]

Ships assisted saving in the colonies by lowering the freight cost of exports and imports, but they also contributed directly to the colonial balance of payments and hence to provincial incomes. Although clearly an export commodity in themselves, ships were not normally included in official estimates of colonial exports. In the 1820s the customs collector in Prince Edward Island adjusted his export totals to account for vessels exported and arrived at the estimates shown in Graph 9.1. If the customs estimates of the value of vessels exported are accurate, then vessel exports had turned the visible trade balance positive.

A cautious re-estimate of the island's subsequent imports and exports suggests that the visible trade balance was likely to have been positive in most years before Confederation (see also Graph 9.2).[17] Islanders were certainly aware of this contribution of ships to their trade balances, and they could even exaggerate its importance: the Charlottetown *Patriot* said that vessel exports in 1875 added $700,000 to the export figure of $1.3 million for that year.[18] New Brunswick's

Graph 9.1
Prince Edward Island's Imports and Exports, 1822–8

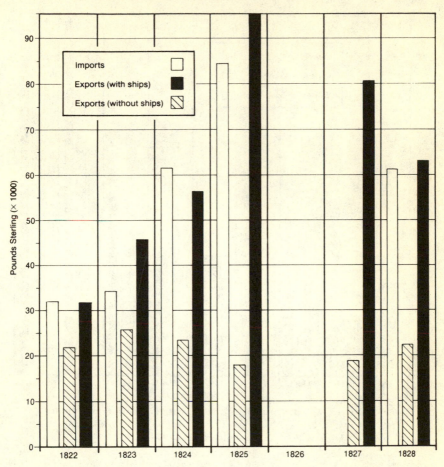

Source: Custom House Returns, *Journals of the House of Assembly*, Prince Edward Island, 1822–9.

trade balance probably remained negative in most years, but by the 1850s ships were probably adding about a third to the real value of provincial exports (Graph 9.3).[19]

These revisions of the trade balance do not take into account earnings of shipowners from external trade, which should also be included in provincial income accounts. Even if annual net earnings were only $3 per ton, New Brunswick's ocean-going fleets probably brought more than £80,000 sterling into the colony in an average year in the

Graph 9.2
Prince Edward Island's Imports and Exports, Selected Years, 1830–70

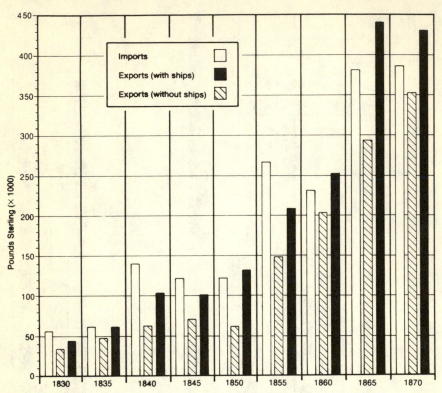

Source: Lewis R. Fischer, "Enterprise in a Maritime Setting: The Shipping Industry of Prince Edward Island, 1787–1914," unpublished research report, Maritime History Group, Memorial University of Newfoundland, 1978, 240.

1860s.[20] For such reasons as this, the controller of customs wrote as follows about shipowning in 1864: "The most advantageous branch of our trade in 1864 has probably been that of shipowning, which although not exceedingly prosperous for some time past, has been the means of introducing into the Colony a large amount of gold or its equivalent in exchange, to pay for our heavy imports during the year."[21] In its contribution to New Brunswick's trade, the shipping sector was second only to timber for most of the nineteenth century.

It is conceivable that, in the absence of either shipbuilding or local shipowning, alternative methods of transportation would have been found, and other contributors to the balance of payments discovered.

Graph 9.3

New Brunswick's Imports and Exports by Decade (Annual Average), 1820s–1860s

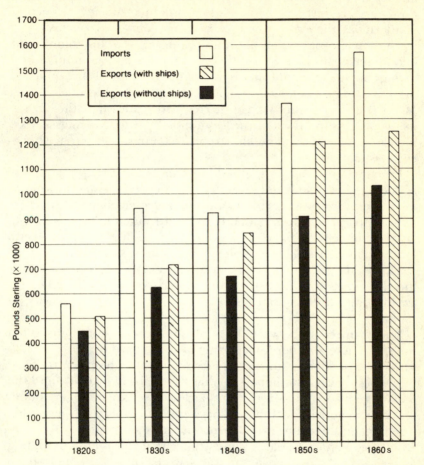

Sources: Colonial Office 193 series (New Brunswick Blue Books); New Brunswick, *Journals of the House of Assembly*; vessel registries for Saint John and Miramichi.
Note: The average for the 1860s is for 1860–6 only.

This kind of issue often arises in economic history, when the historian seeks to isolate the contribution of a particular industry. Long ago Robert Fogel argued that "to establish the proposition that railroads substantially altered the course of economic growth, one must do more than provide information on the services of railroads. It must also be shown that substitutes for railroads could not (or would not) have performed essentially the same role."[22] And years ago it was shown that this logic contained two separate questions: did shipbuilding or shipowning influence the pattern of local economic growth, and did these industries influence growth in ways that only they could do? One can answer the first question without answering the second; furthermore, the second question cannot be answered conclusively.[23]

The actual contribution of the shipping sector to the colonial balance of payments had several effects. It signified an accumulation of savings, in the form of profits, in the hands not only of British investors but also of a colonial merchant class. Shipbuilders, said Peter Mitchell of New Brunswick in 1878, "had made ships the savings banks of some portions of the Dominion."[24] Such "savings banks" increased the merchant's ability to hire labour and to purchase specific colonial products.

Even if many inputs in shipbuilding came from Britain, local linkages existed. The linkages extended well beyond those who worked in the shipyards, as a Pictou County newspaper observed in 1854: "This activity in trade is evidently to be attributed to the amount of ship building going on, which, besides giving employment to several hundred men – carpenters, riggers, blacksmiths, &c., also gives much work to a large number of persons from the county who supply the ship yards with timber, or the merchants with top timber for exportation, thus causing the circulation of large amounts of capital."[25]

The connection between farming and shipbuilding was often noted: "There was hardly a farmer in the province who did not, some time or another, during the winter get out a few floor timbers, foothooks, knees, top timbers, or hardwood logs for plank, and the dollars he made in this way he regarded as so much money found, for these materials for shipbuilding were got out during the winter, when he and his teams would otherwise have been idle."[26] In 1878, J.C. Pope of Prince Edward Island argued that tariffs on shipbuilding materials, by depressing shipbuilding, were "ruinous to the farmers of this Province."[27] Farmers provided labour, timber, foodstuffs, and other inputs in shipbuilding, and the industry became part of the seasonal round of activity in a society characterized by occupational pluralism.

The nature of such exchanges and the movement of labour from one activity to another make it impossible to measure the contribution of shipbuilding exactly. Census data, for instance, may be quite misleading. The 1871 census reported 1,364 hands employed in New Brunswick shipyards, suggesting that shipbuilding and ship material–making accounted for only 8.3 per cent of all industrial employment in New Brunswick.[28]

It is likely, however, that the enumerators recorded only those employed at the time of enumeration; they do not tell us the total number of persons employed in shipyards during the year. Shipyard workers in Nova Scotia numbered 2,058 in 1870, according to the same census, though slightly more tonnage was built in New Brunswick in that year! Fortunately we know from other sources the share of production costs accounted for by wages, and we know how many man-days of labour were invested in the building of a ship. Given the total tonnage produced in New Brunswick in 1870, the census appears to have underestimated labour inputs by at least 20 per cent. Shipbuilding accounted probably for over 12 per cent of industrial wages in that year.[29]

In the 1850s and early 1860s shipbuilding employment was even more important. The shipping registrar estimated that there were at least 2,000 men employed in producing ships and ship materials in Saint John in 1863. In the province as a whole those employed in shipbuilding were likely to be double that number (by comparison, the 1861 census estimated 14,110 people in "industrial class" occupations in the province). Total wages paid to those employed in shipbuilding were probably at least $1 million that year, possibly as much as $1.6 million.[30] This represents a very substantial cash flow in such a small economy: by comparison, the gross value of New Brunswick exports of forest products was only $3 million in 1863.

We cannot determine total payments to labour from shipbuilding, not least because an unknown portion was not in the form of wages. But if we accept that gross provincial product was $35.6 million in 1870, then GPP was probably slightly more than $31 million in the early 1860s; and if labour's share was two-fifths of GPP (as it is in most modern economies), then shipbuilding may have accounted for 10 to 12 per cent of all payments to labour in the economy.[31] This calculation does not take into account the multiplier effect of these payments, or the fact that purchases of local materials such as timber and planking also involved payments to the workers who had cut such timber. And it ignores the cash flow resulting from profits and wages in shipping (rather than shipbuilding). Annual wage payments in a fleet of 200,000 tons were probably about $700,000 in the early 1860s. This cannot be added to the above estimates, of course, because there is no way of knowing what portion remained within New Brunswick's economy.

To estimate the share of national income or gross provincial product accounted for by shipbuilding and shipping is much more difficult. McClelland estimated total shipyard sales in 1870 to be slightly more than 3 per cent of provincial product.[32] Shipbuilding output in that year was below average for the third quarter of the century, however, and the value figure in the census is an underestimate.[33] It is more likely that shipbuilding accounted for at least 5 per cent of provincial product in the third quarter of the century and in peak years, such as 1863–4, for more than 10 per cent.[34] Having arrived at such numbers, there is still room for debate over their significance; while some historians will take them to be small, David Alexander thought them large. As a point of comparison, and despite the debate over the significance of the "wheat boom" in Canada's economy, wheat exports accounted for about 3 per cent of GNP in the first decade of the twentieth century.[35]

Shipping was a separate business, of course, but sales of this transport service cannot be added to shipyard sales in estimating shares of GPP, since shipping used shipyard output as its input. Taken by itself, however, New Brunswick's ocean-going fleet of the early 1870s (about 200,000 tons) earned gross revenues of about $16 to $20 per ton per year, or between 9 and 11 per cent of GPP. Shipowning, as we have already seen, was probably profitable in these years and may in the early 1870s have contributed a quarter of all profits in the province.[36] The evidence suggests that, taken separately or together, shipbuilding and shipowning were substantial industries in New Brunswick; certainly they were much more than "a mere ripple upon the existing economy."

This is merely to confirm what contemporaries often said: that these industries were large. Given the size of the fleets built and owned there, and given that these colonies were major shipowning societies in terms of tonnage built and owned per capita, the idea that these industries were minor contributors to provincial output, profits, and wages is not credible. More important is the specific nature of the interactions between shipping and the society of which it was part. There can be no doubt that these industries generated a substantial cash flow through the economy. They were also a significant part of the profits of merchant capital and so assisted the accumulation of surplus by merchants. Shipyards and sailing ships were artisanal "manufactories," subject to increasing concentration and growing division between capitalist employer and wage labour. Using increasing amounts of iron and other industrial products, and large numbers of wage labourers, shipping moved slowly in the direction of industrial capital.

How far did these industries move their host societies toward more developed industrial capitalism? The question remains unanswered, because the net effects of such industries are very difficult to measure,

Table 9.1
Annual Wage Payments ($) per Employee, New Brunswick and
Nova Scotia, 1870–90

Year	Province	Shipyards	Ship Materials	All Industries
1870	New Brunswick	254	334	211
	Nova Scotia	238	261	204
1880	New Brunswick	241	345	194
	Nova Scotia	274	257	201
1890	New Brunswick	311	309	224
	Nova Scotia	313	306	207

Sources: Canada Census, 1871, 1881, and 1891.

but we must note the ways in which shipping and shipbuilding may have impeded the development of industrial capitalism. Peter McClelland led the way here with his discussion of the productivity of regional industries. McClelland and others have argued that the dominant economic activities in New Brunswick did not lend themselves to sustained growth in productivity and that there may have been a chronic problem of low per-capita incomes in the region as a whole.[37]

If we examine the simplest neo-classical measures of such things, the shipping sector does not appear a major culprit. Wages in shipbuilding and ship material–making were higher than wages in other industries (Table 9.1).[38] Although the figures must not be read as precise estimates of annual average wages, they suggest that wages were relatively high in shipbuilding and also that the differential between wages in shipbuilding and other occupations may have increased over time. If one is looking for sources of low per-capita incomes, one must look to other economic sectors.

If "productivity" is measured in terms of output per worker or output per capital employed, then shipbuilding was a relatively productive industry, even in 1890. Tables 9.2 and 9.3 show value added per worker and per unit of capital invested in shipyards, where value added is simply the gross value of products minus the value of raw materials. Comparisons from one census year to the next may be of little value (especially in the measures of "capital productivity" in Table 9.3). The point is to establish relative magnitudes, and these suggest that shipbuilding was not relatively unproductive.[39] Indeed, when Maritimers shifted capital from wooden shipbuilding to other industries, it seems that they were moving into relatively unproductive industries. It may be, of course, that shipbuilding was not conspic-

Table 9.2
Value Added ($) per Employee in Shipyards and in
All Industrial Establishments, 1870–90

Year	Province	Shipyards	All Industries
1870	New Brunswick	475	432
	Nova Scotia	489	419
1880	New Brunswick	407	374
	Nova Scotia	500	419
1890	New Brunswick	488	425
	Nova Scotia	578	427

Sources: Canada Census, 1871, 1881, 1891.

uously productive but rather that there was a serious problem with the productivity of labour and capital in industries outside the marine sector.

In the context of the Maritimes, shipbuilding yielded a fairly substantial value added from a combination of skilled labour and relatively small inputs of capital. Although productive by the narrow measures used above, the industry was also characterized by low capital intensity. The capital–labour ratio was much lower than in other industries in 1870, and the difference increased over time, at least in New Brunswick.[40] The comparison with Ontario shipyards by 1890, where production of steamships had already begun, suggests that Ontario shipyards were much larger on average, with much higher capital–labour ratios and much higher levels of value added per worker. The capital–labour ratio was more than six times higher in Ontario than in New Brunswick.[41]

Shipbuilding and shipowning were productive and profitable, and they certainly brought a substantial cash flow to the region, but they did not contribute much to a transition to industrial capitalism. Much of the labour employed in these industries was that of skilled craftsmen. It was difficult to displace such labour: the techniques of wooden ship construction did not lend themselves to labour-replacing technologies. By 1870 the industrial transformation was more advanced in other industries, and if employers wished to free themselves from dependence on the volatile, mobile, and highly skilled labour force in shipbuilding and shipping, the easiest path was to invest in other industries.

The problem in shipowning was the extraordinary way in which the industry required the owner of capital to entrust his or her entire assets to a labour force that was beyond immediate supervision and

Table 9.3
Value Added ($) per Capital Invested, Shipyards and
All Industrial Establishments, 1870–90

Year	Province	Shipyards	All Industries
1870	New Brunswick	3.83	1.33
	Nova Scotia	3.36	1.08
1880	New Brunswick	1.69	0.88
	Nova Scotia	1.85	0.84
1890	New Brunswick	3.01	0.72
	Nova Scotia	1.78	0.78

Sources: Canada Census, 1871, 1881, 1891.

control. The problem in shipbuilding was that a large proportion of value was received by labour rather than by capital. The wage levels in Table 9.1 suggest this, but so also does the measure known as surplus value, and its relation to capital. Surplus value is the difference between what workers produce and what they receive for their upkeep; this difference accrues to capital in the form of profits, interest, and rents.

A simple approximation is the result of subtracting wages, productive salaries, and depreciation from value added. If we then divide this amount – the surplus value that accrues to capital – by wages and productive salaries, we get the rate of surplus value, a well-known measure in Marxist economics. The higher this rate, the larger the portion of value added accruing to capital, and the smaller the share going to labour as wages and salaries. A rate of one indicates that value added was divided equally between capital and labour; less than one indicates a smaller share went to capital than to labour.[42]

Table 9.4 gives approximations of surplus value and suggests that the rate of surplus value in shipbuilding was low even in 1870. It was lower than in many other industries, even in the Maritimes. Shipbuilding in the Maritimes appears to have been a poor generator of surplus value, and a relatively high proportion of value realized from production returned to labour rather than to capital, even when the industry was most productive.

The last column in Table 9.4, however, suggests an important qualification: the ratio of surplus value to total capital advanced (the rate of profit) was relatively high in both 1870 and 1880. That the industry survived as long as it did is no surprise: although labour-intensive, it appears to have been relatively profitable, and profit rates alone cannot explain the shift of capital from shipbuilding. The

Table 9.4
Estimates of Surplus Value and Profit Rates in Shipbuilding and
Other Industries, 1870 and 1880

Industry	Capital Invested ($000) (C)	Value Added ($000)	Wages and Salaries ($000) (V)	Surplus Value ($000) (SV)	SV/ V	SV/ (C+V)
1870						
Shipyards						
New						
Brunswick	169.2	648.6	355.9	282.5	0.79	0.54
Nova Scotia	299.4	1,007.3	546.3	443.1	0.81	0.52
Ontario	134.0	229.1	172.2	48.9	0.28	0.16
Cotton Factories						
New						
Brunswick	125.0	55.6	22.7	25.4	1.12	0.17
Ontario	457.0	212.2	87.8	96.9	1.10	0.18
Foundries and Machine Working						
New						
Brunswick	314.2	402.1	205.6	177.6	0.86	0.34
Nova Scotia	307.1	338.4	174.3	145.7	0.84	0.30
Ontario	2,403.5	3,055.2	1,630.9	1,280.2	0.79	0.32
Wool Cloth Making						
New						
Brunswick	52.1	53.8	17.8	32.9	1.85	0.47
Nova Scotia	71.8	41.3	21.2	15.7	0.74	0.17
Ontario	2,254.7	1,882.9	785.9	961.6	1.22	0.32
Sugar Refining						
Nova Scotia	25.0	10.0	6.8	1.7	0.25	0.05
Quebec	400.0	406.8	112.2	270.6	2.41	0.53
All Industry						
New						
Brunswick	5,976.2	7,935.9	3,956.2	3,621.2	0.91	0.36
Nova Scotia	6,041.9	6,531.8	3,237.9	2,931.4	0.91	0.32
Ontario	37,874.0	49,591.9	21,989.2	25,330.4	1.15	0.42
1880						
Shipyards						
New						
Brunswick	224.9	379.7	230.2	136.0	0.59	0.30
Nova Scotia	527.2	976.5	551.6	393.2	0.71	0.36
Ontario	110.9	191.8	139.9	45.3	0.32	0.18
Cotton Factories						
New						
Brunswick	380.0	107.9	40.2	44.9	1.12	0.11
Ontario	1,766.5	878.7	383.0	389.7	1.02	0.18

Table 9.4 – *continued*

Industry	Capital Invested ($000) (C)	Value Added ($000)	Wages and Salaries ($000) (V)	Surplus Value ($000) (SV)	SV/ V	SV/ (C+V)
Foundries and Machine Working						
New						
Brunswick	408.6	323.1	177.9	120.7	0.68	0.21
Nova Scotia	478.5	353.1	181.6	142.8	0.79	0.22
Ontario	4,933.5	3,619.7	1,931.6	1,392.1	0.72	0.20
Wool Cloth Making						
New						
Brunswick	49.3	36.1	18.3	14.8	0.81	0.22
Nova Scotia	155.1	94.9	50.5	35.1	0.70	0.17
Ontario	3,455.5	2,561.5	1,175.6	1,178.5	1.00	0.25
Sugar Refining						
New						
Brunswick	200.0	175.0	75.3	87.7	1.16	0.32
Nova Scotia	350.0	202.0	48.2	132.8	2.75	0.33
Quebec	1,600.0	700.0	240.5	363.5	1.51	0.20
All Industry						
New						
Brunswick	8,425.3	7,451.8	3,958.6	2,987.7	0.75	0.24
Nova Scotia	10,183.1	8,553.3	4,191.3	3,730.9	0.89	0.26
Ontario	80,950.8	66,825.7	31,393.9	30,574.7	0.97	0.27

Sources: Canada *Census*, 1871, 1881; see also Phillip J. Wood, "Barriers to Capitalist Development in Maritime Canada, 1870–1930: A Comparative Perspective," in Peter Baskerville, ed., *Canadian Papers in Business History*, I (Victoria: Public History Group, 1989), 33–57.
Note: Value added is total value of products minus the value of raw materials. The approximation of surplus value is value added minus yearly wages, depreciation, and productive salaries. Depreciation is 6 per cent of the census figure for capital invested. For each industry, productive salaries are the average annual wage times the number of establishments, divided by 2. For all industries, productive salaries are half of 1 per cent of the total value of products. Wages and salaries (v) are the sum of yearly wages and productive salaries. The method and results differ only slightly from those of Phillip Wood. See also note 42.

industry-wide profit rates were only slightly lower in the Maritimes than in Ontario, and it appears that significant differences in profit rates between regions did not appear until after 1890.[43]

Such an industry involved a dependence on skilled labour that capital could do little to avoid. It was possible to increase returns to capital by shedding labour or cutting wages, but only within certain limits. Given their occupational pluralism and the nature of their skills, shipyard workers had other options (including even migration

from the region) which allowed them to resist wage cuts. Shipyard
workers had a tradition of organization: the caulkers, for instance,
could be neither replaced nor easily defeated, and they did not hesitate to strike, as they did in Saint John for several months in 1864.[44]
Like other economic activities in the region, such as fishing, shipbuilding was an industry in which the substitution of capital for labour
was difficult. To the extent that this evidence tells us something about
social relations of production, it indicates a low rate of exploitation
and a reason for the movement of capital into other industries.

Relatively low capital intensity in shipbuilding meant a limited
demand for producer goods and few linkages to new industries in
which many Maritimers were interested. The weakness of these linkages is in itself a major reason for the decline of the industry and
for the absence of laments over that decline. Capital equipment in
shipbuilding included a steam plant, a sawpit (or occasionally a sawmill), blacksmith's equipment, a steam-box used to soften planks, and
an array of axes, adzes, and augers.

Much more likely to generate linkages was the variety of materials
contained in a finished vessel. In 1876 Frank Killam of Yarmouth
estimated that a 1,000-ton wooden vessel contained about sixty tons of
iron. Iron or copper was contained in the fastenings, knees, diagonal
strapping, channel plates, mast fittings (and some masts were iron),
rudder gudgeons, pintles, nails, spikes, chain, anchor, windlass, capstans, pumps, and rigging. By the 1860s, about 20 per cent of the
cost of a vessel came from metal inputs.[45] The resulting demand for
metal products was significant: about $400,000 a year in the 1860s,
in New Brunswick, given an annual average shipyard output of
52,000 tons. The value of output in New Brunswick metal industries
in 1871 was only about $1.7 million. Had shipyards ordered all their
metal inputs from local producers, there would clearly have been a
significant impetus to provincial metal industries.

But most metal inputs were imported, and the low colonial tariffs
on shipbuilding materials encouraged this.[46] The industry could easily import its more sophisticated industrial inputs and sometimes
install them on arrival in England.[47] In the early 1860s about a third
of the cost of a new sea-going ship came from imported materials,
principally the fastenings, chains, anchors, and other metal equipment.[48] By the 1870s it is likely that a larger proportion of the metal
was locally produced. Iron foundries in Nova Scotia and New Brunswick were producing windlasses, capstans, pumps, and other gear,
although the pig iron was still imported. Frank Killam explained that
this had occurred because "we prefer articles of this kind made under

our own inspection; we can then superintend their construction, and can reject any article if it does not suit, which we cannot do if we import it."[49]

Shipbuilding certainly stimulated some growth in iron production and encouraged the appearance of such firms as the Burrell Johnson Iron Co. of Yarmouth. But the direct spin-offs were still limited, because metal inputs were still imported. Asked about the effect of a duty on the "iron and material you now receive duty free," Frank Killam replied that a 20 per cent duty would increase the cost of a ship by $1.75 a ton – which again suggests that imported materials were 20 per cent of the final cost. Even if half of the metal inputs were produced locally by the 1870s, this would represent only 9 per cent of the value of metal industries' output in New Brunswick in the 1870s.[50]

In the 1870s, imports of all ship materials into New Brunswick and Nova Scotia remained substantial, even after a 5 per cent ad valorem duty was applied to some materials, beginning in 1873–4. Graph 9.4 shows annual imports of manufactured ship materials, including anchors, chain cables, lamps, blocks, pumps, steering apparatus, wire rigging, knees, masts, cordage, and sailcloth. In colonial economies with small producer-goods sectors, these imports were substantial. In a single decade Nova Scotians imported $4.2 million in manufactured goods for ships, and New Brunswickers imported $3.6 million. For every dollar of ship's materials produced in the region, $1.40 worth of such goods was imported, and this is if anything an underestimate.[51] The spin-offs from shipbuilding to other industries were limited, not only by the nature of the industry and its inputs but also by the tendency to import manufactured inputs. This tendency resulted from the low tariffs on which the industry insisted, from longstanding connections of merchant capital with British and US suppliers, and from the low cost of inward freights, which the plentiful supply of locally owned tonnage encouraged.

In using manufactured inputs produced elsewhere, shipbuilders contributed to the disarticulated character of the regional economy. In such an economy, units of production are juxtaposed but not highly integrated vis-à-vis each other; the proportion of exchanges with centres outside the region, relative to exchanges within the region, is higher than in more developed capitalist countries.[52] In the Maritimes, linkages from mining, shipbuilding, and agriculture were often realized outside the region. It is impossible to measure precisely the effect of this "loss" of multiplier effects, but one indication of its importance in the Maritimes is the continuing dependence of these provinces on imports, especially of manufactured goods.

Graph 9.4

Ship Materials Imported into Nova Scotia and New Brunswick, 1869–78

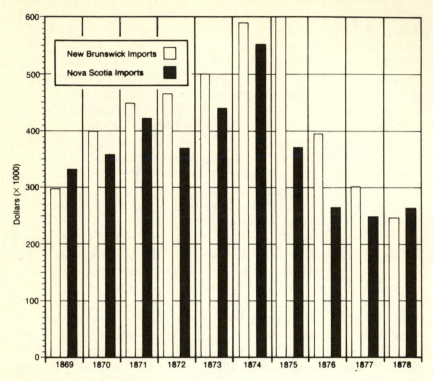

Sources: Tables of Trade and Navigation, Canada, *Sessional Papers*, 1870–9; Canada, *Census*, 1871, 1881. From 1874, ship materials that entered at 5 per cent are added to those entering free.

Table 9.5 gives a few measures of this import dependence, at the point when interprovincial trade flows were still small. Per capita spending on imports was much higher in the Maritimes than in Ontario, for instance, and spending on imported manufactures was about double that of Ontarians. In the Maritimes, a very high proportion of all manufactures came from imports: for the two provinces together imported manufactures were about 35 per cent of the value of domestic industrial products.

Shipbuilders contributed to this import dependence in more ways than one. They imported ship materials, but they also produced ships, which gave them a vested interest in external trade and, very often, spare inward tonnage which helped to lower freight costs and so to keep import prices lower than they might otherwise have been.

Table 9.5
Measures of Imports by Value, Nova Scotia, New Brunswick, and
Ontario, 1870

	Nova Scotia	New Brunswick	Ontario
Total imports per capita ($)	23.1	24.0	16.1
Imports entered for consumption per capita ($)	20.6	22.9	15.1
Manufactured imports per capita ($)	14.3	17.4	7.7
(Manufactured imports/ provincial industrial output) × 100	45	29	11

Sources: Tables of Trade and Navigation, Canada Sessional Papers, 1871, no. 3; Canada Census, 1871.
Note: "Imports of manufactured goods" includes the following: all goods paying 15 per cent ad valorem duty; all goods paying 5 per cent ad valorem duty; drugs, dyes, and oils entering free; manufactures, metal goods, and ship materials entering free; and ale and beer, cigars, coal oil, kerosene, patent medicines, refined petroleum, refined sugar, tobacco, and wine and spirits.

Every year shipowners struggled to find inward cargoes: in an average year in the 1860s and 1870s more than 300,000 tons of shipping entered New Brunswick in ballast, and this figure rose to more than 490,000 tons a year in the 1880s.[53] Not all of this tonnage was locally owned or locally built, but much of it was, and the long-standing interest of merchant capital in bulk exports contributed to this massive spare capacity in inward transportation.

Of course there were exchanges between the shipping sector and other parts of the regional economy. These exchanges, however, were more often within the primary sector and tended to stabilize pre-capitalist social relations and subsistence production. Many exchanges were highly localized and so did not tend toward creation of a regional market. At the level of labour, which moved seasonally between occupations, there was a close integration among shipbuilding, farming, and other occupations.

The principal input in shipbuilding – timber – sustained such integration. About 25 per cent of the costs of new tonnage went toward timber inputs, including boards, plank, spars, knees, and treenails.[54] For New Brunswick, this resulted in an annual average payment of about $520,000 for ship's timber and planking in the 1860s and about $370,000 in the 1870s; for Nova Scotia, about

$408,000 a year in the 1860s and $570,000 in the 1870s. This demand for timber did not account for a very large share of all timber felled, but it was still fairly significant, representing about 12 per cent of all sawmill output in the two provinces taken together in 1870 and about 10 per cent of sawmill output in 1880.[55] Furthermore, these payments did not accrue to a specific branch of the economy, such as sawmilling, since the timber was provided by a range of people – farmers, timber merchants, and even shipyard employees themselves. Since the cutting of ship's timber and planking was labour-intensive, a high proportion of these purchases were probably payments to labour.

Taken together, shipbuilding and shipping gave seasonal employment to large numbers of people and offered cash payments which supplemented the annual incomes of farmers, fishermen, mariners, lumbermen, and their families. To employment in shipbuilding we must add, of course, work in shipping. In mid-summer 1870 about 12,000 people would have been required by the fleets of the Maritime provinces, if all vessels were at sea. Of course only a portion of these workers were residents of the region, but even if two-thirds of the sailors in coastal vessels and only 15 per cent of those in ocean-going vessels were Maritimers, there may have been 4,000 Maritimers at sea in the summer of 1870, earning between $15 and $20 a month. Even if these mariners worked at sea for only four months in the year, we must add another $300,000 to the flow of cash in the regional economy.

These exchanges supplemented incomes in the primary sector of the economy. In doing so, shipping and shipbuilding helped to stabilize labour-intensive staple production and subsistence agriculture. By allowing the import of foodstuffs at low freight costs, the shipping industry further detracted from any incentive to transform agriculture. The result was the persistence of small units of production and highly labour-intensive farming techniques, as compared, for instance, to Ontario.

There was an even more direct relationship between shipping and the fisheries. In fishing, small operators were also very numerous, and the vessel was a type of smallholding itself, the marine equivalent to the family farm. Fishermen worked for shares in the catch rather than wages. In the Maritimes, as in Newfoundland, merchants had little incentive to transform the means of production. More fishermen meant more fish, and labour bore the cost of any decline in prices. Although the statistical evidence is suspect, it appears that labour in the Nova Scotia fishery increased much more rapidly than did fishing boats and vessels between 1850 and 1880.[56] The fishery was becoming more labour-intensive, and very likely a smaller proportion of fishing families could subsist on fishing alone. This must have reinforced the tendency toward occupational pluralism, itself a defence of subsistence and a rejection of dependence on wage labour.

The small schooner allowed easy access to local markets and to fishing and so was part of the productive system in both farming and fishing. The schooner was more than a symbol of independence; it allowed movement between places and occupations. By connecting rural smallholders to markets, it did more to retard than to accelerate the development of capitalism. As early as 1830 the perceptive Capt. Moorsom had noted the connections among occupational pluralism, access to the sea, and the slow development of a capitalist labour market in Nova Scotia. The current depression was caused, he thought, by a "natural indolence which induces a man to rest satisfied if he can 'make out', without being at the trouble of bettering his condition"; and it was caused by "these people having arrived at, and remaining in, that state which, in ignorance of the great principle of the division of labour, makes a man partly depend on land, partly on water, for his subsistence, instead of attending wholly to one, while his neighbour looks wholly to the other."[57]

Joseph Howe also noted the way in which water-borne trade assisted rural smallholders and their "natural antipathy to labour." Around Cornwallis, he said, "the great mass of its population may live, and live well, by working three days a week ... The soil is highly fertile and productive – yielding, with less than ordinary labor, almost all of the necessaries of life in abundance; surrounded by water in every direction, export and import of bulky articles are easily made." In such conditions "every farmer ... ought at least to be independent."[58]

Howe deplored the habits of consumption that independence seemed to allow and saw a connection between access to imports and low farm productivity: "Men own farms – or at all events hold them ... but few labour as assiduously as they could, or derive from their land as much as it might be able to yield ... Almost all expend more for importations, either for personal and household decoration, or to administer to the profusion of their tables, than is consistent with the dignity and character of the Farmer."[59] Beyond Howe's romantic image lay the indistinct divisions of labour and the struggle for self-sufficiency among pre-capitalist farmers. These conditions endured into the last half of the century, assisted by the huge, often locally owned transportation system.

The size of this system of transport explodes the myth of outport "isolation." In the absence of detailed price indices and freight costs, either for towns or for provinces, we cannot estimate the effects of this capacity on incomes or on local production in the Maritimes. But the volume of tonnage entering and clearing the outports allowed these settlements to appear and to survive. On a per capita basis, the volume of seaward transportation was much larger in Nova Scotia than it was in Quebec, for instance. In 1880, by this measure, Arichat, Barrington, and Shelburne were greater ocean ports than Montreal.[60] In Nova Scotia, more ocean-going and international tonnage entered the outports than entered the major entrepôt, Halifax.[61] By lowering the costs of access to markets, shipping tonnage reduced the social and economic costs of dispersed settlement and so retarded the development of urban centres and more concentrated labour markets.

Shipbuilding and shipping encouraged the survival of occupational pluralism and independent commodity production, even as they facilitated the mercantile capture of economic surplus through control of exchange and transportation. The farmers, fishermen, and coastal mariners refused to be separated from the means of their subsistence and means of production.

The extent to which this refusal involved struggles was most clear in the 1900s and 1910s, when schooner-owners battled foreign steamships and new corporate interests in coastal trading: "We have some remnants of the coasting trade left around the coasts of New Brunswick, Nova Scotia and Prince Edward Island; and under the system in vogue for a number of years past that coasting trade has been oppressed by these large corporate interests, who have paid no attention to the local needs of the people, that it is not able to subsist, and will go out of business unless this government remedies the evils that assail it."[62] The battle against steamships occurred at the end of a long struggle to subsist and to preserve the networks of independent commodity production in outport villages.

Of course, wooden ships by themselves did not retard the development of industrial capitalism. What stabilized the mercantile economy was not ships but the system of exploitation of which those ships were a central part. The tendency to import, for instance, was not simply a function of "dependence" on Britain. It resulted from the relations of production on the colonial frontier and the contradictions inherent in these relations. Despite the appearance of wage labour in many sectors, non-capitalist class relations persisted, and movement from wage labour to non-wage production was extensive throughout the century. Mercantile capitalists captured economic surplus, through control of exchange and distribution, partly through ownership or control of a very large shipping sector.

By the 1850s and 1860s many of these merchants also sought to develop local manufacturing, through import substitution and through exploitation of immigrant labour. But exploitation through control of exchange and distribution worked against the transition to industrial capital. Merchants with a vested interest in ships and commodity exchange sought low tariffs in order to import those same goods which others wanted to produce locally, within protected markets. The acquisition of ships allowed merchants to avoid the social and capital costs and risks of manufacturing: thus ship materials could be imported from Britain or the United States, thereby avoiding dependence on a high-wage labour force in the colony itself.

The story of ships' materials is part of a much larger picture. By allowing the import of foodstuffs and agricultural products at low freight costs, the large supply of inward tonnage diminished the incentive to transform agriculture. By supplementing the cash incomes of farmers and lumbermen and their sons, shipping and shipbuilding assisted in the survival of occupational pluralism, rural smallholdings, and low-productivity, labour-intensive agriculture and fishing. Although ships brought immigrants, they also assisted emigration.

In all these ways, merchant shipowning worked toward the survival of independent commodity production and against a basic condition of the transition to industrial capitalism – creation of a larger capitalist labour market. Massive investment in sailing ships was therefore not simply a "diversion" of capital from productive to unproductive sectors. It affected the entire structure of social relations in which the transition to industrial capitalism was occurring. As an experiment with capitalist class relations, shipowning was cautious and ambiguous. Most of the industry's wage labour resided outside the region. Coastal shipping was usually a form of independent commodity production. And even ocean shipping entailed specific obstacles to a rapid transition to industrial capitalism.

It is probably no mere coincidence, therefore, that relatively slow capitalist development in the Maritimes began in the third quarter of the nineteenth century, at the height of the age of sail. In 1850 industry was as well developed in the Maritimes as in Upper Canada (Table 9.6). The evidence suggests that, with the possible exception of iron foundries, industry was larger in the Maritimes, on a per capita basis.

However, there was a larger proportion of industrial investment in wooden shipbuilding in the Maritimes. In the 1850s and 1860s, industrial expansion took place much more rapidly in Ontario (Table 9.7). As Maritimers continued to build their wooden sailing fleets,

Table 9.6
Per Capita Measures of Industry Size in 1850

Industry	No. Establishments per 1,000 Population			No. "Hands" per 1,000 Population		
	NS	NB	Ont.	NS	NB	Ont.
Grist mills	1.1	1.3	0.7	2.1	1.9	1.2
Saw mills	4.2	3.0	1.6	6.5	22.2	3.9
Tanneries	0.9	0.6	0.2	1.4	1.3	0.5
Foundries	0.03	0.06	0.1	0.5	1.2	1.0
Weaving/ carding/ woollens	0.3	0.3	0.2	0.4	0.5	0.9
Breweries	0.1	0.04	0.05	0.2	n.a.	0.1
Other factories	0.5	0.5	0.4	0.7	4.9	n.a.

Sources: Census of Upper Canada, 1851–2; Census of Nova Scotia, 1851; Census of New Brunswick, 1871; Canada, Census, 1871.

Ontarians invested heavily in railways, iron foundries, and machine shops. By 1870 industrial output per capita was 60 per cent greater in Ontario than in the two Maritime provinces.[63] The pattern of all subsequent development began in the age of wood and sail.

What if the shipping sector had survived and made the transition to iron and steel? This is an entirely separate question, which cannot be answered by referring to the effects of shipping and shipbuilding in the era of wood and sail. All too often historians have followed Harold Innis in making incorrect inferences on the basis of the "golden age": since shipping and shipbuilding contributed to staple output in the era of merchant capital, similar industries could have contributed similarly to growth in the twentieth century. The decline of shipping was therefore a "loss" to the region.[64] The comparison with other countries, such as Norway, reinforces the notion, and we hear that Norway "succeeded" where Atlantic Canadians "failed." But these are not the conclusions of historical analysis – they follow from assumptions derived from impressions of an earlier era or of other countries. They are, in short, the stuff of romance.

It is impossible to measure precisely the costs and benefits of an industry that did not exist. Econometric techniques can project the results of investment into the future, given specified assumptions. The results of such methods in historical work will remain inconclusive and unpersuasive, simply because so much that did take place in

Table 9.7
Growth (%) in Factory Employment, 1850–70

Industry	Nova Scotia	New Brunswick	Canada West/ Ontario
Saw mills	60	66	277
Tanneries	46	34	246
Breweries	−55	n.a.	454
Carding/fulling/weaving	−13	1	337
Flour and grist mills	−27	−15	140
Foundries and machine shops	228	169	407
Total provincial population	40	47	70

Sources: Canada, Census, 1871, vol. 4; Kris Inwood, "Economic Growth and Structural Change in Atlantic Canada, 1850–1914," in Lewis R. Fischer and Helge Nordvik, eds., Across the Broad Atlantic: Essays in Comparative Maritime History (Oslo: Norwegian University Press, forthcoming, 1990). We are grateful to Dr Inwood for showing us this very important essay prior to its publication.

the past must be changed in order to project events that did not. Thus to project a steel shipbuilding industry into the Maritimes between 1890 and 1914 requires not simply the addition of an attractive bounty paid to shipbuilders; it also assumes an alteration of the political and economic priorities of both Maritimers and Canadian politicians in order to produce such a bounty. And that is to assume a different society from the one that actually existed. The absence of a steel shipbuilding industry in the Maritimes was not a narrowly missed opportunity. It was part of the distribution of political and economic power in Canada and of the development of industrial capital in the Maritimes.

It is self-evident that a combination of steel shipbuilding and shipowning, if added to industrial capital as it existed in the Maritimes in 1900 or 1911, would have meant a larger industrial base. At this level the argument is mere truism. But what exactly might have been added to the regional industrial base? And at what cost, in terms of forgone opportunities? How much might such industries have contributed to the development of industrial capital in the region?

We can make a few conjectures on the basis of what did occur elsewhere. First, we must assume that Canadian navigation acts effectively reserved a share of cargoes for Canadian-owned tonnage or that other forms of effective protection were implemented. The experience of the first half of the nineteenth century, and of other maritime nations, suggests that the growth of domestic shipowning required some such combination of protection and access to dense shipping markets. In such circumstances Maritimers might have been persuaded to invest in steamships for the Canadian transatlantic grain trade in the "wheat boom" period. This would have meant greater capital accumulation in the Maritimes.

Such shipowning by itself would probably not have yielded significant growth-inducing linkages, still less much direct benefit to labour in the region. First, the presence of such ships in local ownership would not have induced greater movement of goods to and from ports, since the ships could clear from Montreal as easily as from Halifax or Saint John. Second, there was nothing to ensure that employment benefits would be retained in the region. In any case, workers had long since been moving away from seafaring, their places taken by people from other countries, and shipowners clearly preferred to hire Europeans or Asians except at officer ranks.

More important, the presence of such ships in local ownership must certainly have opened a wider division between the interests of shipper and those of shipowner. Given freight rates prevailing before 1914, shipowners would take steps to counteract falling rates of return: they could demand cargo reservation, relief from certain operating costs, and maintenance of freight returns through participation in existing Atlantic shipping conferences. Any or all such steps would have met fierce resistance from capital elsewhere in Canada and from the producers of grain and other products sold in transoceanic markets. There is no need to dwell on the ability of Canadian grain producers to mount vigorous opposition against any form of rate-fixing in transportation. And so to the economic cost of support for such shipowning we must add the political costs of freight-rate maintenance.

But all such considerations would evaporate if benefits were to accrue to both shippers and shipowners. The lesson of the first half of the nineteenth century is that shipowning may flourish, even in times of falling freight rates, if it confers significant benefits to producers and shippers. The timber trade provides the model: where the freight factor – the ocean transport cost as a percentage of the final c.i.f. price – is very high, the addition of new tonnage may lower freight costs, stimulate further production, and even create new demand for the transport end of the production process.

In the 1890–1914 period these conditions did not exist in Atlantic Canada. Freight factors had declined steeply, and those exports having a large oceanic freight factor had declined in relative importance. It is unlikely that significant benefits would accrue to producers or shippers from a significant addition of tonnage in Atlantic Canadian ports. If the owning of many more steamships meant participation in Canada's grain export trade from Montreal, then the argument for a domestic shipping capacity becomes even weaker.

Good freight rate series for Canadian exports do not exist, but we know something about the rates for grain from Montreal to the United Kingdom. These rates fell even more rapidly than most freight indices by the end of the century: from a high of around twelve shillings per quarter in 1873 to between two shillings three pence and four shillings sixpence in the early 1890s.[65] The freight factor for Canadian wheat is unknown, but it probably differed little from the freight factor for wheat from the eastern United States: this fell from a high of 12.4 in 1875 to a range of 3.0 to 3.7 just after the turn of the century, according to Douglass North.[66]

The most significant freight costs of Canadian grain occurred between the place of harvest and the ocean entrepôt. While the addition of Canadian tonnage in Atlantic ports might have stabilized ocean freight rates, it could have yielded only small savings in freight factors and only a marginal benefit to wheat producers. Certainly there was little here to divert the attention of grain growers and politicians from the question of railway freight rates.

If benefits were to accrue from a substantial fleet of Canadian steamships in bulk carrying trades, such benefits were likely to come from shipbuilding and the linkages from this manufacturing industry. We must assume, then, a set of policies to integrate shipowning and shipbuilding: protection for Canadian shipowners and the growth of Canadian exports together induce investment in ships; other policies encourage shipowners to meet this demand from builders located in the Maritimes. The opportunity costs of capital invested in such shipbuilding defy measurement, but we might minimize such costs simply by assuming that the Dominion government redirected a portion of its massively excessive railway subsidies into shipbuilding bounties.[67]

Forward linkages from steel shipbuilding would depend on returns to shipowners and shippers, and such linkages were likely to have been small, given prevailing freight rates and freight factors. Backward linkages would include the stimulus to industries producing materials for ships, including steel plate, boilers, iron, rivets, wood, cordage, and the array of equipment required by a steamship.

Certainly there were potential linkages: in Britain in this period some 30 per cent of all steel output was incorporated in ships.[68] But the spin-offs to iron and steel industries should not be exaggerated: in the steel ship *S.S. Mulgrave*, built at New Glasgow in 1893, only 9 per cent of the final cost came from the imported steel angles and plate.[69] By 1911 the materials used in Ontario shipyards were a smaller fraction of output than in other Canadian industries.[70] Such spin-offs also depended on whether materials were purchased from Canadian suppliers, and certainly a proportion would have been imported. The shipyard projected for Halifax in 1901–2 would have imported both boilers and steel plate.[71] This was to be another enclave industry, an assembly plant using Nova Scotian labour.

The principal benefits from such an industry would have come from the employment of skilled labour and the associated final demand linkages. Steel shipbuilding was a capital-intensive industry, but the presence of skilled labour meant relatively high average wages and a high ratio of wages to total output.[72] The promoters of steel shipbuilding in Halifax in 1901 counted on employing 1,000 workers in their industry. This projection was, of course, overly optimistic, but had it been realized they would have increased manufacturing employment in Halifax County by 22 per cent and in Nova Scotia by about 5 per cent.[73]

More realistically, if the Nova Scotian shipyards had been able to capture a third of the Canadian government shipbuilding program as it existed between March 1918 and March 1920, the province would have had an industry producing $12 million a year and generating $4 million a year in direct wage payments. In other words, the manufacturing base of the Maritime provinces would have been about 4 per cent larger than it actually was.[74]

To carry this speculation further would add little to our conclusions. In the failure to establish a larger iron and steel shipbuilding industry in the Maritimes, there was a forgone opportunity and a "loss" to the region, but this loss must not be exaggerated. Even when the Canadian government shipbuilding program was at its peak in 1918 and 1919, a reasonable share of this investment would have added little to the region's industrial employment and output. It would have brought to the region an industry subject to severe cyclical fluctuations, requiring continuing subsidy and an unyielding effort of lobbying and political commitment to maintain its existence.

All such speculation serves as a reminder of the forces arrayed against the revival of the region's shipping and shipbuilding industries. Those forces included the vested interests of capital in most sectors where output was exported across oceans. Any efforts to maintain a shipbuilding industry in the Maritimes would lead to at least one certain result: the vigorous opposition of capitalists, including those within the region, who relied on the cheapest available shipping services. It would even divide shipowners and shipbuilders, since the former would still prefer the cheaper British vessel.

It would have been very difficult to counteract the differential in price per deadweight ton between ships built in Canada and those produced in Britain. To make the output of shipyards in the Maritimes competitive with the imported British vessel would have required a bounty of about $30 per ton in 1913–14 and over $90 per ton in 1919–20.[75] A lesser subsidy would compel shipowners to demand higher freight rates or a cargo reservation policy which would deny exporters access to cheaper foreign tonnage. Either alternative would have raised the wrath of exporters across the country. Canadian governments rejected both alternatives, and Sir Wilfrid Laurier argued that bounties to the steel industry were no precedent but proved only the folly of such artificial support.[76]

The price difference between British and Canadian tonnage was not the cause of a decline in shipbuilding in Atlantic Canada. We observe this price difference at the end of several decades of decline, when the new industrial capital of the Maritimes was forging links with national markets and national economic development, having lost interest in the integrated shipbuilding and shipowning industries of the age of sail. Their lack of interest was not any simple result of the centrifugal forces of industrial and financial capital in central Canada. It was the result also of a slow transition to industrial capitalism rooted in the structure of exploitation and the specific social relations of production that evolved in Atlantic Canada through the nineteenth century. The merchant marine declined in the context of a complex social totality, the internal structures of which set the limits and the possibilities of human action.

The survival of a large national-flag merchant marine was not in the interest of industrial capital in Canada. The merchant marine survives only if we posit a very different historical logic and a different development path for Canada. The absence of a Canadian merchant marine remains an anomaly, but only if we reject entirely the logic of industrial capital and its market mechanisms.

There are development models that do not assume the accumulation of capital to be the primary goal of economic activity. If goods and services are the social product of labour, then transportation is fully part of this social product, the part that produces value by effecting changes of location. In this logic there may be many technological differences, but no economic distinction, among the mining of coal, the felling of timber, the harvesting of wheat, and the shipping of goods across oceans, since all such activities add value by effecting changes in location.

If shipping is conceived as part of the process of production, and control of this process is vested in producers themselves, then the planning of production may involve every stage from producers' acquisition of skills to the distribution of output in a foreign market. And such planning may find that the building and operating of a merchant marine meet the criteria of social need. There are, after all, countries – including some with capitalist economies – that dictate that high proportions of their product be carried in vehicles, at sea no less than on land, that are built and operated by workers of their own country.

We do not know whether any such model would have included a Canadian merchant marine, because these are the alternatives that Canada forswore. In discovering the paths that our forbears chose, and the alternative economic logic that they rejected, we learn what we are and what we have lost.

CHAPTER TEN

Postscript:
A Comparative Perspective

The decline of Atlantic Canada's merchant marine took place within the specific historical conditions of development in British colonies that had recently become provinces of Canada. This is not to suggest that the development of shipping industries in other countries has no place in our story. At one level, the growth of shipping elsewhere, and the long-term decline in international freight costs, were necessary conditions – although hardly sufficient – for the decline of Canada's merchant marine: obviously, if a supply of ocean-going tonnage had not been available from elsewhere, the incentive to maintain a larger tonnage in Canada would have been greater. At another level, however, other nations' experiences are part of our analysis. Awareness of what happened elsewhere guides our understanding of events in Canada. If most other shipping industries had declined in the decades before 1914, our story would have been very different.

We cannot escape comparative history, even if we can escape the superficiality of comparative advantage. The conditions of growth in other countries may help us to specify the conditions that were absent in Atlantic Canada. This kind of analysis is limited, however, by the inevitable ignorance of historians schooled in the history of a single country and by the absence of comparable evidence about more than a few countries. Our essay in comparative history is postscript rather than conclusion, not because it is unimportant but because it is tentative. It is offered in the belief that comparative analysis can enrich all historical inquiry: by travelling to other societies we learn a little about them and a great deal more about ourselves.

Observing the merchant shipping of other societies brings into startling relief the peculiarity of what happened in the Maritime provinces of Canada in the late nineteenth century. Table 10.1 presents annual growth rates for the world, for major maritime nations,

Table 10.1
Growth of Merchant Shipping Tonnage, Various Countries, 1880–1900

Country	Annual Growth (%)	Country/ Province	Annual Growth (%)
United States	−2.40	Maritime provinces	−5.21
United Kingdom	1.74	Quebec	−2.59
Norway	0.30	Ontario	0.31
Sweden	1.37	British Columbia	12.30
Germany	2.77	Canada	−3.38
France	0.61		
Italy	−0.21	Newfoundland	1.31
Spain	3.62		
Russia	1.48		
Japan	11.95		
World	1.36		

Sources: Keith Matthews, "The Shipping Industry of Atlantic Canada: Themes and Problems," in Keith Matthews and Gerald Panting, eds., *Ships and Shipbuilding in the North Atlantic Region* (St John's: Maritime History Group, 1978), 9–18; Sarah Palmer, "The British Shipping Industry 1850–1914," in Lewis R. Fischer and Gerald Panting, eds., *Change and Adaptation in Maritime History: The North Atlantic Fleets in the Nineteenth Century* (St John's: Maritime History Group, 1985), 90. Figures for Spain from A. Gomez-Mendoza, "Government and the Development of Modern Shipbuilding in Spain, 1850–1935," *Journal of Transport History*, 9, no. 1 (March 1988), 19–35.

and for a few Canadian provinces between 1880 and 1900. What happened in the eastern provinces of Canada was almost unique: only in the United States was there another significant decline in merchant tonnage. And the Maritime provinces were soon out of step with the United States, too, for between 1900 and 1914 the decline of the American merchant marine was arrested, while the collapse in the Maritimes continued.

There was no single path toward growth, and even the transition to steam shipping occurred at very different rates in different countries. The experience of Finland suggests that shipowning could continue even without a rapid transition to steam.[1] More important, the history of world shipping in the twentieth century shows that there is no necessary connection between growth in shipowning and a domestic capacity to build ships.[2] Indeed, the massive shipbuilding complex in Britain could work to the advantage of shipowners elsewhere, at least where ships were allowed to sell freely between countries, and in some countries, such as Sweden, growth depended critically on the large amounts of second-hand British steam tonnage entering world markets. Sweden accomplished the transition from sail to steam before the First World War and, in the process, managed to put a majority of Swedish external trade into Swedish hulls.[3]

Although shipowning could exist without shipbuilding, British shipowners benefited from close connections with domestic shipbuilders. The dominance of the British merchant marine, and its relatively rapid transition to iron and steam, depended critically on this interaction between shipowning and shipbuilding capital.[4] No such interaction occurred in Atlantic Canada. But even superficial examination of the British case reveals a series of conditions that were absent, not only in Canada but in most other countries.

A century before, in the 1790s and early nineteenth century, British shipowning had witnessed certain changes in ownership and management that Atlantic Canada never saw: shipowning emerged as a distinct occupation on a large scale, separated from the traditional functions of the merchant; ownership became very concentrated, especially in major ports such as Liverpool; management in shipping became specialized and professional, beyond the small-scale management that a family firm normally provided.[5]

All this *preceded* the "revolution in commercial organization" represented by the development of liner companies.[6] These companies began in the era of sailing ships and dominated many trades by the 1870s. British liner companies had few large rivals, even by that decade. These companies were a powerful influence on shipbuilding and on government. No such industrial corporations appeared in Atlantic Canadian shipping. The contrast reinforces our emphasis on shipowning as an adjunct of merchant capital in Atlantic Canada.

Other conditions in Britain could not be reproduced in any other shipowning country, whatever its stage of industrial development. Here was an industrializing and island society located at the heart of the world's trade: world seaborne trade increased by about seven times between 1840 and the late 1880s; even in 1914 no less than 40 per cent of seaborne trade still touched on Britain.[7] The removal of the Navigation Acts increased opportunities for foreign carriers in British trades – but by the 1880s British tonnage accounted for over 72 per cent of entrances to ports in the United Kingdom.[8]

British shipowners depended on the massive demand for shipping services in their own "home trades," in colonial trades, and in trade with Europe. The sample of non-Canadian crew agreements compiled by the Atlantic Canada Shipping Project confirms the importance of European trades, especially for British steamers (there are 18,811 voyages in the sample).[9] No less than 43 per cent of the

Table 10.2

General Voyage Patterns for British Sailing and Steam Tonnage
(% of Total Tonnage by Route), 1863–1900

Voyage Description	Sail	Steam
North Atlantic	10.5	31.8
West Indies/North Atlantic and West Indies	3.0	1.6
Mediterranean/North Atlantic and Mediterranean	4.9	11.1
West coast of South America	6.7	0.8
East coast of South America	3.8	4.6
India/Indian Ocean	17.1	6.5
British coastal	10.2	4.7
European coast/Europe–United Kingdom/ United Kingdom–Europe	6.6	10.6
Africa (south of Sahara)	1.1	1.1
Europe–South America–North America	0.9	1.0
US Gulf	1.9	4.9
East Indies	3.4	1.1
Baltic–other Europe/Baltic–North Atlantic	4.3	8.3
Black Sea	1.6	8.3
Australia	12.3	2.2
Other Pacific Rim	11.0	0.8
Other/unknown	0.7	0.6

Source: Non-Canadian Crew List Sample, Maritime History Archive, Memorial University of Newfoundland; see note 9.

voyages by steamers were in British coastal waters or continental European waters between the Baltic and the Black Sea (see Table 10.2). As Robin Craig and others have often pointed out, there was nothing in Canada comparable to the huge outward freights in coal, for instance, to which British shipowners had immediate access.

Whatever the reasons for British dominance, most of the world's shipping was registered outside the United Kingdom.[10] A very different set of conditions, even in countries less advanced industrially, could result in a growing merchant marine. And the case of Japan suggests that it was not necessary to be located close to the dense European market in order to have a shipping industry. However, if a country lacked such proximity and lacked such large coastal and overseas trades as were possessed by Britain and the United States, then the prerequisites for growth were likely to be very different. The

British case did not offer a model – although it certainly could inspire imitators and competitors.

Although there was no single path toward growth, the experience of other countries may suggest certain minimal conditions for growth. These conditions include, we suggest, close integration of capital in shipping with both commercial capital engaged in major overseas trades and with state policy. This condition was present in most if not all of those countries in Table 10.1; it was conspicuously absent in British North America, where a nascent bourgeoisie was fragmented along regional lines and where the maritime capital of the old Atlantic colonies was imperfectly linked to the industrial and commercial capital of central and western provinces.[11]

The country furthest removed from Europe exhibited such integration in the context of a very distinctive pattern of development. In Japan both the state and major commercial firms viewed shipping as a "strategic industry" that required "huge subsidies," because of the role shipping was assumed to have in military, economic, and national development.[12] The growth of shipowning for overseas trades coincided with, but also encouraged, the movement from commercial to industrial capital. The seisho of the 1870s – large mercantile firms involved in trade, services, and financing – evolved into the zaibatsu of the 1890s: large, functionally related enterprises in commerce, mining, finance, and industry, including shipbuilding. Government backing was "crucial" to the growth of the NYK and to the diversification of Mitsubishi into heavy industry, William Wray argues.[13] The state gave Mitsubishi its first fleet of steamers, restricted competition, assisted the company in battles with foreign competitors, and encouraged rapid movement toward monopoly in national shipowning.[14]

These circumstances contained the potential for conflict of interest between shippers and shipowners, but interests of the large corporation, itself both shipper and shipowner, and of the state overlapped. Thus the shipowner could have an interest in low freight rates: "The social gain from low rates, which was the government's goal, could also bring long-term benefit to the NYK by making exports more competitive, thereby providing more cargo for the company. In critical cases involving competition with foreigners the increasing competitiveness of Japanese products facilitated the strategy of risk sharing in which the NYK formed alliances with Japanese shippers."[15]

The point is not that Canadian capitalists and their governments could have or should have done anything like this. The point is that, given the specific regional and historical evolution of industrial capitalism in Canada, nothing even remotely comparable occurred in Canada. Every one of the conditions present in Japan was missing in Canada, and the contrast helps to confirm our emphasis on the slow and disarticulated development of mercantile capital in the Maritime colonies.

State support varied from one shipping nation to another, but in most countries it was substantial and sometimes it appears to have been central to growth.[16] In Spain the building of modern shipyards was one of the spin-offs of naval and colonial policies, and by helping to stabilize demand the state "accelerated the concentration of yards in a few large units of production which enjoyed economies of scale and facilitated the absorption of modern technology."[17] The subsidized industrialization of shipbuilding was a major reason for the growth of a largely Spanish-built merchant fleet before the First World War.

More striking was the series of subsidy laws enacted in France, which combined support for shipbuilding with aid to shipowners. Subsidies to shipbuilders were designed to eliminate the difference in building costs between France and England, and bounties to shipowners were intended to increase national participation in French carrying trades. Thus the law of 1881 gave a per-ton bounty for each 1,000 nautical miles covered, and the bounty for a transatlantic passage by a 1,000-ton ship was more than enough to cover the wage costs for the passage.[18]

Even in Britain "there was never a time when the position of the merchant marine was left entirely to competitive ability."[19] Government support included postal subsidies, loans, payments for use of auxiliary cruisers, hire of troop transports in wartime, Admiralty contracts, payments by colonial administrations, and the support of an elaborate maritime law. Sidney Pollard also argues that modern marine engineering began in the Admiralty, in government-aided technical schools, and in the close relations between the Admiralty and private builders, although Robin Craig, Britain's pre-eminent historian of merchant shipping, rejects Pollard's argument.[20] Although the British government paid no per-mile carrying bounty, mail subsidies "enabled British shipyards and shipping companies to establish a lead which was not surpassed for a century."[21] The major British mail lines, and their continental European competitors, received subsidies many times larger than their profits in the late nineteenth century.[22]

The Canadian government paid mail subsidies and steamship subventions in this period, but the amounts were small and not reserved for Canadian-registered vessels.[23] Even more important, and directly relevant to the evidence cited earlier in this book, these subsidies were designed not to assist the Canadian merchant marine so much as to assist trade and to help coastal communities lying beyond the reach of rail lines. The annual report of the Department of Trade and Commerce in 1926 summarized the aims: "Subsidies paid to ocean lines assist materially in the development of Canadian export trade; while the assistance granted in this way to coasting vessels enables services to be supplied to localities which are in many cases far from any railway or other regular means of communication, and whose populations are often dependent entirely upon subsidized boats for their connections with the rest of the country."[24]

What does this tell us about Atlantic Canada? There is much more here than a lesson about the dependence of national merchant marines on carefully designed state support. The entire complex of relations between the state and maritime capital was different in other shipping nations. Canada lacked its own navy and the stimulus that a navy might have given to domestic shipbuilding, and it is no surprise that the prospect of a navy softened even Wilfrid Laurier's opposition to shipbuilding bounties.[25]

Canada also lacked the kind of consensus between capital and state that might yield a maritime strategy. There was nothing like the nationalist quest for autonomy that fuelled the development of shipping in Japan, where the defenders of autarky could insist that Japan use ships and trade to "resist the countries of the world."[26] There was nothing like the attitude of the French politicians who believed that freights earned by foreign ships in French ports were an annual "tribute" of 345 million francs paid to foreigners.[27] There was nothing like the "vehement nationalist propaganda for the sea" that swept over Germany and linked the interests of shipowners with those of exporters. This "maritime enthusiasm," says Walter Kresse, was far more important than the millions of marks given in mail subsidies.[28]

Even where state subsidy was less important, we are forced to give priority to the expectations and mental horizons generated in the social relations of production of specific regions. The growth of merchant shipowning in the Scandinavian countries depended on far more than proximity to European shipping markets. In these countries, as in Canada, regions that once saw the building and owning of wooden ships were vulnerable to decline in the "real rupture" between the owning of wooden sailing ships and the owning of steamers.[29] There were many other parallels with Atlantic Canada, but the differences stand out. Shipping was "integrated into the local economy"; shipping and shipbuilding accounted for much larger shares of Scandinavian economic output than these industries did in

Canada; external trades depended heavily on the domestic fleets; and there was no imperial motherland from which to borrow law, tradition, and shipping services. "Knowledge about shipping matters was widespread among a wide segment of the local population."[30] The British lead in steam technology encouraged not gloomy predictions about the inevitable demise of Scandinavia's local industries but rather growing determination to follow the British example.[31] There was no regional and historic disjuncture between maritime capital and capital involved in developing a vast continental hinterland. Instead there was "an environment that offered limited scope for alternative investments."[32]

As David Alexander told us many years ago, it was not to the credit of Atlantic Canada that a shipping industry arose there in the first place, but equally it is not to the region's discredit that it disappeared. The conditions required for the growth of a large merchant marine were transplanted from across the Atlantic and did not survive integration into the industrial capitalism of the North American continent. There was little that Maritime Canadians could have done, by themselves, to preserve a merchant marine. Those who were most affected by decisions over the fate of their industries – the working people of maritime Canada – were not consulted. In the framework of regionally fragmented development, capital and the state acted together and built a great coastal nation with a small merchant navy.

Sample Gross Revenue Calculations, 1863, 1873 (Chapter 6)

1 TIMBER

Vessel name: *British Lion*
Tonnage: 1,279
Port of registry: Windsor
Passage: Saint John–Liverpool
Date of arrival: 10 August 1863
Cargo: 3,695 deal ends, 34,268 deals, 3,370 boards, 3,433 pieces scantling, 10,000 pieces palings, 4 half cords lathwood, 53 tons pig iron
Freight rate per standard: 85 shillings (average for July 1863)
Total number of standards (@ 120 deals per standard, and assuming 1 deal end = 2/3 deal): 305.9 standards
Total deal revenue: £1,300 sterling
Number of deals per ton: 29
Estimated total gross revenues (since there were twenty-nine deals per ton, rest of cargo = 38 per cent of gross revenues, assuming vessel fully laden): £2,096.8 sterling

2 PETROLEUM

Vessel name: *Onesiphorus*
Tonnage: 230
Port of registry: Saint John
Passage: New York–London
Date of arrival: 25 February 1863
Cargo: 1,613 barrels refined petroleum, 1 case and 300 half-cases benzine
Freight rate: 8 shillings 3 pence [8/3] per barrel for refined oil (January freights ranged from 8/0 to 8/6.)
Total gross revenues: £665.4 sterling (including nothing for benzine)

3 COTTON

Vessel name: *Zimi*
Tonnage: 962
Port of registry: Saint John
Passage: New Orleans–Liverpool
Date of arrival: 6 March 1873
Cargo: 2,976 bales cotton, 3,120 staves
Freight rate: 5/8 d [pence] per pound (New Orleans rates varied from 5/8 to 11/16 in January and February 1873.)
Number of pounds of cotton shipped: 1,383,840 (assuming 465 pounds per bale)
Total gross revenue: £3,603.7 sterling

4 GRAIN

Vessel name: *Brothers*
Tonnage: 537
Port of registry: Yarmouth
Passage: New York–London
Date of arrival: 19 December 1873
Cargo: 31,547 bushels wheat
Freight rate: 9 shillings per quarter (Freights from New York to Cork for orders ranged from 8/6 to 10/6 for wheat in November 1873.)
Number of quarters shipped: 3,943.37 (1 quarter = 8 bushels.)
Total gross revenues: £1,774.5 sterling

5 GUANO

Vessel name: *Forest King*
Tonnage: 888
Port of registry: Halifax
Passage: Callao–London
Date of arrival: 21 October 1873
Cargo: 1,350 tons guano
Freight rate: 68 shillings per ton (June–July average)
Total gross revenue: £4,590 sterling

6 RICE

Vessel name: *Prince Eugene*
Tonnage: 1,328
Port of registry: Saint John
Passage: Bassein–Liverpool

Date of arrival: 13 January 1873
Cargo: 20,400 bags rice
Freight rate: 75 shillings per ton
Number of bags per ton: According to R.W. Stevens an East India bag = 1.5 cwt; at
Moulmein, 14 bags clean rice = 1 ton.
Total gross revenue: £5,464.3 sterling
(Actual gross revenue from Moran-Galloway Ledger, Moran Papers, New Brunswick
Museum: £5,856 sterling)

7 MOLASSES

Vessel name: *Persia*
Tonnage: 285
Port of registry: Windsor
Passage: Matanzas–Liverpool
Date of arrival: 24 March 1863
Cargo: 516 hds 24 tierce 76 brls molasses
Freight rate: 48 shillings per ton (Freight rates were 45–50 shillings in January and
February.)
Stowage: We assume freight rates to be by liquid tun; one Havana hogshead = 110
gallons and 252 gallons = 1 tun. A tierce is either 1/2 or 2/3 hogshead.
Total gross revenue: £566 sterling

SOURCES

United Kingdom bills of entry for Liverpool and London; *Mitchell's Maritime Register*;
New York *Maritime Register*; R.W. Stevens, *On the Stowage of Ships and Their Cargoes*, 3rd
edition (London: Longmans, 1863), 6th edition (London: Longmans, 1873); Moran
Papers, New Brunswick Museum; Colin Campbell Papers, Dalhousie University
Archives.

Average Gross Revenue, Selected Commodities (Chapter 6)

Table B.1

Average Gross Revenue per Registered Ton for Single Passages with Selected Commodities, 1863, 1873, and 1883

Cargo	1863	1873	1883
Timber			
Gross revenue ($)	326,406	387,597	91,076
Total tonnage	48,763	45,152	16,791
No. passages	52	53	16
Gross revenue ($) per ton	6.69	8.45	5.42
Cotton			
Gross revenue ($)		789,159	187,094
Total tonnage		49,864	16,125
No. passages		61	21
Gross revenue ($) per ton		15.83	11.60
Petroleum			
Gross revenue ($)	14,908	153,054	70,660
Total tonnage	3,122	14,596	13,302
No. passages	9	30	12
Gross revenue ($) per ton	13.42	10.49	5.31
Grain			
Gross revenue ($)	55,777	48,702	13,937
Total tonnage	4,486	3,790	2,014
No. passages	5	5	2
Gross revenue ($) per ton	12.43	12.85	6.92
Guano			
Gross revenue ($)	204,728	91,584	
Total tonnage	7,653	4,089	
No. passages	5	4	

Table B.1 – *continued*

Cargo	1863	1873	1883
Molasses			
Gross revenue ($)	31,370		
Total tonnage	3,568		
No. passages	12		
Gross Revenue ($) per ton	8.79		
Rice			
Gross Revenue ($)		338,543	
Total tonnage		16,792	
No. passages		15	
Gross revenue ($) per ton		20.16	

Sources: United Kingdom bills of entry; see also Appendix A.

Returns on Six Nova Scotia Vessels, 1867–92 (Chapter 6)

Table C.1
Returns, 1873–90, on Barque *Harold*, 960 Tons, Built 1873

Year	Depreciated Value ($) of Vessel	Annual Depreci- ation ($)	Net earnings ($)	Earnings Minus Depreci- ation ($)	% Return on Depre- ciated Assets	% Return on Initial Capital
1873	33,600	3,024	n.a.			
1874	30,576	2,752	n.a.			
1875	27,824	2,504	n.a.			
1876	25,320	2,279	3,212*	2,072	8.2	6.2
1877	23,041	2,074	9,440	7,366	32.0	21.9
1878	20,967	1,887	9,881	7,994	38.1	23.8
1879	19,080	1,336	6,496	5,160	27.0	15.4
1880	17,744	1,597	5,304	3,707	20.9	11.0
1881	16,147	1,453	3,792	2,339	14.5	7.0
1882	14,694	737	1,432	697	4.7	2.1
1883	13,959	698	3,952	3,254	23.3	11.8
1884	13,261	663	2,768	2,105	15.9	6.3
1885	12,598	630	2,080	1,450	11.5	4.3
1886	11,968	598	0	−598	−5.0	−1.8
1887	11,370	568	0	−568	−5.0	−1.7
1888	10,802	540	2,280	1,740	16.1	5.2
1889	10,262	513	760	247	2.4	0.7
1890	9,749	487	2,518	2,031	20.8	6.0
Average annual return					15.0	7.9

Source: Dickie Letters, Dalhousie University Archives.
Note: Depreciation rates used here are 9 per cent a year to 1882 and 5 per cent a year thereafter. In a letter of 25 March 1881 J.E. Dickie says: "If I can buy an eighth of this vessel for $15 per register ton, do you want the half of it?"
*For half of the year only.

Table C.2

Returns, 1877–90, on Ship *Colchester*, 1,384 Tons, Built 1876

Year	Depreciated Value ($) of Vessel	Annual Depreci- ation ($)	Net earnings ($)	Earnings Minus Depreci- ation ($)	% Return on Depre- ciated Assets	% Return on Initial Capital
1877	52,252	5,748	7,744	1,966	3.8	3.8
1878	46,504	5,115	8,682	3,567	7.7	6.8
1879	41,389	4,553	12,496	7,943	19.2	15.2
1880	36,836	4,052	6,304	2,252	6.1	4.3
1881	32,784	3,606	6,280	2,674	8.2	5.1
1882	29,178	1,459	8,424	6,965	23.9	13.3
1883	27,719	1,386	16,528	15,142	54.6	29.0
1884	26,333	1,317	4,064	2,747	10.4	5.3
1885	25,016	1,251	4,069	2,818	11.3	5.4
1886	23,765	1,188	599	−589	−2.5	−1.1
1887	22,577	1,129	0	−1,129	−5.0	−2.2
1888	21,448	1,072	2,927	1,855	8.6	3.6
1889	20,376	1,019	8,781	7,762	38.1	14.9
1890	19,357	968	2,016	1,048	5.4	2.0
Average annual return					13.6	7.5

Source: Dickie Letters, Dalhousie University Archives.

Note: Depreciation is estimated at 11 per cent to 1881 and 5 per cent thereafter. In July 1881 J.E. Dickie bought four shares in the vessel for $2,000; by this measure the vessel would be worth $32,000 (J.B. Dickie to J.E. Dickie, 20 June and 12 July 1881).

Table C.3
Returns, 1881–9, on Barque *Linden*, 913 Tons, Built 1881

Year	Depreciated Value ($) of Vessel	Annual Depreci- ation ($)	Net earnings ($)	Earnings Minus Depreci- ation ($)	% Return on Depre- ciated Assets	% Return on Initial Capital
1881	31,500	1,040*	0	−1,040	−3.3	−3.3
1882	30,640	3,046	3,462**	416	1.4	1.3
1883	27,414	2,741	3,480	739	2.7	2.3
1884	24,673	2,467	4,232	1,765	7.2	5.6
1885	22,206	2,221	4,651	2,430	10.9	7.7
1886	19,985	1,599	2,450	851	4.3	2.7
1887	18,386	1,471	878***	142	0.8	0.5
1888	16,915	1,015	4,423	3,408	20.1	10.8
1889	15,900	954	6,970	6,016	37.8	19.1
Average annual return					9.1	5.2

Source: Dickie Letters, Dalhousie University Archives.
* One-third of the year only.
** The vessel was stranded and severely damaged shortly after launching. Repairs, which cost $8,000, were paid from the first voyages in 1882. The earnings for 1882 cited above are estimated from remittances received by J.E. Dickie after repair costs were paid. Letters from J.B. Dickie to J.E. Dickie, 13 December 1881; 17 April 1882; 14 October 1882; and 28 December 1882.
*** There appears to be a letter missing in 1887. J.E. Dickie received a remittance of $109.80 on his eight shares in April; but between 21 April 1887 and 29 January 1889 there was only one further remittance, a mere $75.50. The results above probably underestimate the real returns for this vessel.

Table C.4
Returns, 1887–9, on Ship *Selkirk*, 1,757 Tons, Built 1886

Year	Depreciated Value ($) of Vessel	Annual Depreci- ation ($)	Net earnings ($)	Earnings Minus Depreci- ation ($)	% Return on Depre- ciated Assets	% Return on Initial Capital
1887	52,710	4,744	1,071*	−1,301	−2.5	−2.5
1888	47,966	4,317	7,493	3,176	6.6	6.0
1889	43,649	3,928	16,170	12,242	28.0	23.2
Average annual return					10.7	8.9

Source: Dickie Letters, Dalhousie University Archives.
Note: Depreciation is estimated to be 9 per cent a year. The vessel made a passage from Saint John to Liverpool in the autumn of 1886 but used the proceeds to pay for metalling. One 1887 remittance is missing: Martin Dickie's letter of 30 December 1887 mentions a remittance that is due, but there is no mention of this remittance in subsequent letters.
* Half year only.

Table C.5

Returns, 1885–92, on Barque *Avoca*, 1,487 Tons, Built 1885

Year	Depreciated Value ($) of Vessel	Annual Depreci- ation ($)	Net earnings ($)	Earnings Minus Depreci- ation ($)	% Return on Depre- ciated Assets	% Return on Initial Capital
1885	45,801	1,367*	2,308	948	2.1*	2.1
1886	44,441	3,999	4,598	599	1.3	1.3
1887	40,442	3,640	6,826	3,186	7.9	7.0
1888	36,802	3,312	9,236	5,924	16.1	12.9
1889	33,490	3,014	14,207	11,193	33.4	24.4
1890	30,476	1,829	8,658	6,829	22.4	14.9
1891	28,647	1,719	2,026	307	1.1	0.7
1892	26,928	1,617	3,576	1,959	7.3	4.3
Average annual return					11.6	8.5

Source: Aylward Papers, MG no. 36, Public Archives of Nova Soctia. Depreciation is estimated at 9 per cent to 1889 and 6 per cent thereafter.
* One third of a year.

Table C.6
Returns, 1867–84, on Ship *John Mann*, 1,043 Tons, Built 1867

Year	Depreciated Value ($) of Vessel	Annual Depreci- ation ($)	Net earnings ($)	Earnings Minus Depreci- ation ($)	% Return on Depre- ciated Assets	% Return on Initial Capital
1867	38,168	1,718*	3,974	2,256	5.9	5.9
1868	36,450	3,280	3,974	694	1.9	1.8
1869	33,170	2,985	5,482	2,497	7.5	6.5
1870	30,185	2,717	n.a.			
1871	27,468	2,472	3,037	565	2.1	1.5
1872	24,996	2,250	12,550	10,300	41.2	27.0
1873	22,746	2,047	14,947	12,900	56.7	33.8
1874	20,699	1,863	7,137	5,274	25.5	13.8
1875	18,836	1,695	8,213	6,518	34.6	17.1
1876	17,141	1,543	4,462	2,919	17.0	7.6
1877	15,598	1,404	8,261	6,857	44.0	18.0
1878	14,194	1,277	10,232	8,955	63.1	23.5
1879	12,917	1,163	7,285	6,122	47.4	16.0
1880	11,754	1,058	8,217	7,159	60.9	18.8
1881	10,696	963	7,245	6,282	58.7	16.5
1882	9,733	876	915	39	0.4	0.1
1883	8,857	797	6,477	5,680	64.1	14.9
1884	8,060	725	3,511	2,786	34.6	7.3
Average annual return					33.3	13.5

Source: Thomas Aylward Notebook, cited in Charles Armour and Thomas Lackey, *Sailing Ships of the Maritimes* (Toronto, 1975), 94.
Note: The vessel was launched on 1 June 1867; on 11 June, Thomas Aylward bought four shares for $2,385.50. The vessel was sold on 1 November 1884 for $7,000. Annual depreciation was about 9 per cent.
* Half-year.

Notes

CHAPTER ONE

1 Frederick William Wallace, *Wooden Ships and Iron Men* (London: Hodder and Stoughton, 1924); *In the Wake of the Wind Ships* (Toronto: Musson Book Co., 1927).
2 Frederick William Wallace, *Roving Fisherman: An Autobiography* (Gardenvale, Que.: Canadian Fisherman, 1955).
3 See especially Stanley T. Spicer, *Masters of Sail: The Era of Square-Rigged Vessels in the Maritime Provinces* (Toronto: Ryerson Press, 1968); Spicer, *Sails of the Fundy: The Schooners and Square-Riggers of the Parrsboro Shore* (Hantsport, NS: Lancelot Press, 1984); John Congdon Crowe, *In the Days of the Windjammers* (Toronto: Ryerson, 1959); Claude K. Darrach, *From a Coastal Schooner's Log* (Halifax: Nova Scotia Museum, 1979); Feenie Ziner, *Bluenose, Queen of the Grand Banks* (Philadelphia: Chilton Book Co., 1970); Andrew Horwood, *Newfoundland Ships and Men* (St John's: Macey's Publishing, 1971); Cassie Brown with Harold Horwood, *Death on the Ice* (Toronto: Doubleday, 1974); Cassie Brown, *A Winter's Tale: The Wreck of the Florizel* (Toronto: Doubleday, 1976); R.J. Cunningham and K.R. Mabee, *Tall Ships and Master Mariners* (St John's: Breakwater Books, 1985); Charles Armour and Thomas Lackey, *Sailing Ships of the Maritimes* (Toronto: McGraw-Hill Ryerson); *On the High Seas: The Diary of Capt. John W. Froude of Twillingate* (St Johns: Jesperson Press, 1983); Benjamin Doane, *Following the Sea* (Halifax: Nova Scotia Museum, 1987); Harry D. Roberts with Michael Nowlan, *The Newfoundland Fish Boxes: A Chronicle of the Fishery* (Fredericton, NB: Brunswick Press, 1982); Nicolas De Jong and Marven E. Moore, *Launched from Prince Edward Island* (Charlottetown: PEI Heritage Foundation, 1981); George Whiteley, *Northern Seas Hardy Sailors* (New York: W.W. Norton, 1982); Jessie L. Beattie, *The Log Line: The Adventures of a Great Sailing Captain* (Toronto: McClelland and Stew-

art, 1972); Clement W. Crowell, *Novascotiaman* (Halifax: Nova Scotia Museum, 1979).

4 "Economic Growth in the Atlantic Region, 1880 to 1940," in David G. Alexander, *Atlantic Canada and Confederation; Essays in Canadian Political Economy* (Toronto: University of Toronto Press, 1983), 74.

5 See Judith Fingard, *Jack in Port: Sailortowns of Eastern Canada* (Toronto: University of Toronto Press, 1982); Eric W. Sager, *Seafaring Labour: The Merchant Marine of Atlantic Canada, 1820–1914* (Kingston and Montreal: McGill-Queen's University Press, 1989); Eric W. Sager and Lewis R. Fischer, *Shipping and Shipbuilding in Atlantic Canada, 1820–1914* (Ottawa: Canadian Historical Association Booklet, 1986); Richard Rice, "Sailortown: Theory and Method in Ordinary People's History," *Acadiensis*, 13, no. 1 (Autumn 1983, 154–68.

The Atlantic Canada Shipping Project produced six volumes of conference proceedings: Keith Matthews and Gerald Panting, eds., *Ships and Shipbuilding in the North Atlantic Region* (St John's: Maritime History Group, 1978); Lewis R. Fischer and Eric W. Sager, eds., *The Enterprising Canadians: Entrepreneurs and Economic Development in Eastern Canada, 1820–1914* (St John's: Maritime History Group, 1979); David Alexander and Rosemary Ommer, eds., *Volumes Not Values; Canadian Sailing Ships and World Trades* (St John's: Maritime History Group, 1979); Rosemary Ommer and Gerald Panting, eds., *Working Men Who Got Wet* (St John's: Maritime History Group, 1980); Lewis R. Fischer and Eric W. Sager, eds., *Merchant Shipping and Economic Development in Atlantic Canada* (St John's: Maritime History Group, 1982); Lewis R. Fischer and Gerald panting, eds., *Change and Adaptation in Maritime History: The North Atlantic Fleets in the Nineteenth Century* (St John's: Maritime History Group, 1985).

See also Eric W. Sager and Lewis R. Fischer, "Atlantic Canada and the Age of Sail Revisited," *Canadian Historical Review*, 68, no. 2 (June 1982), 125–50; Rosemary Ommer, "The Decline of the Eastern Canadian Shipping Industry, 1880–1895," *Journal of Transport History* (1984), 25–44.

6 In 1879 Joseph Tasse, MP, estimated that Canada was seventh or eighth among the shipping nations of the world. He pointed out that many vessels registered in Canada were not owned in Canada and that a large proportion of our registered tonnage consisted of coastal vessels of a kind often not included in the official totals of other shipping nations. Canada, House of Commons *Debates*, 1 May 1879, 1670–71.

7 Annual data appear in Keith Matthews, "The Shipping Industry of Atlantic Canada: Themes and Problems," in Matthews and Panting, eds., *Ships and Shipbuilding*, 9–18.

8 Data on shipbuilding output appear in Richard Rice, "Measuring British Dominance of Shipbuilding in the Maritimes, 1787–1890," in Matthews and Panting, eds., *Ships and Shipbuilding*, 148–55.

9   Fernand Braudel, "History and the Social Sciences: The *Longue Durée*," in Fernand Braudel, *On History*, trans. Sarah Matthews (Chicago: University of Chicago Press, 1980), 27–8.

10 Peter D. McClelland, "Commentary on Demand and Supply in Shipping and Regional Economic Development," in Fischer and Sager, eds., *Merchant Shipping and Economic Development*, 113–17.

11 A good summary of this approach is in R.O. Goss, "Economics and Canadian Atlantic Shipping," in Fischer and Sager, eds., *Merchant Shipping and Economic Development*, 89–112.

12 Opportunity cost refers to the cost involved in forgoing a benefit from one alternative when choosing another. The concept is basic in neoclassical economics, since it posits a rational process of decision-taking in which the returns from an alternative are compared to the real cost of undertaking it, including the costs both of actual outlays and of forgoing other opportunities. The critical difficulty lies, of course, in estimating putative returns from a choice not taken.

13 Lewis R. Fischer and Helge W. Nordvik, "From Namos to Halden: Myths and Realities in the History of Norwegian Seamen's Wages, 1850–1914," *Scandinavian Economic History Review*, 35, no. 1 (1987), 41–63.

14 See William D. Wray, *Mitsubishi and the N.Y.K., 1870–1914; Business Strategy in the Japanese Shipping Industry* (Cambridge, Mass.: Council on East Asian Studies, 1984).

15 "From the viewpoint of the economic historian," says Douglass North, "this neoclassical formulation appears to beg all of the interesting questions," in large part because "the costs of acquiring information, uncertainty, and transactions costs do not exist." North, *Structure and Change in Economic History* (New York: W.W. Norton, 1981), 5.

16 Martin Hollis and Edward J. Nell, *Rational Economic Man: A Philosophical Critique of Neo-Classical Economics* (Cambridge: Cambridge University Press, 1975), 13–16, 211.

17 See also note 15 above.

18 "In future Canada will be able to best the world in the manufacture of steel ships ... From the nature of things shipbuilding can be done in Canada cheaper than anywhere else in the world. The cost of skilled labour in Canada will remain higher, but to conterbalance this I confidently anticipate that a very skilled class of workmen will spring up"; Halifax *Herald*, 10 February 1902.

    A letter of Harry Crowe of Halifax to G.B. Hunter makes clear that Hunter was, if anything, more optimistic than Halifax businessmen about the prospects for selling Nova Scotian–built ships in international markets: H. Crowe to G.B. Hunter, 5 June 1902, Harry Crowe Letterbooks, Public Archives of Nova Scotia. We are indebted to David Frank for these references.

19 The four vessels built by Halifax Shipyards as part of the Canadian Government Shipbuilding Programme to April 1921 cost $196 per ton. The cost of all 63 vessels in the program was $192 per ton. Report of the Deputy Minister of Marine and Fisheries, Canada *Sessional Papers*, 1922, LVIII, 13.

20 A.H. MacAdam, vice-president, National Shipbuilding Corp., New York, to C.C. Ballantyne, 2 June 1920, National Archives of Canada, RG 42, vol. 307, file 51666. MacAdam was referring to the experience of shipbuilders in Trois-Rivières, Quebec, and he added that the labour market in Canada was "wonderful."

21 In July 1920 the Department of Maritime and Fisheries prepared a List of Shipyards in the Dominion of Canada, which estimated deadweight tonnage capacity per annum. Of the 440,500-ton national capacity, Halifax Shipyards and Nova Scotia Steel and Coal Co. accounted for 62,000 tons. Four shipyards in British Columbia accounted for 150,000 tons, while Quebec accounted for 110,000 tons and Ontario for 118,500 tons. National Archives of Canada, RG 42, vol. 307, file 51666.

Relatively high labour costs accounted for much of the price of differential between British Columbia and other regions. One indication of costs is the tenders received by the Dominion government to build the 200-foot steamer *Estavan*, for service on the Pacific coast. The tender of the B.C. Marine Railway Co. was $455,000; that of Collingwood Shipbuilding of Ontario was $260,000; L.P. Brodeur in House of Commons *Debates*, 31 March 1911, 6487.

22 Production function refers to the relationship between the quantity of a good produced and the quantities of inputs required to produce it. There are a number of equations in neo-classical economics to express this relationship.

23 Eric W. Sager and Gerry Panting, "Staple Economies and the Rise and Decline of the Shipping Industry in Atlantic Canada, 1820–1914," in Fischer and Panting, eds., *Change and Adaptation in Maritime History*; 1–45.

24 M.H. Watkins, "A Staple Theory of Economic Growth," in W.T. Easterbrook and M.H. Watkins, eds., *Approaches to Canadian Economic History* (Toronto: McClelland and Stewart, 1967), 55.

25 James M. Gilmour, *Spatial Evolution of Manufacturing: Southern Ontario, 1851–1891* (Toronto: University of Toronto Press, 1972), 31.

26 Prince Edward Island Customs Returns, 1825, in Colonial Office series 231 (PEI Blue Books). The officials who gathered the export figures recalculated exports to include the value of ships built in Prince Edward Island and sent elsewhere: total exports for 1825 were valued at 95,426 pounds, of which ships accounted for 77,470 pounds.

27 Watkins refers to Quebec-built ships as "staple exports" in "A Staple Theory," in Easterbrook and Watkins, eds., *Approaches*, 69.

28 Kris E. Inwood, "Local Control, Resources and the Nova Scotia Steel and Coal Company," Canadian Historical Association *Historical Papers* (1986), 254–82.

29 See, for instance, Douglas McCalla and Peter George, "Measurement, Myth and Reality: Reflections on the Economic History of Nineteenth Century Ontario," *Journal of Canadian Studies*, 21, no. 3 (Fall 1986), 71–86; Ian M. Drummond, Louis P. Cain, and Marjorie Cohen, "CHR Dialogue: Ontario's Industrial Revolution," *Canadian Historical Review*, 69, no. 3 (September 1988), 283–314.

30 Douglass C. North, "Conference Summary," in Fischer and Sager, *Merchant Shipping and Economic Development*, 235.

31 The literature on dependency theory and development theory is now very extensive. For summaries see Colin Simmons, "Economic Development and Economic History," in Barbara Ingham and Colin Simmons, *Development Studies and Colonial Policy* (London: Frank Cass, 1987), 3–99; Magnus Blomstrom and Bjorn Hettne, *Development Theory in Transition* (London: Zed Press, 1984); Ronald H. Chilcote, *Theories of Development and Underdevelopment* (Boulder: Westview Press, 1984); Ronaldo Munck, *Politics and Dependency in the Third World: The Case of Latin America* (London: Zed Press, 1984); David Harrison, *The Sociology of Modernization and Development* (London: Unwin Hyman, 1988).

   Among Marxist critiques of the dependency approach are Geoffrey Kay, *Development and Underdevelopment: A Marxist Analysis* (London: Macmillan, 1975); E. Laclau, "Feudalism and Capitalism in Latin America," *New Left Review*, no. 67 (May–June 1971); E. Laclau, *Politics and Ideology in Marxist Theory* (London: Verso, 1979); R. Brenner, "The Origins of Capitalist Development: A Critique of Neo-Smithian Marxism," *New Left Review*, no. 104 (July–August 1977), 27–92; and Bill Warren, *Imperialism: Pioneer of Capitalism* (London: Verso, 1980).

32 Ian M. Drummond, *Progress without Planning: The Economic History of Ontario from Confederation to the Second World War* (Toronto: University of Toronto Press, 1987). The explanation in this work rests heavily on technological diffusion; see the comments of Louis Cain and Marjorie Cohen in Drummond, Cain, and Cohen, "CHR Dialogue," 300–14.

33 T.W. Acheson, "The Great Merchant and Economic Development in Saint John, 1820–1850," in P.A. Buckner and David Frank, eds., *Atlantic Canada before Confederation* (Fredericton: Acadiensis Press, 1985), 200–1.

34 Ian McKay, "The Crisis of Dependent Development: Class Conflict in the Nova Scotia Coalfields, 1872–1876," in Gregory S. Kealey, ed., *Class, Gender, and Region: Essays in Canadian Historical Sociology* (St John's: Committee on Canadian Labour History, 1988), 16.

35 Michael Clow, "Politics and Uneven Capitalist Development," *Studies in Political Economy*, no. 14 (Summer 1984), 134.

36 Marx's comments on transportation appear in *Capital*, II, chapter 6 (New

York: Vintage Books, 1981), 225–9. "The term 'use-value' denotes a power, and, derivatively, things which have that power ... The use-value of a thing is its power to satisfy, directly or indirectly, a human desire ... Exchange-value is a property of use-values which possess commodity status. The exchange-value of a commodity is its power of exchanging against quantities of other commodities." These definitions are from G.A. Cohen, *Karl Marx's Theory of History: A Defence* (Princeton: Princeton University Press, 1978), 345, 347.

37 Surplus value is the difference between the use value of labour, which goes to the capitalist employer, and the value returned to labourers in the form of wages. On the assumption that only the expenditure of labour creates economic value, it follows that workers do not receive the whole value of what they produce, and a portion of the value produced is appropriated by the employer as surplus value.

38 In Marxism the "mode of production" refers to two analytically separate but related dimensions in the social process of production and reproduction. It refers to the relations of production, the specific set of relations between human beings as the social product of labour is created and distributed; and the forces of production, the specific set of technology, technique, and labour applied in production.

39 Marx, *Capital*, III (New York: International Publishers, 1967), 327–8; cf. Steven Antler, "The Capitalist Underdevelopment of Nineteenth Century Newfoundland," in Robert J. Brym and R. James Sacouman, eds., *Underdevelopment and Social Movements in Atlantic Canada* (Toronto: New Hogtown Press, 1979), 186. On Marx's approach to development see also Ivan Vujacic, "Marx and Engels on Development and Underdevelopment: The Restoration of a Certain Coherence," *History of Political Economy*, 20, no. 3 (Fall 1988), 471–98.

40 Florencia E. Mallon, *The Defense of Community in Peru's Central Highlands: Peasant Struggle and Capitalist Transition, 1860–1940* (Princeton: Princeton University Press, 1983), 7.

41 Norman Long and Bryan Roberts, *Miners, Peasants and Entrepreneurs; Regional Development in the Central Highlands of Peru* (Cambridge: Cambridge University Press, 1984), 247.

42 Ibid., 67–8, 87.

43 Instances of such dependence in shipping appear in Eric W. Sager, *Seafaring Labour: The Merchant Marine of Atlantic Canada, 1820–1914* (Montreal and Kingston: McGill-Queen's University Press, 1989), chapter 2, 44–73.

44 Kay, *Development and Underdevelopment*, 86.

45 See, for instance, Rosemary E. Ommer, "From Outpost to Outport: The Jersey Merchant Triangle in the Nineteenth Century," PhD thesis, McGill

University, 1979; Ian McKay, "Industry, Work and Community in the Cumberland Coalfields, 1848–1927," PhD thesis, Dalhousie University, 1983; David A. Sutherland, "The Merchants of Halifax, 1815–1850: A Commercial Class in Pursuit of Metropolitan Status," PhD thesis, University of Toronto, 1975; Graeme Wynn, *Timber Colony: A Historical Geography of Early Nineteenth Century New Brunswick* (Toronto: University of Toronto Press, 1981); G. Porter and H.C. Livesay, *Merchants and Manufacturers: Studies in the Changing Structure of Nineteenth Century Marketing* (Baltimore: Johns Hopkins University Press, 1971); James E. Vance, Jr, *The Merchant's World: The Geography of Wholesaling* (Englewood Cliffs, NJ: Prentice-Hall, 1970); A.R.M. Lower, *'Great Britain's Woodyard': British America and the Timber Trade, 1763–1867* (Montreal: McGill-Queen's University Press, 1973); T.W. Acheson, *Saint John: The Making of a Colonial Urban Community* (Toronto: University of Toronto Press, 1985); L.D. McCann, "The Mercantile-Industrial Transition in the Metal Towns of Pictou County, 1857–1931," *Acadiensis*, 10, no. 2 (Spring 1981), 29–64; James F. Shepherd and Gary M. Walton, *Shipping, Maritime Trade and the Economic Development of Colonial North America* (Cambridge: Cambridge University Press, 1972).

46 R.T. Naylor, *Canada in the European Age 1453–1919* (Vancouver: New Star Books, 1987), xv. Although our context is very different from theirs, there is still much to be learned about the "janus face" of merchant capital from Elizabeth Fox-Genovese and Eugene D. Genovese, *Fruits of Merchant Capital: Slavery and Bourgeois Property in the Rise and Expansion of Capitalism* (Oxford: Oxford University Press, 1983).

47 Naylor, *Canada in the European Age*, 280.

CHAPTER TWO

1 One report suggests that nearly all the Poole vessels engaged in the Newfoundland trade were built in Newfoundland: D.W. Prowse, *A History of Newfoundland from the English, Colonial, and Foreign Records* (Belleville, 1972), 165n.

2 Stanley T. Spicer, *Masters of Sail: The Era of Square-Rigged Vessels in the Maritime Provinces* (Toronto, 1968), 16.

3 Lawrence A. Harper, *The English Navigation Laws: A Seventeenth Century Experiment in Social Engineering* (New York, 1939), 389–90.

4 Robert Craig and Rupert Jarvis, *Liverpool Registry of Merchant Ships* (Manchester 1967).

5 12 & 13 Vict. cap. 29.

6 Lord Sheffield estimated that a total of six vessels were built in all the British North American colonies in 1769; in 1770 there were four vessels, and in 1771, fifteen. In these three years ten vessels were built in Nova

Scotia, for a total of 450 tons: House of Commons *Journals*, XLVII, 1792, 356; see also Richard Rice, "The Rise of Shipbuilding in British North America, 1787–1855," PhD thesis, University of Liverpool, 1978, 39.

7 For the immediate effect on Nova Scotian trade see David A. Sutherland, "The Merchants of Halifax, 1815–1850: A Commercial Class in Pursuit of Metropolitan Status," PhD thesis, University of Toronto, 1975, 19–24.

8 Gerald S. Graham, *Sea Power and British North America 1783–1820: A Study in British Colonial Policy* (Cambridge, Mass., 1941), Appendix C.

9 Between 1788 and 1792 an annual average of 14,500 tons cleared Nova Scotia and New Brunswick for the West Indies, compared to an annual average of 4,700 tons clearing for the United Kingdom: calculated from Public Record Office, Customs 17; Rice, "The Rise of Shipbuilding," 45.

10 Between 1800 and 1814 a total of 266,693 tons cleared Nova Scotia and New Brunswick for the British West Indies – an annual average of 17,798 tons. The tonnage entering Nova Scotia and New Brunswick from the British West Indies was smaller – 165,127 tons between 1800 and 1814, or 11,000 tons a year – but bilateral trading was still very substantial.

The volume of trade between the West Indies and the United Kingdom was much larger: many vessels were engaged in a trilateral Britain-Maritimes–West Indies pattern, but a majority of the tonnage clearing from the Maritimes to the West Indies probably returned directly on the same route.

11 This was a reversal of the pattern of the late 1780s, when more tonnage came from Britain to the British North American colonies than returned directly home: Graham, *Sea Power*, 61.

12 Between 1800 and 1808, 114,000 tons cleared the United Kingdom for Nova Scotia and New Brunswick. In the same years 158,972 tons entered inward to Britain from Nova Scotia and New Brunswick. These figures and those in note 10 are from Graham, *Sea Power*, Appendix C. Graham also notes that "most British merchants were loath to send their larger ships systematically on a triangular voyage – Great Britain to the United States to the West Indies and return, or the reverse." Ibid., 58.

13 According to Gary Walton, "The evidence strongly suggests that specialized trade routes were common . . . This specialization is seen in terms of ownership by route as well as route regularity. Moreover, shuttle routes appear to be the main pattern . . . while triangular routes appear to be of minor importance." Gary M. Walton, "New Evidence on Colonial Commerce," *Journal of Economic History*, 28 (1968), 364.

14 Colonial Office, series 193, List of Vessels Clearing the Naval Office in Saint John, 1 July 1808 to 5 January 1810. These lists report 36 vessels clearing for the West Indies, of which 22 were registered in New Brunswick.

15 Calculated from the total for vessels passing Sambro Light House and

recorded in Light House Papers, Public Archives of Nova Scotia, RG 31–105, volume 2. Of fifty-one clearances from Halifax for the West Indies between 1 July and 31 December 1820, thirty-four were by vessels registered in Nova Scotia: from Colonial Office, series 221, List of Vessels Cleared at the Naval Office, Port of Halifax.

16 Graham, *Sea Power*, 231.

17 Calculated from figures on shipbuilding output in Rice, "The Rise of Shipbuilding," Appendix A.

18 Ibid., 53.

19 There were 3,648 tons newly registered in Prince Edward Island between 1795 and 1806. Of these only 218 tons were transferred to the United Kingdom. The most important market was Newfoundland. This analysis is based on ship registries for Prince Edward Island.

20 Calculated from Rice, "The Rise of Shipbuilding," Appendix A; Rice, "Measuring British Dominance," Appendix 1; Brian R. Mitchell and P. Deane, *Abstract of British Historical Statistics* (Cambridge, 1962), Transport 2, 220–2.

21 A.H. Imlah, *Economic Elements in the Pax Britannica* (New York, 1969), Table 23, 175.

22 In 1815 a total of 2,159,065 tons cleared outward from the United Kingdom in foreign trades; by 1852 this total was 8,242,702 tons, which suggests a growth rate of 3.7 per cent a year: from a return of tonnage entering and clearing in the foreign trade in British *Parliamentary Papers*, 1852–53, XCVIII, 302.

23 Calculated from Mitchell and Deane, *Abstract*, Transport 2, 220–2. This is the growth rate for the years 1820–50 estimated from $\log Y_t = a + b_t$.

24 Calculated from ibid., Transport 1.

25 In 1815, 34.8 per cent of tonnage clearing in the foreign trade from Britain was accounted for by foreign tonnage; by 1852 this proportion was 38.7 per cent: *Parliamentary Papers*, 1852–53, XCVIII, 302.

26 In 1846, 178,584 tons were on registry in Sunderland; only 2,661 tons had been built in the colonies. Sunderland was a major shipbuilding centre, producing about a quarter of all tonnage built in Britain in the early 1830s: Select Committee on Manufactures, Commerce and Shipping, *Parliamentary Papers*, 1833, VI, Appendix I, 718.

27 This is the simple correlation of annual totals of tonnage built in British North America and tonnage built and first registered in the United Kingdom; the latter figures are from Mitchell and Deane, *Abstract*, 220–1.

28 Craig, "British Shipping and British North American Shipbuilding in the Early Nineteenth Century," in H.E.S. Fisher, ed., *The Southwest and the Sea* (Exeter: Exeter University Press, 1968), 27.

29 Several correlation coefficients have been calculated. The correlation

between tonnage built and first registered in the United Kingdom and tonnage built in all British North America (using Craig's figures in "British Shipping") yields $r = +0.84$ for 1814–51. Correlating tonnage built and first registered in the United Kingdom, using Mitchell and Deane's figures, and tonnage built in the three Maritime colonies, using Rice's data, yields $r = +0.78$ for 1814–50, but the relationship strengthens over time, because correlating annual changes for 1827–48 yields $r = +0.73$, so that $r^2 = +0.53$.

Using these same series, if annual changes in the Maritimes' shipbuilding output is lagged by one year, the correlation of annual changes yields $r = +0.80$ for 1815/14–1830/29, or $r^2 = +0.64$; between 1831/30 and 1848/47 $r = +0.44$ when the Maritimes' output is lagged by one year, but $r = +0.73$ if the Maritimes' output is *not* lagged!

Correlating tonnage built in New Brunswick and tonnage built and first registered in the United Kingdom for 1815–50 yields $r = +0.85$; correlating annual *changes* in these two series yields $r = +0.67$ for 1815/14–1848/47, and lagging the New Brunswick data by one year lowers the result to $r = +0.40$. But the one-year lag once again produces a stronger result between 1815/14 and 1830/29, when $r = +0.64$.

For Prince Edward Island, the correlation with shipbuilding in the United Kingdom yields $r = +0.70$ for 1815–50, but correlating annual changes (with no lag) produces $r = +0.61$ for 1815–48.

The correlation between Nova Scotia tonnage and United Kingdom-built tonnage for 1815–50 was $+0.82$.

The correlation between Newfoundland- and United Kingdom – built tonnage for 1815–50 was $+0.01$.

30 Letter of G.F. Young to W.E. Gladstone, 28 May 1844, in *Parliamentary Papers*, 1846, XLV, 354–8.

31 Craig, "British Shipping," 22.

32 Sometimes the decision was made by the builder's agents in Liverpool. Thus in 1829 R. Addison of Liverpool informed Ward & Son of Saint John that he had not sold its vessel the *Emerald* because "it is *totally impossible* to sell the vessel except by forcing her off at a mere nominal value," and so he had ballasted her with salt and coals and sent her to New Brunswick for another cargo of timber: Addison to Ward, 14 March 1829, Ward Papers, packet 19, New Brunswick Museum.

33 Total tonnage clearing United Kingdom ports for British North America in 1845 was 917,423; of this 593,116 tons were in ballast. In 1846 978,590 tons cleared for British North America, of which 605,253 tons were in ballast: *Parliamentary Papers*, 1847, LX, 155.

34 At one point the Transport Office was employing 290,000 tons: "Return

of the Greatest Number of Hired Transports," *Parliamentary Papers*, 1826, XXII, 305.

35 Correlating annual *changes* in loads of timber exported from New Brunswick to Britain with annual changes in tonnage entering the United Kingdom from New Brunswick between 1800 and 1819 (omitting 1809–13, when data are missing) yields $r = +0.97$ and $r^2 = +0.94$.

36 Log $Y_t = 2.508 + 0.0309t$, and the antilog of 0.0309 is 1.074.

37 The correlation between loads of timber from British North America to the United Kingdom and newly built tonnage in Canada and the Maritimes yields $r = +0.79$ for 1806–49. There are problems, however, with the timber export figures, and timber was exported in various forms, not all of which can be added together. The omission of deals, deal ends, and sawn lumber in the 1840s is unfortunate because these were increasing in importance.

38 *Parliamentary Papers*, 1852–53, XCVIII, 302.

39 Between 1835 and 1839 an annual average of 2 million tons entered US ports, and only 7 per cent was non-British or non-US tonnage (*Parliamentary Papers*, 1847, LX, 145). In the same years an annual average of 651,000 tons entered Britain from British North America, with probably 46–50 per cent of it accounted for by vessels built in British North America (*Parliamentary Papers*, 1840, XLIV, 306–12). British North America–built tonnage in the British North America–United Kingdom passage represented the equivalent of about 15 per cent of all entrances into US ports.

40 The data in Graph 2.6 are from British *Parliamentary Papers*, 1866, LXV, 19; 1865, L, 239; 1864, LV, 19; 1863, LXIII, 19; 1862, LIV, 119; 1861, LVIII, 19; 1860, LX, 420; 1859, XXVIII, 389; 1857–8, LIV, 379; 1857, XXXIX, 54; 1856, LI, 366; 1855, XLVI, 281; 1854, LX, 47; 1852–3, XCVIII, 297; 1852, XLIX, 13; 1851, LI, 209; 1850, LIII, 391; 1849, LI, 483.

41 *Parliamentary Papers*, 1854–5, XLVI, 280.

42 Letter of 11 October 1832, House of Assembly *Journals*, Prince Edward Island, Appendix C.

43 Rice, "The Rise of Shipbuilding," 93, using *Parliamentary Papers*, 1840, LXXV, 2–20, 58–82.

44 Arthur R.M. Lower, *Great Britain's Woodyard: British America and the Timber Trade, 1763–1867* (Montreal, 1973), 259–60; McClelland, "The New Brunswick Economy," Tables XVIII, XX, XXIII, 73–86.

45 McClelland, "The New Brunswick Economy," Table XXVII, 97.

46 On timber duties see Graeme Wynn, *Timber Colony: A Historical Geography of Early Nineteenth Century New Brunswick* (Toronto: University of Toronto Press, 1981), 30–3.

47 Ibid., 53.

CHAPTER THREE

1 "The transportation industry forms on one hand an independent branch of production, and thus a special sphere of investment of productive capital. On the other hand, it is distinguished from other spheres of production by the fact that it represents a continuation of a process of production within the process of circulation and for its benefit." Marx, *Capital*, II (Chicago, 1933), chapter 6, 172. "Users of freight transport perceive transport as a cost in their overall production function and seek to minimise it wherever possible," says K.J. Button, *Transport Economics* (London: Heinemann, 1982), 4; cf. R.W. Faulks, *Principles of Transport* (London: I. Allan, 1973), 16.

2 Douglass C. North, "Ocean Freight Rates and Economic Development 1750–1913," *Journal of Economic History*, 18, no. 4 (December 1958), 537–55. On productivity see Douglass C. North, "Sources of Productivity Change in Ocean Shipping, 1600–1850," *Journal of Political Economy*, 76 (September–October 1968), 953–70; C. Knick Harley, "Ocean Freight Rates and Productivity, 1740–1913: The Primacy of Mechanical Invention Reaffirmed," *Journal of Economic History*, 48, no. 4 (December 1988), 851–76.

3 R.S. Craig, "British Shipping and British North American Shipbuilding in the Early Nineteenth Century," in H.E.S. Fisher, ed., *The Southwest and the Sea* (Exeter, 1968) 21–2; David Williams, "Merchanting in the First Half of the Nineteenth Century: The Liverpool Timber Trade," *Business History* 8 (1966), 111–12; Simon P. Ville, *English Shipowning during the Industrial Revolution* (Manchester: Manchester University Press, 1987), 2–3, 18.

4 Williams, "Merchanting," 112.

5 Ralph Davis, *The Rise of the English Shipping Industry in the Seventeenth and Eighteenth Centuries* (London, 1962), 91–6.

6 On the timber trade and its regulation see Graeme Wynn, *Timber Colony: A Historical Geography of Early Nineteenth Century New Brunswick* (Toronto: University of Toronto Press, 1981); on truck see Rosemary Ommer, " 'All the Fish of the Post': Resource Property Rights and Development in a Nineteenth Century Inshore Fishery," *Acadiensis*, 9, no. 2 (Spring 1981), 107–23. On the theory of colonial exploitation see Steven D. Antler, "The Capitalist Underdevelopment of Nineteenth Century Newfoundland," in Robert J. Brym and R. James Sacouman, *Underdevelopment and Social Movements in Atlantic Canada* (Toronto, 1979); Antler, "Colonial Exploitation and Economic Stagnation in Nineteenth Century Newfoundland," PhD thesis, University of Connecticut, 1975.

7 The few schooners in Newfoundland having auxiliary gasoline motors were included with auxiliary steamers. The same vessel may appear in

the totals for more than one port. The unit of analysis is the first registry of a vessel in each port, and many vessels were first registered in one port, then transferred to another, and in the latter they are also counted as a first registry. This procedure is appropriate because our focus is on investment patterns.

8 In the 1820s the mean tonnage of vessels newly registered in Saint John (172 tons) was 142 per cent greater than that of vessels newly registered in Halifax (71 tons). The mean tonnage of Saint John vessels (495 tons) was 150 per cent greater than that of Halifax vessels (198 tons). Estimated from Registry Data Files.

9 On sealing steamers see Chesley W. Sanger, "Technological and Spatial Adaptation in the Newfoundland Seal Fishery during the 19th Century," MA thesis, Memorial University, 1973; Levi Chafe, *History of the Newfoundland Seal Fishery from the Earliest Available Records down to and Including the Voyage of 1923* (St John's: Trade Printers and Publishers 1924); James E. Candow, *Of Men and Seals: A History of the Newfoundland Seal Hunt* (Ottawa: Canadian Parks Service, 1989).

10 The measurement of tonnage changed in 1836 and 1854. The effect of the 1854 change differed among vessels of different tonnage classes, but certainly we are not overestimating tonnages after 1854. William Smith, the New Brunswick registrar, wrote as follows: "The new tonnage built last year, viz. 38,330 tons Register, would represent about 41,000 tons old, or carpenter's measurement, which is the tonnage by which vessels are usually bought and sold." Customs Returns for 1859, Colonial Office series 193, New Brunswick Blue Books, 1860. In the Appendices of the *Journals of the House of Assembly* of Prince Edward Island for 1858, 1859, 1860, and 1861 there are "Accounts of Vessels Launched and Registered at this Port," giving pre-1854 and post-1854 tonnages for each vessel. For vessels of 250 to 499 tons, the pre-1854 tonnage was 22 per cent higher than the post-1854 tonnage ($n = 66$). For vessels of 500 to 999 tons, the old measurement was on average 5 per cent higher than the new ($n = 10$).

11 A second tonnage measurement, also entered on the registries, deducted from gross tonnage the area of all non-cargo spaces, such as crew's quarters, fuel bunkers, and machinery spaces. This second measure, net registered tonnage, was a much more accurate measure of carrying capacity. The difference between gross and net registered tonnage was much less in sailing vessels than in steamers.

12 The tonnage of the newly registered ship in the 1840s was 559; by the 1880s the ship was on average 1,559 tons. David Alexander, "The Port of Yarmouth, Nova Scotia, 1840–1889," in Keith Matthews and Gerald Panting, eds., *Ships and Shipbuilding in the North Atlantic Region* (St John's: Maritime History Group, 1978), 82–3.

13 If we break tonnage into nine ranges (1–9, 10–49, 50–99, 100–149, 150–249, 250–499, 500–999, 1,000–1,499, and 1,500+), to know a vessel's tonnage class in the Saint John fleet was to improve one's chances of guessing its rig by 40 per cent (lambda with rig dependent = 0.42). A very similar result was found for the Yarmouth fleet from 1840 to 1889: David Alexander and Gerald Panting, "The Mercantile Fleet and Its Owners: Yarmouth, Nova Scotia, 1840–1889," *Acadiensis*, 7, no. 2 (Spring 1978), 6 n. 2. The relationship is not closer because the tonnage of most rigs increased over time so that each rig moved through two or more tonnage classes.

14 On the shift from two to three masts see David R. MacGregor, *Merchant Sailing Ships 1815–1850* (London, 1984), 26, 30; on studding-sails see John Harland and Mark Myers, *Seamanship in the Age of Sail* (London, 1984), 155–72.

15 "These little vessels cannot draw out to the westward anything like as fast as heavier ones, and the loss of ten days can never be made up again," wrote Robert Quirk to J.M.C. Stumbles, 13 April 1881, Duncan Letterbooks vol. 362, Public Archives of Prince Edward Island.

16 Harland and Myers, *Seamanship*, 46. Similarly the giant steel sailing ships of the early twentieth century were capable of faster sailing than the smaller wooden clippers of the 1850s. See also Howard I. Chapelle, *The Search for Speed under Sail 1700–1855* (New York, 1967), 29.

17 Chapelle, *The Search for Speed*, 25–7.

18 Harland and Myers, *Seamanship*, 84.

19 Her length–breadth ratio was 5.07. See Charles Armour and Thomas Lackey, *Sailing Ships of the Maritimes* (Toronto, 1975), 58–9. An "extreme clipper" (Chapelle's term) had a higher ratio. McKay's *Lightning*, for instance, had a ratio of 5.7 in registered dimensions: Chapelle, *The Search for Speed*, 379. On clippers see also David R. MacGregor, *Fast Sailing Ships: Their Design and Construction, 1775–1875* (London: Conway Maritime Press, 1988).

20 Chapelle, *The Search for Speed*, 398ff.

21 The story of these freak vessels is told in David Williams, "Bulk Carriers and Timber Imports," *Mariner's Mirror*, 54 (1968), 373–82.

22 Select Committee on Manufactures, Commerce and Shipping, *Parliamentary Papers*, 1833, VI, 526: James Gilmour explained to this committee how he persuaded masters to make three passages in a season.

23 Select Committee on the Commercial Marine, *Parliamentary Papers*, 1844, VIII, 309.

24 Ibid., 336; cited in Richard Rice, "The Rise of Shipbuilding in British North America, 1787–1855," PhD thesis, University of Liverpool, 1978, 134.

25 G.F. Young, Chairman of the Committee of the General Shipowners'

Society, to W.E. Gladstone, 28 May 1844, *Parliamentary Papers*, 1846, XLV, 354–8.

26 The reputation went back even to eighteenth-century vessels from the thirteen American colonies: Davis, *The Rise of the English Shipping Industry*, 374; Marshall Smelser and William J. Davisson, "The Longevity of Colonial Ships," *American Neptune*, 33 (1973), 16–19. On the durability of softwood and naval vessels built of softwood see Robert Albion, *Forests and Sea Power: The Timber Problem of the Royal Navy, 1652–1862* (Cambridge, Mass., 1926), 391–8; Select Committee on Foreign Trade, *Parliamentary Papers*, 1820, III, 436–8; Select Committee on Foreign Trade, *Parliamentary Papers*, 1821, VI, 55; Rice, "The Rise of Shipbuilding," 135–6.

27 The calculation includes vessels that were condemned, broken up, lost at sea, or supposed lost or for which the entry merely reads "no longer exists." The estimate excludes all vessels transferred to registry elsewhere or registered de novo in Saint John.

28 Report of the Select Committee to Inquire into the Shipwrecks of Timber Ships, *Parliamentary Papers*, 1839, IX, 226.

29 Ibid., 351ff. British North American vessels clearing were slightly over six years old on average, whereas British vessels were 17.5 years old.

30 See the evidence of Charles Graham, secretary of Lloyds, to the Select Committee on Shipwrecks, citing Lloyds surveyors: "I generally find them strained aloft, particularly their waterway seams, with the butts of their blank shears and shear steaks, and the knee fastenings which pass through the latter, and not unusually find their stanchions started and blank shears split, and which must have admitted much water when at sea in bad weather, so much so as to have caused the ship to have water-logged ... The which straining and looking aloft is, in my opinion, generally occasioned by the heavy deck-loads that are brought on them." The beams of upper and lower decks were frequently sprung and broken, "as well as the straining the knee-fastenings, the wood of which (if North American softwood) is not hard enough to hold the bolts." *Parliamentary Papers*, 1839, IX, 241.

31 Calculated from annual data on shipping registered in the United Kingdom and ships built and first registered in Britain, 1820–49 (omitting 1827), in B.R. Mitchell and P. Deane, *Abstract of British Historical Statistics* (Cambridge, 1962), 217–21.

32 In Saint John, for instance, net physical capital formation was 41 per cent of gross investment in the 1830s, but it was negative in the next two decades. Over the long period from 1826 to 1877 (a peak in fleet size) the proportion was 12.7 per cent. In Halifax, however, where much less tonnage was transferred to registry elsewhere, the proportion was 20.4 per cent from 1826 to 1874.

33 Capital consumption was less rapid among steamships: in the 1870s and 1880s net investment in steam tonnage in the United Kingdom was 57 per cent of gross investment. See Eric W. Sager and Lewis R. Fischer, "Patterns of Investment in the Shipping Industries of Atlantic Canada, 1820–1900," *Acadiensis*, 9, no. 1 (Autumn 1979), 31–3.

34 O.J. Firestone estimated net capital formation to be 33 per cent of gross in the Canadian economy in 1870 and 38 per cent in 1890: O.J. Firestone, *Canada's Economic Development 1867–1953* (London, 1958), 112.

35 Brodie McGhie, testifying to the Select Committee on Foreign Trade, *Parliamentary Papers*, 1821, VI, 36. John Spence told the Select Committee on Manufactures, Commerce and Shipping that 300 of 1,000 timber ships were suitable for any trade: *Parliamentary Papers*, 1835, VI, 421, cited in Rice, "The Rise of Shipbuilding," 125 n. 64.

36 Letter of John Cooke of Derry, 1838, in Cecil J. Houston and William J. Smyth, "New Brunswick Shipbuilding and Irish Shipping: The Commissioning of the *Londonderry*, 1838," *Acadiensis*, 16, no. 2 (Spring 1987), 95. See also the account of the building of the *Waterloo* (which vessel lasted thirty-seven years) at St Martin's New Brunswick: J. Russell Harper, "St. Martin's Men Build a Ship in 1814," *American Neptune*, 21 (1961), 279–91.

37 Vessels built by the Wrights were often on contract: Richard Rice, "The Wrights of Saint John: A Study of Shipbuilding and Shipowning in the Maritimes, 1839–1855," in David S. Macmillan, ed., *Canadian Business History: Selected Studies 1497–1971* (Toronto 1972), 317–37. A large proportion of the vessels of the Millidge family were built on contract, and there are several contracts in the Peake-Brecken collection in the Public Archives of Prince Edward Island. See also the 1834 contract in Stanley T. Spicer, *Masters of Sail: The Era of Square-Rigged Vessels in the Maritime Provinces* (Toronto: Ryerson Press, 1968), 147–8.

38 In 1824 George Brown of Liverpool, referring to the sale of a vessel called *W. Wallace*, told the Wards that "if she had had oak in her stem, stern & transoms she would have readily reckn'd £1 p ton more for birch is with us decidedly objectionable above water altho' perhaps there may be more prejudice than is necessary against it." Letter of 21 November 1824, Ward papers, Packet 20, New Brunswick Museum.

39 Letters of Ward and Sons to Gibbs, Bright and Co., Liverpool, 15 December 1840 and 28 April 1841, and letter to Capt. Philip Masters of 24 August 1843, Ward Papers, Packet 3 (Letter Book 1839–44), New Brunswick Museum. The letter of 15 December also says that a Lloyds classification is desired on condition that it be done "without putting us to the expence of many things that by their regulations we consider as altogether useless being added to this Ship."

40 Letters of 7 June 1826 and 5 July 1826 from Ward and Sons to Richard

Addison, Ward Papers, Packet 19 (regarding the brig *Jane*); and the building agreements of the 1820s and 1830s in the Peake Papers, Public Archives of Prince Edward Island, Acc. no. 2881.

41 Charles Graham, secretary of Lloyds, testifying to the Select Committee on Shipwrecks, *Parliamentary Papers*, 1839, IX, 236.

42 Letter of James Robertson, 10 December 1850, in I.D. Andrews, *Report on the Trade and Commerce of the British North American Colonies with the United States and Other Countries* (Washington, DC, 1851), 451–3. Lloyds surveyors reports held in the National Maritime Museum, Greenwich, show ratings of from A4 up to A7 for New Brunswick vessels in the mid-1850s. By the 1860s and 1870s the A7 rating was much more common.

43 Annual Return of Trade and Navigation, New Brunswick, *Journals of the House of Assembly*, 1865, 6.

44 Of the tonnage built in New Brunswick in 1865, the Saint John Customs Office reported as follows: 34,785 tons were classed 7A1 at British Lloyds; 3,035 tons classed 5A1 at Lloyds; 8,920 tons classed 4A1 at Lloyds; 437 tons classed 7A1 at Bureau Veritas; 11,995 classed 5A1 at Bureau Veritas; 479 tons classed 4A1 at Bureau Veritas; 5,823 tons (mainly small schooners and woodboats) were not classed. "Annual Returns of Trade and Navigation for the Year 1865," New Brunswick, *Journals of the House of Assembly*, 1866.

45 From "An Account of All the New Vessels Registered in New Brunswick in the Year 1857," New Brunswick, *Journals of the House of Assembly*, 1858, Appendix, cccxliv-cccxlv. A separate table includes thirteen vessels sent from Saint John on governor's pass, without being registered in Saint John. Several vessels built outside Saint John were being classed 7A1, and one vessel, built in Moncton, was being built to 8A1 standards.

The following table (number of vessels built or first registered in New Brunswick by Lloyds class, 1857) summarizes the data. The summary is of the Lloyds class to which vessels were being built under the inspection of Lloyds surveyors. Some vessels may not have earned the classification to which they were being built. Most unclassed vessels were woodboats and small schooners. Saint John includes Carleton, Courtenay Bay, Indiantown, Kennebecasis, Portland, and Sand Point.

	8A	7A	6A	4A	Unclassed
Saint John	–	39	–	1	5
Miramichi/					
Richibucto	–	9	–	4	5
Outport	1	18	1	14	46
Nova Scotia	–	–	–	2	3
Total	1	66	1	21	59

46 Lloyds surveyors' reports, National Maritime Museum, Greenwich, England. In 1863 an unnamed reporter for the Saint John *News* toured that city's shipyards and reported in detail on the thirty vessels he found under construction. Of 28,073 tons being built, 17,180 tons (61 per cent) were being built to class A7. Most of the rest were being built to class A4. The A4 ships were being built mainly of spruce; the A7 ships contained larger quantities of hackmatack and southern oak. From a typescript by an unnamed reporter, Shipbuilding about Saint John 1863, indexed under that title in the Saint John Public Library.

47 Frank Killam, cited in House of Commons *Journals*, X, 1876, Appendix 3, 165–6.

48 "It is well known to persons connected with shipbuilding operations that there is a marked difference in the manner of constructing ships now compared with former years; and that the alterations made ... tend greatly to increase their durability, enhance their value, and reduce the cost of building ... In former times the keel of a ship was made in three heights with a shoe above and another below, and it was difficult if not impossible to secure them ... At the present day the keel is made in two heights, and the floors rest upon the main keel and are supported by the keelson bolts which pass down through the keel each floor, and, with the thick garbord stakes on each side bolted horizontally through the keel in each other, render the destruction of the whole of the keel at the same time almost an impossibility." From Shipbuilding about Saint John 1863.

49 Eric Lawson, of Bowen Island, British Columbia, has been studying Canadian shipbuilding for many years. The *Egeria* was a square-rigger built at the Kennebecasis shipyard of Thomas Edward Millidge. At the time of writing the hull still exists, at Port Stanley, Falkland Islands.

50 "We have impressed on all of our builders the absolute necessity of salting thoroughly," wrote James Duncan to Sir James Malcolm, 13 August 1875, Duncan Letterbooks vol. 359A, Public Archives of Prince Edward Island.

51 Killam was testifying to the Select Committee on the Causes of the Present Depression: House of Commons *Journals*, X 1876, Appendix 3, 166.

52 Recaulking and remetalling were important for both durability and sea-worthiness. Remetalling a hull might occur every three or four years. Referring to the barque *Snow Queen*, Capt. Everett McDougall wrote to the owners: "The vessel's metal is in a very bad condition, being on now nearly 3 1/2 years, and she can't possibly sail. In fact if it is left on much longer, there will not be much of it left to take off." McDougall to Frieze and Roy, 20 February 1888, Frieze and Roy Papers, Dalhousie University Archives.

53 "We kept them pretty well at par," said the Liverpool shipowner George Kendall of Americans in the cotton trade, "by having North American

ships; but we could do nothing with the States, if it was not for the North American ships; we could not sail British ships in that trade." Select Committee on the Commercial Marine, *Parliamentary Papers*, 1844, VIII, 332, cited in Rice, "The Rise of Shipbuilding," 93.

"Without those ships we could not as a nation successfully compete with our neighbours on the continent of Europe, nor should we have the least chance in the cotton ports of America," wrote William Pope in *Remarks on Shipbuilding in British America* (Liverpool, 1845).

54 Select Committee on the Commercial Marine, *Parliamentary Papers*, 1844, VIII, 405.

55 John J.B. Hutchins, *The American Maritime Industries and Public Policy, 1789–1914* (Cambridge, Mass., 1941), 191, 202.

56 There is a good description of a Miramichi shipyard in Spicer, *Masters of Sail*, 115–17.

57 William Smith, controller of customs, stated that a new vessel built in 1862 to class 7A1 and costing £10,000 sterling would include £3,000 worth of imported materials and that "the New Brunswick Government duties ... would be about £130." New Brunswick, House of Assembly *Journals*, 1863, "Annual Returns of Trade and Navigation."

58 Much of the preceding is from the testimony of Frank Killam, House of Commons *Journals*, X, 1876, Appendix 3, 164–6.

59 See the responses of several New Brunswick and Nova Scotian merchants and officials in "Fifth Report of the Select Committee on Fisheries, Navigations, &c.," House of Commons *Journals*, 1869, II, Appendix 3, 110–12 (beginning with the answer of Hon. J. Ferguson). James Robertson of Moncton, for instance, answered as follows: "Five and six years' vessels fitted for sea, $30; seven years class for about $34 per ton."

60 Yarmouth vessels seem to have cost more than other Nova Scotian vessels: Frank Killam quoted a price of $45 per ton in 1876 (see note 58), but he also noted that prices were falling.

61 The ship *George T. Hay*, built at Spencer's Island, Nova Scotia, in 1887 cost $31.77 per ton outfitted. Thomas Mosher of Avondale, Nova Scotia, contracted to build a 707-ton barquentine in 1889 for $35.19 per ton outfitted. The ship *E.J. Spicer* (1880) cost $37.10 per ton. These examples are from Spicer, *Masters of Sail*, 152. The *N.B. Lewis*, built at Salmon River, Digby County, Nova Scotia, in 1880, cost "approximately" $40,000, or $30.12 per ton, "fully rigged for sea": Clement W. Crowell, *Novascotiaman* (Halifax, 1979), 66.

62 Spicer, *Masters of Sail*, 41.

63 The ten leading building locations for each fleet supplied the following proportions of new tonnage: Yarmouth, 61.8 per cent; Windsor, 81.3 per cent; Pictou, 87.8 per cent; and Miramichi, 85.3 per cent.

64 David Alexander and Gerald Panting, "The Mercantile Fleet and Its Owners: Yarmouth, Nova Scotia, 1840–1889," *Acadiensis*, 7, no. 2 (Spring, 1978), 6.

65 The following table shows the proportion (%) of new tonnage accounted for by the largest five building locations by period and tonnage class (Saint John):

Period	500–999 tons	1,000–1,499 tons	1,500 + tons
1840s	68.3	90.4	–
1850s	61.4	65.5	100 (four places)
1860s	42.3	70.7	100 (four places)
1870s	45.2	61.2	93.0
1880–1914	66.5	71.5	80.3

Source: Saint John vessel registries. Most of the 1,500 + vessels after 1900 were built in Scotland. The number of building locations supplying a majority of tonnage diminished as vessel size increased.

66 See, for instance, Basil Greenhill and Ann Giffard, *Westcountrymen in Prince Edward's Isle: A Fragment of the Great Migration* (Newton Abbot, 1967).

CHAPTER FOUR

1 An effort was made to distinguish all unique individuals named as owners on the registries, and a code was assigned to each. Usually if two shareholders having the same name lived in different places, it was assumed that they were different individuals. Distinctions were sometimes difficult to make, and the figures must be considered estimates, especially for St John's registries, where the recurrence of surnames makes identification of owners (other than merchants) very difficult:

The number of unique owners for each port was as follows: Halifax, 8,966 (1820–1914); Saint John, 6,274 (1820–1914); St John's, 5,020 (1820–1914); Charlottetown, 2,255 (1820–1914); Yarmouth, 3,066 (1840–1914); Windsor, 1,605 (1849–1914); Pictou, 871 (1840–1914); and Miramichi, 854 (1828–1914).

2 Shares in registered vessels were divided into 64ths, and the registry states how many 64ths each owner held at the time of registry. For each owner we calculate "tonnage owned" in each vessel by multiplying the vessel's gross tonnage by the number of shares and dividing by 64. If two or more owners held an unspecified portion of shares among them, each portion is assumed to be equal (thus if two owners share

32/64ths of a 1,000-ton vessel, and the division of the 32 shares between them is unspecified, each is given 250 tons).

3 Including only vessels of 500 tons and more, about 773,000 tons were newly registered in eight major ports between 1820 and 1849. Of this total, 90 per cent was owned by merchants and only 1.7 per cent by small owner-operators (mariners, farmers, planters, fishermen, and traders).

4 Thus in Halifax 55 per cent of all tonnage in vessels of less than 250 tons was owned by traders, fishermen, mariners, or farmers on second or subsequent registry in the port. In Saint John the comparable figure was 40 per cent, and in Charlottetown it was 47 per cent.

5 *New Monthly Magazine*, 1 September 1818.

6 Colonial Office, series 221, List of All Ships Cleared Outwards in the Port of Sydney, Cape Breton, 5 July–15 October 1804. These Naval Office records report the name of the master and the name of the owner; in 59 of 86 clearances the owner was the same as the master; at least 52 clearances were by vessels owned by a resident of Cape Breton. The Halifax figures are from Colonial Office series 221, List of Vessels Cleared at the Naval Office, Port of Halifax, from 1 July 1820 to 31 December 1820. Of 219 clearances, 78 were by vessels where the owner was the master (and the total does not include vessels owned by S. Cunard and operated by Edward Cunard). Many of the owner-operators were American.

7 See Eric W. Sager, *Seafaring Labour: The Merchant Marine of Atlantic Canada, 1820–1914* (Montreal: McGill-Queen's University Press, 1989), especially chapters 4, 6, and 8. But see also Marcus Rediker, *Between the Devil and the Deep Blue Sea: Merchant Seamen, Pirates, and the Anglo-American Maritime World, 1700–1750* (Cambridge: Cambridge University Press, 1987).

8 T.W. Acheson, *Saint John: The Making of a Colonial Urban Community* (Toronto: University of Toronto Press, 1985), 53, 63.

9 Ibid., chapter 3; T.W. Acheson, "The Great Merchant and Economic Development in Saint John 1820–1850," *Acadiensis*, 8, no. 2 (Spring 1979), 3–27.

10 Acheson, *Saint John*, 54.

11 Esther Clark Wright, *Saint John Ships and Their Builders* (Wolfville, NS: printed by the author, 1976), 52–5; Acheson, *Saint John*, 78.

12 The Millidge shipyard was at Kennebecasis. T.E. Millidge's father was Thomas Millidge, a shipowner, and his maternal grandfather was James Simonds. Millidge was related, therefore, to the Simonds and to the Gilberts, both owners of prominent merchant firms.

13 Compare, for instance, Acheson's list of great merchants in *Saint John*, 274 n 8, with the lists of shipbuilders in Wright, *Saint John Ships*, 172–97. Clearly there was little overlap.

14 G.A. White, *Halifax and Its Business* (Halifax: Nova Scotia Printing, 1876), 65.

15 On Halifax merchants see David A. Sutherland, "The Merchants of Halifax, 1815–1850: A Commercial Class in Pursuit of Metropolitan Status," PhD thesis, University of Toronto, 1975.

16 From 1840 to 1850 at least twenty-one of the thirty-nine new major shipowners took part in the formation of businesses other than merchant-shipowning. About half of those listed as founders of public companies in Yarmouth were shipowners. Elisha W.B. Moody, Benjamin Rogers, and Thomas Killam were in the Marine Insurance Association; Moody and Rogers were in the Commercial Wharf Co. in the 1850s; the Killams and their relatives founded the Yarmouth Steam Navigation Co. in the 1850s; the Killams were also involved with the Nova Scotia Electric Telegraph Co.

17 Major owners who began before mid-century included Ezra Churchill; Shubael Dimock (shipbuilder); Nicholas Mosher (mariner and shipbuilder); and Bennett Smith and his brothers (shipbuilders). Merchant-shipowners rather than shipbuilders tended to be creators of the public companies, including the Avon Marine Insurance Co. and the Kerosene Gaslight Co.

18 J.G.B. Hutchins, *The American Maritime Industries and Public Policy, 1789–1914* (Cambridge, Mass.: Harvard University Press, 1941), 239–40.

19 Roche to Edward Twining, 24 June 1838, William Roche Letterbook, Public Archives of Nova Scotia.

20 Roche to G. Mitchell, 13 July 1837, Roche Letterbook.

21 Roche to Messrs Winter & Preston, Demerara, 13 December 1836, Roche Letterbook.

22 Roche to Capt. Donally, 5 November 1835, Roche Letterbook.

23 Roche to Capt. Hore, 18 June 1838, Roche Letterbook.

24 Roche to Capt. Hore, 5 November 1837, Roche Letterbook.

25 Report of the Select Committee on Manufactures, Commerce and Shipping, British *Parliamentary Papers*, 1833, VI, 526.

26 See the discussion of merchant capital in G.A. Cohen, *Karl Marx's Theory of History: A Defence* (Princeton: Princeton University Press, 1978), 299–302.

27 Newman, Hunt and Company to Newman and Company, Newfoundland; Newman, Hunt and Company Records, Newfoundland Letter Book 1858–1865, no. 41, f. 340, Provincial Archives of Newfoundland and Labrador; we are indebted to James. K. Hiller for this reference.

CHAPTER FIVE

1 The main problem with official figures is that registrars did not always know when a vessel actually went out of service. Conscientious registrars cleansed their registries periodically, and when they did so the official

figures indicate a large number of disposals. We have corrected for this in our estimates of tonnage on registry, by applying an average vessel life to all cases where disposal information is missing or inadequate. The averages applied are in most cases the average by rig and by decade. Thus if a schooner registered in Saint John in the 1840s has no more disposal information than "Registry closed 1865," this vessel is assigned the average life of all Saint John schooners registered in the 1840s whose actual service lives were known. The results certainly do not overestimate tonnage on registry, and our estimates are usually (although not always) lower than the official figures.

Users of these registries might wish to refer to a series of unpublished research papers written by David Alexander for the Atlantic Canada Shipping Project in 1976 and 1977, contained in the Maritime History Archive, Memorial University of Newfoundland; for instance, David Alexander, "The Average Registry Life of Yarmouth Vessels, 1840–1889," Maritime History Group Research Paper: Yarmouth Vessels No. 6, December 1976. For other problems of registry analysis see Richard Rice, "Measuring British Dominance of Shipbuilding in the Maritimes, 1787–1890," in Keith Matthews and Gerald Panting, eds., *Ships and Shipbuilding in the North Atlantic Region* (St John's: Maritime History Group, 1978), 111–55.

2 The Nova Scotia ports of registry in the eighteenth and nineteenth centuries, with their opening dates, were Halifax (1787), Shelburne (1787–1823, 1859–   ), Sydney (1787), Liverpool (1840), Pictou (1840), Yarmouth (1840), Arichat (1842), Digby (1849), Guysborough (1849), Lunenburg (1849), Windsor (1849), Parrsborough (1850), Annapolis (1858), Baddeck (1858), Pugwash (1858), Ship Harbour–Port Hawkesbury (1858), Amherst (1874), Maitland (1874), Port Medway (1874), Weymouth (1874), Barrington (1875), Londonderry (1875), and Truro (1875). The major New Brunswick registries were always those in Saint John and Miramichi, but vessels were also registered in St Martin's.

3 By the 1890s, for instance, official figures for Newfoundland suggest that over 100,000 tons were on registry in St John's; our computer file suggests that there were about 80,000 tons on registry. The date of actual disposal of small vessels was often unknown to the registrar. Our method, by applying an average to these unknowns, may result in an underestimate of total tonnage; the official figures are certainly an overestimate.

4 "The would-be short-term owner became a full-time shipowner by default," wrote Peter McClelland in "The New Brunswick Economy in the Nineteenth Century," PhD thesis, Harvard University, 1966, 206. This was only part of McClelland's argument, and he was referring only to New Brunswick.

5 If we estimate the contributions of each port to the total growth for the

eight ports (rather than growth of official tonnage on registry for the region), then Saint John's contribution was 32 per cent, Yarmouth's 27 per cent, Windsor's 15 per cent, and Halifax's 9 per cent.

6 The equation is $\log Y_t = 5.285 - 0.0003t$ with a very small negative correlation coefficient, which suggests a very low growth rate (-0.07 per cent a year).

7 The equation for 1849–79 is $\log Y^t = 5.228 + 0.0404t$, which suggests a growth rate of 9.8 per cent a year.

8 The growth rate for the United Kingdom is estimated from B.R. Mitchell and P. Deane, *Abstract of British Historical Statistics* (Cambridge: Cambridge University Press, 1962), 218.

9 The growth rate for gross tonnage added to the eight major registries was 0.9 per cent a year for 1849–74, although the equation yields a poor fit to the data ($r = +0.25$). Between 1820 and 1849 the growth rate was 5.5 per cent a year, with a much better fit ($r = +0.81$). Some portion of this earlier growth might result from the appearance of new registries (especially Pictou and Yarmouth in 1840), but this is unlikely to have inflated the growth rate very much, since most vessels owned in Pictou or Yarmouth prior to 1840 were registered in Halifax. It is instructive to look only at the dominant port, Saint John: there gross investment grew by 4.6 per cent a year from 1820 to 1849; the growth rate was 0.1 per cent a year from 1849 to 1874.

10 In the 1840s average vessel life (excluding vessels transferred to other registries or registered de novo) was 10.3 years; this increased to 12.9 years for vessels built in the 1870s and 14.9 years for vessels built in the 1880s. See Table 3.5.

11 T.W. Acheson, "The Great Merchant and Economic Development in Saint John, 1820–1850," in David J. Bercuson and Phillip A. Buckner, *Eastern and Western Perspectives* (Toronto, 1981), 102.

12 This is growth in world trade at constant prices: Simon Kuznets, *Modern Economic Growth: Rate, Structure and Spread* (New Haven, Conn., 1966), Table 6.3, 306.

13 Between 1850 and 1860 total tonnage entering and clearing ports in the United Kingdom increased at an annual average rate of about 5.5 per cent; the annual growth rate between 1860 and 1870 was 4.0 per cent. Calculated from William Page, *Commerce and Industry*, originally published 1919 (New York, 1968) II, no. 63, 162.

14 Total world tonnage grew by about 47 per cent in the 1850s and 26 per cent in the 1860s: A.W. Kirkaldy, *British Shipping: Its History, Organisation and Importance*, originally published 1914 (London, 1970), Appendix XVII.

15 In 1850, 8.1 per cent of world tonnage was steam-powered; the proportion rose to 10.9 per cent in 1860 and 15.8 per cent in 1870: ibid.

16 The United Kingdom had about 20.1 per cent of world trade in the 1840s

and 25.1 per cent in the 1860s. British colonies had about 4.5 per cent in the 1840s and about 6.3 per cent in the 1860s; the United States about 7.3 per cent in the 1840s and about 8.3 per cent in the 1860s. The European share remained at about 70 per cent in the 1840–70 period. Kuznets, *Modern Economic Growth*, Table 6.3, 306–7.

17 For a useful summary see Jeffrey J. Safford, "The Decline of the American Merchant Marine, 1850–1914: An Historiographic Appraisal," in Lewis R. Fischer and Gerald Panting, eds., *Change and Adaptation in Maritime History: The North Atlantic Fleets in the Nineteenth Century* (St John's: Maritime History Group, 1985), 53–85.

18 Harold U. Faulkner, *American Economic History* (New York, 1924), 255; Safford, "The Decline of the American Merchant Marine," 54.

19 US Bureau of the Census, *The Statistical History of the United States from Colonial Times to the Present* (New York, 1976), series Q417–32 and Q506–17.

20 *Novascotian*, 31 January 1839, cited in David A. Sutherland, "The Merchants of Halifax, 1815–1850: A Commercial Class in Pursuit of Metropolitan Status," PhD thesis, University of Toronto, 1975, 339.

21 Cited in Sutherland, "The Merchants of Halifax," 415.

22 Ibid., 416–17.

23 The appendices of the Prince Edward Island House of Assembly *Journals* give annual breakdowns of vessels "belonging to PEI," distinguishing "foreign trade" from "coasting trade." The *Journals* for 1833 to 1835, giving such returns for the years 1832–5, suggest that in those four years an annual average of 1,985 tons were employed in foreign trades and 6,276 tons in coasting. In some years in the 1840s tonnage in foreign trades exceeded tonnage in coasting. In 1851 the tonnage in foreign trades was equal to tonnage in coasting. In 1853, 10,907 tons went in foreign trades and 14,883 was in coasting. In 1854, 25,673 tons went in foreign trades and 15,023 tons was in coasting. Obviously the distinctions are rough and arbitrary, because the same vessels could be employed in both local coasting trades and in foreign trades in the same year. The value of the island's exports to the United States increased from an annual average of £2,596 in 1845–9 to £20,176 in 1850–4.

24 *Church Times*, 16 November 1849; see also *Novascotian*, 10 December 1849. Returning from the West Indies via an American port is one reason why the total tonnage entering Nova Scotia directly from the British West Indies (an annual average of 30,400 tons between 1855 and 1866) was so much less than the total tonnage clearing Nova Scotia for the British West Indies (51,200 tons a year between 1855 and 1866).

25 In 1860, for instance, seventeen New Brunswick vessels carrying deals entered Eastport and cleared from there for the United Kingdom; official figures reported the cargoes as exports to the United States. See William

Smith's annual report in "Customs House Returns," New Brunswick House of Assembly *Journals*, 1862.

26 Keith Matthews, "The Canadian Deep Sea Merchant Marine and the American Export Trade, 1850–1890," in David Alexander and Rosemary Ommer, eds., *Volumes Not Values: Canadian Sailing Ships and World Trades* (St John's: Maritime History Group, 1979), 217.

27 William Smith, New Brunswick registrar of shipping, in his report "Annual Returns of Trade and Navigation," New Brunswick House of Assembly *Journals*, 1864.

28 McClelland, "The New Brunswick Economy," 127.

29 Ibid., Table XL, 143.

30 The total value of field crops in 1851 (estimated in 1871 dollars) was $4,393,000; total value for 1871 was $7,633,000. New Brunswick's population was 193,800 in 1851 and 285,600 in 1871. New Brunswick *Census*, 1851, and Canada *Census*, 1871, IV; McClelland, "The New Brunswick Economy," 50.

31 In 1865, for instance, 47.4 per cent of New Brunswick imports and 57.8 per cent of Nova Scotia imports by value consisted of manufactures and miscellaneous products (not including wines and liquors). A further 39.5 per cent of New Brunswick imports and 29.6 per cent of Nova Scotia imports consisted of agricultural products. S.A. Saunders, *The Economic History of the Maritime Provinces* (Fredericton: Acadiensis Press, 1984), Appendix Table 3, 103.

32 Between 1828 and 1869 real per capita exports fell by about 1 per cent a year (export values were deflated using the Rousseaux price index).

33 See Kris Inwood, "Economic Growth and Structural Change in Atlantic Canada, 1850–1910," in Lewis R. Fischer and Helge Nordvik, eds., *Across the Broad Atlantic: Essays in Comparative Maritime History* (Oslo: Norwegian University Press, forthcoming, 1990).

34 Cf. Douglass C. North, *The Economic Growth of the United States 1790–1860* (Englewood Cliffs, NJ: Prentice-Hall, 1961), 6.

35 McClelland, "The New Brunswick Economy," 34–54.

36 Rusty Bitterman's reconstruction of farm production and consumption in Cape Breton suggests that nearly half of the households of Middle River failed to provide for their subsistence needs on their farms in 1871: Bitterman, "Economic Stratification in a Cape Breton Agricultural Community in the Nineteenth Century: A Production/Consumption Approach," undergraduate essay, 1985; "Middle River: The Social Structure of Agriculture in a Cape Breton Community," MA thesis, University of New Brunswick, 1987; and "The Hierarchy of the Soil: Land and Labour in a 19th Century Cape Breton Community," *Acadiensis*, 18, no. 1 (Autumn 1988), 33–55.

37 Cf. Steven D. Antler, "Colonial Exploitation and Economic Stagnation in Nineteenth Century Newfoundland," PhD thesis, University of Connecti-

cut, 1975; Antler, "The Capitalist Underdevelopment of Nineteenth Century Newfoundland," in Robert J. Brym and R. James Sacouman, eds., *Underdevelopment and Social Movements in Atlantic Canada* (Toronto, 1979), 179–202; see also Graeme Wynn, "The Maritimes: The Geography of Fragmentation and Underdevelopment," in L.D. McCann, ed., *A Geography of Canada: Heartland and Hinterland* (Scarborough, 1982), 156–213.

38 "We have latterly thought it to our advantage to charter our vessels and on the whole have done as well as by trading on our own account," wrote James Duncan to Sir James Malcolm, 1 August 1871, Duncan Letterbooks vol. 356, Public Archives of Prince Edward Island. The choice was still being made in the 1870s.

39 New Brunswick, *Journals of the House of Assembly*, Custom House Returns, 1867.

40 *Novascotian*, 24 June 1850, citing an article in the *Courier*.

41 Le Marchant to Newcastle, Nova Scotia House of Assembly *Journals*, 1854, Appendix I.

42 Sir John Harvey to Colonial Secretary Grey, 31 October 1849, cited in Sutherland, "The Merchants of Halifax," 436–7.

43 Custom House Returns, House of Assembly *Journals*, 1867.

44 Ibid., 1863, 1864.

45 Ibid., 1863.

46 The ten ports in order of importance were Liverpool, Saint John, New York, London, Cardiff, Antwerp, Dublin, Le Havre, Newport, and Bristol.

47 The twenty ports in order of importance were New York, Saint John, Sydney (Nova Scotia), Rio de Janeiro, Sandy Hook, Liverpool, Cardiff, Quebec, Philadelphia, Bombay, Montevideo, New Orleans, Baltimore, Delaware Breakwater, Boston, Buenos Aires, Tybee, Havana, Aden, and Savannah. Together they accounted for 56 per cent of intended destinations.

48 Eastern US and Gulf ports accounted for 23 per cent of all entrances into port by vessels in the Crew Agreement samples for the four major ports in the 1863–78 period; 44.8 per cent of all passages either began or ended in eastern US or Gulf ports. In the next period (1879–90) 55.5 per cent of passages began or ended in eastern US or Gulf ports.

For the Yarmouth fleet, David Alexander estimated the average annual growth rate of entrances into port by region in 1863–79 and estimated each region's contribution to total world growth in entrances. He concluded that US ports contributed 50.8 per cent of all growth in this period: David Alexander, "Output and Productivity in the Yarmouth Ocean Fleet, 1863–1901," in Alexander and Ommer, eds., *Volumes Not Values*, 75.

A similar analysis, using the Windsor voyage file, and using tonnage entering port rather than number of entrances as the unit of analysis, showed that 35 per cent of all tonnage entering port between 1863 and 1878 entered ports in the eastern United States or US Gulf; these regions contributed an estimated 44.7 per cent of growth in all world tonnage-entrances between 1863 and 1878.

A similar analysis on the Halifax fleet revealed that British North American and West Indies ports were relatively more important, and US ports less important, than they were for the Windsor fleet. Note that coastal and colonial agreements are not included. Ocean voyages beginning in North America may be under-estimated; but our sample of voyages by deep-sea vessels is very large.

49 The six routes were British North America–United Kingdom, eastern United States–United Kingdom, and eastern United States–northern Europe, and the return passage on those three routes. The data in maps 5.1, 5.2, and 5.3 are from the Crew Agreements for Saint John, Yarmouth, Halifax, and Windsor. For further analysis and information on the size of the samples see the essays in Alexander and Ommer, eds., *Volumes Not Values*. For Yarmouth, for instance, David Alexander estimated that the computerized sample probably contained over 70 per cent of all voyages by Yarmouth vessels of 250 tons or more.

50 See C.K. Harley, "The Shift from Sailing Ships to Steamships, 1850–1890: A Study in Technological Change and Its Diffusion," in N. McCloskey, ed., *Studies on a Mature Economy: Britain after 1840* (London, 1971), 215–34; Harley, "Aspects of the Economics of Shipping, 1850–1913," in Fischer and Panting, eds., *Change and Adaptation in Maritime History*, 169–86; and Harley, "Ocean Freight Rates and Productivity, 1740–1913: The Primacy of Mechanical Invention Reaffirmed," *Journal of Economic History*, 48, no. 4 (December 1988), 851–76.

51 Gerald S. Graham, "The Ascendancy of the Sailing Ship, 1855–1885," *Economic History Review*, 9 (1956–7), 74–88.

52 Of all new tonnage in vessels of 500 tons and more registered in the eight ports between 1900 and 1914, 25.8 per cent (34,535 tons) was registered in St John's; these were mainly coastal steamers and steamers used in the seal hunt.

53 A series of correlation coefficients was calculated, using tonnage on registry in eight ports, including only vessels over 250 tons and vessels not transferred within three years of first registry (this is the best measure of ocean tonnage retained on local registries by local owners). The correlation coefficients between ocean tonnage on registry and freight rate indices are as follows:

Index	1869–99	1879–99
North	$r = +0.39$	$r = +0.66$
Norwegian	$r = +0.22$	$r = +0.45$
Isserlis	$r = +0.32$	$r = +0.65$

Taking the more sensitive measure – the correlation between annual changes in two time series – produces negative coefficients for the correlation between tonnage and the first two freight rate series listed above. Lagging the tonnage change by a year produces a small positive coefficient in each case: +0.11 (North); +0.22 (Norwegian). If net investment in shipping is treated as a dependent variable, and if freight rates are the independent variable, the relationship between the two is weak.

54 Estimating growth rates from logarithms (log $Y_t = a + bt$) suggests that US export freight rates fell at a rate of −3.16 per cent a year between 1873 and 1899; the Isserlis index fell by −2.48 per cent a year; and the Norwegian US east coast index fell by −2.46 per cent a year.

55 In 1870, total tonnage in the major merchant fleets of the world was 16,765,205 tons; by 1900 the total was 26,205,398 tons: A.W. Kirkaldy, *British Shipping: Its History, Organisation and Importance* (London, 1914), Appendix XVII.

56 Between 1880 and 1900, the US merchant marine grew by about 27 per cent; total Canadian tonnage fell by 50 per cent. Both figures include river, lake, and coastal tonnage. The more appropriate comparison, however, may be between US tonnage registered for foreign trades (i.e. excluding river and lake tonnage) and ocean-going fleets in the Maritimes: US tonnage declined by 38 per cent over the two decades, while Maritimes tonnage declined by 74 per cent.

57 Sail-powered tonnage in the world's major fleets totalled 8,435,874 tons in 1910; the total in 1850 was 8,300,378 tons: Kirkaldy, *British Shipping*, Appendix XVII.

CHAPTER SIX

1 The registry is number 87 in 1863. Her gross tonnage was 271, and she was built in Truro. The registry lists James Dickie as owner of sixteen shares (there were seven other shareholders), but John's letter to James on 4 November 1863 makes clear that they each had eight shares: Dickie Letters, Dalhousie University Archives.

2 J.B. Dickie to J.E. Dickie, 19 November 1863, Dickie Letters.

3 J.B. Dickie to J.E. Dickie, 8 May 1868, Dickie Letters.

4 J.B. Dickie to J.E. Dickie, 17 April 1872, Dickie Letters.

5 *Reasons for an Augmentation of at Least Twelve Thousand Mariners, to Be Employed in the Merchants' Service and Coasting Trade* (1759), cited in Ralph Davis, *The Rise of the English Shipping Industry* (London, 1962), 387.

6 The literature is voluminous, but I am indebted to Douglass C. North, *Structure and Change in Economic History* (New York: Norton, 1981).

7 Marx, *Capital*, III (Harmondsworth: Penguin Books, 1981), 127. The detailed discussion of profit appears in this volume, especially chapters 1–4, 8–12, 17, and 22–24.

8 On the rate of profit see ibid., chapter 2.

9 Ibid., 134.

10 Robert Evans, Jr, " 'Without Regard for Cost': The Returns on Clipper Ships," *Journal of Political Economy* (1964), 32–43.

11 "Norwegian ships are supposed by many to be the cheapest sailed vessels in the world, owing to the frugal habits of their people," wrote William Smith in 1863: New Brunswick, "Annual Returns of Trade and Navigation," House of Assembly *Journals*, 1863.

12 William Smith, in ibid., 1863, 1864.

13 In using this method we are deeply indebted to Robin S. Craig and Richard O. Goss for their advice and encouragement. See R.O. Goss, ed., *Advances in Maritime Economics* (Cambridge, 1977), and Goss, "Economics and Canadian Atlantic Shipping," in Lewis R. Fischer and Eric W. Sager, eds., *Merchant Shipping and Economic Development in Atlantic Canada* (St John's: Maritime History Group, 1982), 89–112.

No method of estimating shipping profits can be exact. Our first method attempts to reduce hypothetical reconstruction to a minimum. Unfortunately freight rate data for some commodities are too scarce to be reliable. Often vessels carried a mix of cargoes, and in such cases it is difficult to estimate gross revenues. The main disadvantage with this method is that it misses major trades in which Canadian vessels were active, such as those to northern European ports.

14 The years selected require justification. Freight rates were higher in the early 1860s than in the late 1850s, but 1863 was not an untypical year. US export freight rates in 1863 (see Graph 5.12) were very slightly below the average for seven years centred on 1863 (1860–6); 1863 freight rates were slightly above the seven-year average, using Matthews's index (Graph 5.13). Freight rates in 1873 were at a peak, but this year was chosen deliberately in order to arrive at estimates of the maximum potential earnings in the 1870s. In 1883 freight rates were in the middle of the decline between the mid-1870s and mid-1880s. The indices of Isserlis and North (Graph 5.15) suggest that rates were 21 to 26 per cent below the average for the last half of the 1870s. Although freight rates went much lower, by 1883 investment in shipping in the Maritimes was already declining rapidly.

15 Clement W. Crowell, *Novascotiaman* (Halifax, 1979), Appendix E, 382–3. Moving west across the Atlantic, or outside the North Atlantic, vessels could earn something by carrying empty petroleum barrels, railway ties, salt, or coal.

16 Canadian *Sessional Papers* include estimates of port costs for several vessels in 1879 and 1880: barquentine *Flora* (571 tons) in Baltimore, Philadelphia, New York, and Halifax; barque *Erinna* (1,130 tons) in New York and Halifax; ship *Esther Roy* in Philadelphia and Halifax; ship *William*

Douglas (1,263 tons) in New York and Halifax; barque *W.J. Stairs* (1,060 tons) in Baltimore and Halifax; and a hypothetical 800-ton grain ship at New York, Baltimore, Philadelphia, and Boston.

Charges included tonnage tax, harbour master's fee, pilotage, towage, wharfage, stevedoring, elevator charges, customs clearance, consular fees, health officers' fees, hospital fees, and (in the case of grain vessels) brokerage commission. Costs were much higher in US ports than in Halifax, but the average for all fifteen port stops was $1.09 per ton. See *Sessional Papers*, 1881, IX, no. 61. Port charges for ports of call, where cargo was neither loaded nor unloaded, would be much less.

If there were three cargo-loading and unloading port calls in a year, total port costs for a 1,000-ton vessel would be $3,270 a year. If the figures for annual wage costs were $3,500, insurance $2,500, repairs $2,000, victualling $1,500, brokerage costs $1,500, and office and other costs $800, then total operating costs would be $15,070, or $15.07 per ton per year. Total costs excluding depreciation would be about four times the wage bill. See also note 17.

17 Killam's estimates were as follows.

(1) The annual wage bill was $4,500, assuming that a full crew was eighteen or nineteen men. This estimate is certainly high, or Killam was assuming that the vessel was employing men for twelve months in the year. If the vessel employed a full crew for nine months, which is more plausible, and if able seamen were being paid on average £3 sterling a month, petty officers between £4 and £6 a month, and officers £7 pounds, then the total monthly wage payments would be about £84, and the annual wage payments about $3,700. Very likely Killam was assuming the costs of crew hired in relatively high-wage North American ports.

(2) He assumed annual supplies of $2,500. This must include much more than victualling. Canadian vessels took on victuals in many ports and tried to avoid provisioning in high-cost North American ports. As a general rule victuals cost a shilling per man per day in British ships; this translates into an annual victualling bill of $1,250, assuming a 1,000-ton vessel fully manned for nine months.

(3) Annual repair and renewal costs were $3,000, not including depreciation.

(4) He assumes insurance costs of 10 per cent: $2,500 if the vessel were valued at $25 per ton. A new vessel might be insured at her full value, closer to $35 or $40 per ton, but many vessels were underinsured. See Killam's testimony in "Report of the Select Committee on the Causes of the Present Depression," House of Commons *Journals*, X, 1876, Appendix 3.

(5) Killam did not mention port charges, and these could vary a great deal, but port costs including stevedoring could be anywhere from $600

to $1,000 for a 1,000-ton vessel in a US port, and if we assume two such American ports and one or two European ports in a year, total port costs of $2,000 to $3,000 are reasonable.

18   Average annual disbursements (not including insurance) for the barque *Douglas Campbell* (845 tons) were $13.30 between 1876 and 1881, and this included two remetallings. Between 1875 and 1882 annual average disbursements for the *Susan L. Campbell* were $14.25 per ton, including two remetallings. Both vessels operated within the North Atlantic: see Colin Campbell Papers, Dalhousie University Archives.

From 1876 to 1889 the barque *Snow Queen* had operating costs of $13.85 per ton: calculated from the *Snow Queen* accounts, Dalhousie University Archives. Between 1886 and 1893 the *N.B. Lewis* (1,328 tons) incurred costs of $14.87 per ton annually, including insurance and office expenses, or $12.05 per ton, excluding insurance and office expenses: Crowell, *Novascotiaman*, 384.

On five passages between New York and London in 1887, total disbursements of the ship *Charles S. Whitney* (1,754 tons) were only $8.80 per ton, not including insurance: Spicer, *Masters of Sail*, 196.

19   The *N.B. Lewis* cost about $40,000 when new in 1880 and sold for $13,000 in 1893, which suggests a depreciation rate of about 9 per cent (Crowell, *Novascotiaman*, 384). The *Queen of the Fleet* (941 tons) as launched in 1876 and sold in 1895 for £600, which suggests a depreciation rate of 12 per cent (Charles Armour and Thomas Lackey, *Sailing Ships of the Maritimes* [Toronto: McGraw-Hill Ryerson, 1975], 135). The *William D. Lawrence* cost $107,453 in 1874 and sold in 1883 for £6,500, which suggests a rate of 13 per cent (Armour and Lackey, *Sailing Ships*, 126). The ship *John Mann* (1,043 tons) cost $38,168 when new in 1867 and sold for $7,000 in 1884, which suggests a rate of 9.5 per cent (Armour and Lackey, *Sailing Ships*, 94). These rates are on the high side because they reflect the low selling prices in the 1880s and 1890s.

The barque *Harold* (960 tons) was built in 1873, and in 1881 J.B. Dickie thought her worth $15 per registered ton, which suggests a depreciation rate of 10 per cent (J.B. to J.E. Dickie, 25 March 1881, Dickie Letters, Dalhouse University Archives).

A note about insurance appraisals in the Osmond O'Brien Papers states: "Vessels are appraised (1/2 value estimated as follows) viz. New Vessels $14 per ton" and at seven years $6 per ton, at ten years $4.50 per ton, and at sixteen years $3 per ton, which figures suggest a depreciation rate of 9 per cent a year (note of 22 October 1892, Osmond O'Brien papers, Dalhousie University Archives, MS-4 120 G2).

The Norwegian shipowner Peter Jebsen was concerned to estimate accurately the depreciation of his sailing vessels, and his annual flat rate appears to have approximated 7 per cent (the percentage is estimated from his depreciated book value of the barque *Ellida* from 1868 to 1880: Lewis R. Fischer and Helge W. Nordvik, "From Broager to Bergen: The Risks and Rewards of Peter Jebsen, Shipowner, 1864–1892," *Sjofartshistorik Arbok* (Bergen, 1986), 59.

20 The average annual gross return per ton was estimated as follows. Gross revenues for timber were $6.69 per ton (Appendix B); it was assumed that vessels made 2.2 such passages per year; potential annual gross revenues were therefore $14.72 per ton. It was assumed that vessels with grain and petroleum made an average of two voyages a year; vessels with guano one voyage; and vessels with molasses 2.2 voyages. In the final average each commodity is weighted as follows: timber, 55 per cent; petroleum, 12 per cent; grain, 10 per cent; guano, 6 per cent; and molasses, 17 per cent. This is roughly the proportion of these commodities entering Liverpool and London, although of course many commodities are omitted. The result if anything underestimates the share of grain and overestimates the low-value cargoes (timber and molasses) being carried by vessels from the Maritimes. The resulting overall weighted average was $18.73 a year.

Operating costs begin at $12 per ton per year because so many vessels were still operating from Maritimes ports, where port charges were lower than in US ports (see notes 17 and 18). In calculating depreciation, it is assumed that average costs per ton were $40 when new. This is somewhere between the costs of new vessels classed 4A1 and new vessels classed 7A1 (see Graph 3.1). Obviously annual returns for the 4A1 vessel would be higher than those suggested in Graph 6.1: in the first year of her life, the range would be from 7.4 per cent to 16.9 per cent for the 4A1 vessel costing £7 per ton when new.

21 The cargoes used in the analysis were timber from New Brunswick, cotton from US Gulf ports, petroleum from the eastern United States, grain from the eastern United States, guano from South America, and rice from Rangoon. Annual gross revenues appear in Appendix B. The proportions were as follows: timber, 10 per cent; cotton, 33 per cent; petroleum, 25 per cent; grain, 20 per cent; guano, 4 per cent; rice, 8 per cent. These percentages reflect the relative importance of these cargoes entering Liverpool and London in Atlantic Canadian vessels in 1868, 1873, and 1878, but the share of cotton cargoes has been reduced slightly: cf. Sager and Panting, "Staple Economies and the Rise and Decline of the Shipping Industry in Atlantic Canada, 1820–1914," in Lewis R. Fischer and Gerald Panting, eds., *Change and Adaptation in Maritime History: The North Atlantic Fleets in the Nineteenth Century* (St John's: Maritime History Group, 1985), 26–7 (Table 6: cargoes carried to UK by Four Major Fleets: 1868, 1873, 1878).

Again it is assumed that westbound passages brought a small revenue, sufficient to offset 10 per cent of annual costs or to increase annual gross earnings by 6 to 8 per cent. New tonnage is again valued at $40 a ton, and the depreciation rate is 7 per cent.

22 Our estimates of profit measure returns to capital that survived; we have not taken into account the fact that many capital assets in this industry sank before they could earn a profit. But the proportion of all tonnage in service that was lost in each year was between 3 and 3.5 per cent in the 1870s and 1880s. Vessels lost at sea had often served a near-normal life; and the average age of vessels lost at sea increased significantly between the 1860s and the 1880s (from nine to thirteen years for Yarmouth vessels; from nine to twelve years for Saint John vessels). Even if we make a deduction for annual losses, rates of return remain high. The effect of such losses on shipowners' perceptions of risk cannot be discounted, however.

23 Gross revenues for the fifty-one passages appear in Appendix B. We assume a marginal increase in vessel use (2.2 passages a year with timber; 1.6 with cotton; 2.1 with petroleum; and 2.1 with grain). During the 1880s the chances of completing two passages a year fell, however, as steamers moved into the cotton and grain trades particularly. We assume annual costs of $11 to $13 per ton. The cost of new tonnage had fallen, but we assume an initial cost of $38 per ton and annual depreciation of 9 per cent.

24 One cost may not be deducted, of course: that of money borrowed in order to purchase the shares. There is no way of knowing how common such debt charges were. And the same problem applies to any investment, and so to the landward investments with which shipping investment must be compared in this period.

25 The evidence for the first four vessels comes from the Dickie Letters in the Dalhousie University Archives. Between 1875 and 1886 James Dickie received cheques from his brother John B. Dickie of Truro, who was managing owner of the vessels. When John died in 1886, his son Martin took over as managing owner. What survives are the letters that accompanied each divident payment.

The Dickie Letters are sufficiently detailed that we can reconstruct the trades in which the vessels were deployed. The barques *Harold* and *Linden* and the ship *Colchester* all began by carrying timber from the Maritimes and grain and petroleum from the eastern United States to Britain or Europe. In the mid-1880s the *Colchester* went into trades to the east coast of South America, and the other two vessels soon followed. These vessels were, therefore, part of a general trend. The ship *Selkirk* began in the oil trade in 1887 but soon went into the Far East trades, carrying case oil to the Pacific, timber from British Columbia, and rice from Yokohama.

The Dickie vessels were not unusually lucky. The *Harold* performed well for thirteen years until major repairs and remetalling meant that there were no net earnings for over two years. The *Linden* was less fortunate: she was stranded en route to Saint John after being launched, and repairs cost $8,000 (paid for from her first passages). In 1887 she was detained for some time in France because of smallpox among the crew. The *Colchester* was a sound vessel, but in 1887 Martin Dickie stated that Capt. Dart's "brain seemed to be parboiled in liquor" and the vessel lost money in the mid-1880s. The vessels were remetalled and recaulked every four or five years.

26 The standard deviation for the post-1880 sample was 16.8.

27 Martin Dickie to J.E. Dickie, 25 November 1886, Dickie Letters.

28 Martin Dickie to J.E. Dickie, 18 March 1889 and 8 February 1890, Dickie Letters. The builder was William Cameron of South Maitland.

29 Martin Dickie to J.E. Dickie, 27 May 1887, Dickie Letters.

30 Robert G. Moran to James Moran, 13 February 1878, Moran Papers, New Brunswick Museum.

31 G.W. Owen, writing from Auckland, New Zealand, to L.C. Owen, 28 February 1887 and 10 October 1887, Owen Papers, Public Archives of Prince Edward Island, Acc. no. 2744.

32 Peter Mitchell, MP, in House of Commons *Debates*, 18 February 1878, 363.

33 In 1885 C.H. Fairweather presented a paper to the Saint John Board of Trade in which he said: "In years past the yield from vessel property was 20 per cent." In 1885 "profits are almost nil, or say not over a fourth or fifth" of their peaks in the previous decade. *Saint John Trade Reporter*, February 1885.

34 Willis Report, Canada *Sessional Papers*, 1885, no. 37, 42.

35 Quirk to James Moller and Co., 1 April 1881, Duncan Papers, item 362, Public Archives of Prince Edward Island.

36 Letters of 4, 7, and 11 April from Quirk to Moller, Duncan Papers, item 362.

37 Quirk to Capt. Robert Dunn in the *James Duncan*, 4 April 1881, Duncan Papers.

38 Quirk to Mrs Phoebe Dunn, 8 June 1882, Duncan Papers.

39 Quirk to Paul Gerhard of New York, 15 March 1881, Duncan Papers.

40 Quirk to R.M.C. Stumbles, 23 March 1881, Duncan Papers.

41 Quirk to R.M.C. Stumbles, 5 May 1881, Duncan Papers.

42 The ratio is average sea days per voyage divided by average port days

per voyage. "Average sea days" is equal to average voyage duration (the entire voyage from opening to termination of the crew agreement) minus "average port days," where "port days" is equal to the product of the average number of ports of call per voyage times the average time in ports of call plus one average turn-around time at voyage's end.

43 In 1873 James Duncan decided not to put vessels in the coal trade because "the voyages are so short" and "they are so often in port"; "we believe these long voyages will net the most money even if the vessels come back in ballast." Letter of 15 April 1873, Duncan Letterbooks vol. 358, Public Archives of Prince Edward Island.

44 See Eric W. Sager, *Seafaring Labour: The Merchant Marine of Atlantic Canada 1820–1914* (Montreal: McGill-Queen's University Press, 1989), chapter 7.

45 The steepest decline (2.4 per cent a year) was in the Yarmouth fleet, and the slowest (1.8 per cent a year) was in the Saint John fleet.

46 Most sailors were paid in pounds sterling, but some were paid in dollars. In the averages depicted here, dollars are converted to pounds sterling at $4.86 and the average is weighted by the numbers who received wages in each currency. Dollar wages were generally much higher than sterling wages; the post-1874 decline occurred despite the fact that the proportion of all sailors receiving wages in dollars increased over time. The trends were similar in other fleets, but in the Windsor fleet wages were slightly higher because of the slightly larger proportion of crews receiving dollar wages: see Sager, *Seafaring Labour* Graph 14. Average wages in the Windsor fleet fell by 29 per cent between 1874 and 1885. The decline in real terms was not so steep, of course, because this was a period of deflation.

47 In a previous analysis we used tonnage entering port as a surrogate for output. Thus for the Yarmouth fleet, from 1863 to 1879, REV + SV + FRW = 7.4 per cent a year, where REV is the rate of growth of all vessel-entrances into port deflated to take into account an increasing proportion of entrances in ballast, where SV is the rate of growth of average tonnage and FRW is the rate of growth of the Isserlis freight rate index, deflated by the Canadian Taylor import price index.

Over the same period the annual growth rate of man-months of labour employed was 4.1 per cent, and total wage payments grew by 5.1 per cent a year. In the first period of decline (1879–90) REV + SV + FRW = −1.6, while man-months showed an annual rate of −5.8 per cent and total wages had an annual rate of −4.6 per cent. See Eric W. Sager, "Labour Productivity in the Shipping Fleets of Halifax and Yarmouth, Nova Scotia, 1863–1900," in Rosemary Ommer and Gerald Panting, eds., *Working Men Who Get Wet* (St John's: Maritime History Group, 1980), 180.

48 Sager, *Seafaring Labour*, especially chapters 6 and 7.

CHAPTER SEVEN

1 Of all new tonnage registered in the seven major ports of the Maritimes between 1900 and 1914, 54.6 per cent was owned by shipping companies. Many of these were companies named after the steamship being registered.

2 Of all newly registered tonnage in seven major ports in the Maritimes in the 1850s, the small operators (mariners, traders, fishermen, and farmers) held only 11.8 per cent in the 1850s. Between 1820 and 1849 their share of new tonnage had been 24.1 per cent. In the 1870s their share was 13 per cent; in the 1880s and 1890s it rose to 18 per cent.

3 Of all newly registered tonnage in St John's between 1900 and 1914, 51 per cent was owned by merchants. A further 20 per cent was owned by smallholders – traders, mariners, planters, or fishermen.

4 Of all tonnage newly registered in Yarmouth between 1840 and 1914, slightly over 52 per cent was held at first registry by people called shipowners; the share held by merchants was 22 per cent. In Saint John, by contrast, 57 per cent of new tonnage was held by merchants and 4 per cent by "shipowners."

5 The R.G. Dun Collection in the Baker Library, Boston, tends to confirm this: reference is often made to the condition and performance of the shipping investments of major shipowners in our sample, but other commercial activities clearly have priority.

6 This is the proportion of 141,605 tons for which ownership is known in the seven major ports. Merchants held a further 19.4 per cent, and shipowners held 7 per cent. In Newfoundland, of 149,659 steam-powered tons registered up to 1936, only 35 per cent was held by shipping companies; merchants held 28 per cent and shipowners 7 per cent. Thus mercantile ownership was still significant, even with the new technology.

7 Fifteen steamships, totalling 45,953 gross tons, were registered in Saint John in 1907; each ship was registered in the name of an incorporated company.

8 The major shipowner is defined as any owner who held more than 1,000 gross tons of newly registered tonnage.

9 In analysing incorporators, we are suggesting something about intentions and aspirations of investors; we imply nothing about the success or viability of businesses, since many of the newly incorporated companies may never have operated.

10 Over time, the joint stock company became more common. There was a significant increase in the number and proportion of incorporations in secondary manufacturing, as the following table of Nova Scotia incorporations between 1850 and 1889 suggests:

% of total for decade

Decade	Primary	Secondary	Tertiary	Finance	Total no.
1850s	22	10	50	18	50
1860s	39	12	27	21	66
1870s	41	27	26	6	172
1880s	25	30	42	3	179
1850–89	33	24	35	8	467

Source: Nova Scotia, *Statutes,* held in the library of the Nova Scotia Legislature.

11 Thus of all incorporations in the financial sector between 1850 and 1889, 97 per cent had at least one major shipowner among the incorporators. By comparison, only 28 per cent in the primary sector involved at least one major shipowner; 39 per cent in secondary manufacturing did so, as did 41 per cent in the tertiary sector.

12 For instance, major shipowners of Halifax were mentioned in the statutes 152 times. These contacts with new companies occurred in all decades, but 51 per cent were before 1870, and another 31 per cent occurred in the 1870s, when incorporating activity and tonnage on registry peaked in the same years.

13 All dates here indicate the quinquennium of last investment in newly registered tonnage.

Those connected with the Bank of Yarmouth included Amasa Durkee (whose new shipping investments continued until the quinquennium 1875–9); Samuel Killam (whose new shipping investments continued until 1865–9); J.C. Farish (to 1880–4); John Flint (to 1875–9); and Andrew Lovitt (to 1875–9).

Incorporators of the Burrell Johnson Iron Co. included Joseph Burrell (whose shipping investment continued to 1870–4); Nathaniel Churchill (to 1875–9); Freeman Dennis (to 1875–9); Hugh D. Cann (to 1885–9); Abel C. Robbins (to 1875–9); and Aaron Goudey (to 1875–9).

Incorporators of the railway included Frank Killam (to 1880–4); Thomas M. Lewis (to 1875–9); Joseph R. Kinney (to 1875–9); Augustus F. Stoneman (to 1900–4); John K. Ryerson (to 1870–4); William Townsend (1865–9); George B. Doane (1875–9); Samuel M. Ryerson (1875–9); Thomas Killam Jr (1875–79); John W. Lovitt (to 1870–4); John Young (to 1870–4); and Loran E. Baker (to 1890–4).

Most major shipowners were involved with marine insurance and other insurance companies. Shipowners also founded the Building and Loan Society, the Commercial Wharf Co., the Gaslight Co., the Gold Mining and Quartz Co., the Mountain Cemetery Co., the Nova Scotia Electric Telegraph Co., the Nova Scotia Telephone Co., the Skating Rink Co., the Woollen Mills Co., the Yarmouth and Boston Steamship Co., the Yarmouth Duck and Yarn Co., the Yarmouth Iron Works, and the Yarmouth Street Railway Co., and several commercial firms.

14 Thus Allan Haley invested in new shipping between 1875–9 and 1890–4: his interests included the Shipowners Marine Insurance Co., founded 1877; the Nova Scotia Fire Insurance Co., 1878; Windsor Plaster Co., 1878; Windsor Temperance Reform Club Hall, 1878; Maritime Reaper and Mower Co., 1881; Nova Scotia Telephone Co., 1887; Yarmouth Street Railway, 1887; Cumberland Land Reclamation Co., 1888; and Hants Mineral Oil and Mining Co., 1889.

15 These companies included Black Brothers and Co., Chebucto Marine Railway, Eldorado Gold Mining, Globe Gold Mining, Halifax Electric Light Co., Halifax Gas Light Co., Halifax Railway Co., Morning Herald Publishing and Printing Co., North Sydney Marine Railway, Northern Head Coal Co., Stadacona Gold Mining, Starr Manufacturing Co., Strait of Canso Marine Railway, Truro Gaslight Co., United Mining Association.

16 In about 5 per cent of cases it was not possible to determine whether the shipowner and incorporator were the same individual; these cases have been omitted from the count.

17 If we deduct shipping companies and individuals not resident in Saint John from the total of 358 major owners (those who put 1,000 tons or more of newly registered tonnage on the Saint John registry), we are left with 269 major owners, who registered 63.4 per cent of all new tonnage. Of all major owners, almost 60 per cent of the 358 (or 78 per cent of the 269) were involved in one or more incorporations. Incorporating activity of the major owners is as follows (the following may be compared with Table 7.2, which includes major and minor owners):

	Pre-1860		Post-1860	
	No.	%	No.	%
Manufacturing	44	12.8	23	7.5
Mining	35	10.2	20	6.5
Timber/boom	19	5.5	18	5.9
Railways	43	12.5	55	18.0
Finance	90	26.2	68	22.2
Public service	48	14.0	76	24.8
Ferries/marine	26	7.6	27	8.8
Land transport	24	7.0	8	2.6
Agric./land	10	2.9	6	2.0
Trading	4	1.2	5	1.6
Total	343		306	

18 The following table gives estimates of the number of directorships held by major Saint John shipowners in each sector between 1860 and 1890:

	Manufacturing and mining	Finance	Service and commercial	Marine
Number	74	97	105	14
% of total	25.5	33.4	36.2	4.8

Sources used for this compilation include the major directories for Saint John, such as *Chubb's Almanac, McAlpine's Gazette, McAlpine's St. John Directory*, and *The New Brunswick Almanac and Register*, and newspapers, especially the *Colonial Empire*, the *Royal Gazette*, and the Saint John *Star*. We assume that our survey has yielded most of the directorships for companies based in Saint John. Of the 269 major shipowners resident in Saint John, at least 101 held one or more company directorships.

19 Dun suggests that Jacob V. Troop and Howard D. Troop preferred to have their real estate mortgaged because they "get the money @ 6%" and could make a profit by deploying it elsewhere. R.G. Dun Collection, vol. 9, 557κ, 8 October 1875. Between the 1860s and the 1880s Howard Troop was an incorporator of hotels, insurance companies, a telegraph company, a dry dock company, a music academy, and a publishing company.

20 R.G. Dun Collection, vol. 9, 238J and 265, December 1871.

21 Ibid., 560, 613, June and October 1875.

22 Of twenty-eight major shipowners from the Halifax registry for whom detailed probate records have been found, the average estate was $172,733. The average amount in real estate was $33,600. The twenty-eight individuals were Jonathan Allison, Thomas Bayne, Stephen Binney, Martin P. Black, William L. Black, Robert Boak Jr, Daniel Cronan, Edward Cunard, Charles DeWolf, William B. Fairbanks, George E. Francklyn, Alfred G. Jones, Thomas Kenny, Thomas Kinnear, Henry Lawson, John Lithgow, Isaac Mathers, James A. Moren, Jeremiah Northup, James B. Oxley, James Phelan, William J. Stairs, John Strachan, John Taylor, George J. Troop, George Vigus, Benjamin Weir, and Joseph Weir.

23 Of the major owners who were each responsible for 5,000 tons or more of newly registered shipping, we have probate records for sixteen. These sixteen, with the last years of their new-vessel registration, are: George Carvill (1875); William Davidson (1871); John Haws (1856); Thomas Hilyard (1870); George King (1866); James Kirk (1850); James H. Moran (1879); John Robertson (1867); Francis Ruddock (1868); Joseph Ruddock

(1859); Robert Stackhouse (1866); William Thomson (1886); John Walker (1866); Fred A. Wiggins (1863); Stephen Wiggins (1856); and John Wishart (1856). The total assets in probate were valued at $2,486,266. Of this, 29 per cent was in real estate, and 67 per cent in cash, stocks, or bonds. Wills and inventories are in the Public Archives of New Brunswick, in Fredericton.

24 Charlottetown *Patriot*, 6 February 1879 (the article was about the decline of shipping and shipbuilding).

CHAPTER EIGHT

1 Douglass C. North, *Structure and Change in Economic History* (New York: W.W. Norton, 1981), 6–7

2 Seven years ago James M. Gilmour pointed out this possibility to me, and I have not forgotten what he said.

3 A very useful summary is by Jeffrey J. Safford, "The Decline of the American Merchant Marine, 1850–1914: An Historiographic Appraisal," in Lewis R. Fischer and Gerald E. Panting, eds., *Change and Adaptation in Maritime History: The North Atlantic Fleets in the Nineteenth Century* (St John's: Maritime History Group, 1985), 53–85.

4 "For it may be little more than a truism to state that the individuals that are best adapted to survive have a better chance of surviving than those not so well adapted to survive." T.H. Morgan, cited in Francis Hitching, *The Neck of the Giraffe, or Where Darwin Went Wrong* (London: Pan Books, 1982), 104.

5 Much of the discussion begins with F.A. Hayek, "Economics and Knowledge," *Economica*, 4 (February 1937), 33–54, and Hayek, *Individualism and Economic Order* (London: Routledge and Kegan Paul, 1949). Much of the literature is cited in Israel M. Kirzner, *Perception, Opportunity and Profit: Studies in the Theory of Entrepreneurship* (Chicago: University of Chicago Press, 1979).

6 Martin Dickie to James E. Dickie, 21 January 1887, Dickie Correspondence, Dalhousie University Archives.

7 Undated article from the *Yarmouth Tribune*, cited in *Halifax Herald*, 3 January 1881.

8 The implications of all of this for Marxism are worth noting: see, for instance, Mark Poster, *Foucault, Marxism and History: Mode of Production versus Mode of Information* (Oxford: Polity Press, 1984); Julius Sensat, *Habermas and Marxism: An Appraisal* (London: Sage Publications, 1979); Walter L. Adamson, *Marx and the Disillusionment of Marxism* (Berkeley: University of California Press, 1985). See also Gregory Clark, "Economists in Search of Culture: The Unspeakable in Pursuit of the Inedible?" *Historical Methods*, 21, no. 4 (Fall 1988), 161–4.

9 "Report of the Select Committee on the Causes of the Present Depression," House of Commons *Journals*, 1876, X, Appendix 3, 164.

10 Peter Mitchell, MP, in House of Commons *Debates*, 18 February 1878, 363. Mitchell's remarks went unquestioned, even by Frank Killam, who spoke earlier in the same debate.

11 Canada *Sessional Papers*, 1885, no. 37, 42.

12 House of Commons *Debates*, 1888, 389.

13 House of Commons *Debates* 2 March 1893, 1606.

14 Ibid.; 1606 (Mr Gillmor).

15 Ibid.

16 See, for instance, Joseph Howe, *Speech of the Hon. Joseph Howe on Intercolonial Railroads, and Colonization, Delivered at Halifax, Nova Scotia, May, 1851* (Halifax, 1851).

17 Joseph Howe to Thomas Baring, 31 December 1861, cited in Rosemary Langhout, "Developing Nova Scotia: Railways and Public Accounts, 1849–1867," *Acadiensis*, 14, no. 2 (Spring 1985), 8 n 17.

18 Ibid., 8.

19 See, for instance, Edmund Flynn of Richmond, Nova Scotia, in the debate on Halifax as a winter port: House of Commons *Debates*, 20 December 1880, 160.

20 C.H. Fairweather in a speech to the Saint John Board of Trade, 22 January 1885, reported in the *Saint John Trade Reporter*, February 1885.

21 Short two- and three-line fillers were omitted from the count. Articles were subdivided into leaders, editorial-page articles, and miscellaneous and into three categories by length of article. Of 1,364 short articles, only sixteen had as a principal topic local or Maritimes shipowning, and only fourteen, local shipbuilding; of 517 articles of medium length, only ten had shipowning or shipbuilding as principal topics; of 256 long articles, only two had shipowning or shipbuilding as principal topics.

22 *Yarmouth Herald*, 14 February 1867.

23 Of 649 articles in the fifty-two issues in the sample, only sixteen had local shipowning or shipbuilding as a principal topic.

24 Saint John *Globe*, 18 January 1867.

25 Ibid., 10 December 1867.

26 "The Outlook for the Future," Saint John *Daily Sun*, Supplement, 3 April 1889, 13.

27 Thomas Kenny, president of the Merchants' Bank of Halifax, cited in "Report of the Select Committee on Inter-Provincial Trade," Canada *Sessional Papers*, 1883, Appendix no. 4, 22.

28 *Yarmouth Tribune*, cited in the *Halifax Herald*, 3 January 1881. There was the occasional reminder in the press that wooden shipping was not yet dead. "Although iron ships have gradually superceded those built of

wood in the British Islands ... the question between wood and iron is still an open one with many intelligent shipowners and shipmasters ... The question of ultimate superiority is still an open question": an article in the *New York Shipping List*, quoted in Saint John *Daily Telegraph*, 2 October 1875, and found in a Scrapbook on Saint John Industries, Shelf 46, New Brunswick Museum.

29   Note also that the opponents of Confederation in 1867 also assumed that manufacturing growth would occur, alongside the traditional marine-based industries. They argued, however, that Canadian control of Dominion tariffs, and "throwing our markets open to Canadian manufactures," would "destroy" manufacturing industry in the Maritimes: *Morning Chronicle*, 22 July 1867, cited in Delphin A. Muise, "The Federal Election of 1867 in Nova Scotia: An Economic Interpretation," *Collections of the Nova Scotia Historical Society*, XXXVI (1968), 340–1.

30   R.T. Naylor, *The History of Canadian Business*, II (Toronto: James Lorimer, 1975), 283.

31   See, for instance, Jones, Mitchell, Davies, Forbes, and others in House of Commons *Debates*, 28 February 1876.

32   John V. Ellis of Saint John in House of Commons *Debates*, 14 March 1890, 1963.

33   William Welsh (Queen's, Prince Edward Island) in House of Commons *Debates*, 18 April 1888, 908.

34   House of Commons *Debates*, 14 June 1887, 989.

35   A.G. Jones in House of Commons *Debates*, 14 June 1887, 992.

36   George Robertson of Saint John in *Royal Commission on Transportation: Evidence*, I, 1904–5, 74–5 (in National Archives of Canada, RG 33–3).

37   Ibid., 75 and 465.

38   Ibid., 328. The speaker was Mayor Crosby of Halifax.

39   Ibid., 287. The speaker was R.J. Matheson of Dartmouth.

40   Ibid., 86 and 238–41.

41   Bertram died before the commission finished its work, but the final report recommended a shipbuilding bounty of $5 per ton on all wooden vessels built in Canada and $6 per ton on all iron or steel vessels of 500 tons or more.

42   I. Matheson and Co. of New Glasgow built the 122-foot steel-hulled *Mulgrave* in 1893. The plates, frames, anchors, and chains were imported from Britain. We are indebted to Larry McCann for this information.

43   Cantley clearly believed that it was possible to build steamships and cruisers for a Canadian navy in Nova Scotia: "Most of the people in this part of the Dominion are of the opinion that Halifax is an ideal place to build cruisers." Letter of 24 December 1909 to J.C. MacGregor, Thomas Cantley Papers, Public Archives of Nova Scotia, MG 1, vol. 167. Cantley drafted more than one memorial on the subject. He noted that "shipyards

have practically no protection"; that Canada has been "unsuccessful to a mortifying extent in developing water transportation"; and that, by comparison, direct aid to railways was massive. Canada required protection even against British ships, protection for the ship repair business, free import of building materials, building bounties, and a naval building program. Cantley was also confident that steel plate could be manufactured in Nova Scotia and that labour could be supplied, although he recognized that the development of so complex an industry would take several years. Thomas Cantley, "Resources of the Province of Nova Scotia as Regards Steel Ship Construction," and "Shipbuilding in Canada: A Memorial Presented to the Canadian Government, April 1913," Cantley Papers, vol. 167, no. 7.

44 J.B. Black read a motion from the Maritime Board of Trade in House of Commons *Debates*, 14 January 1907, 1448. One of the more detailed cases for a shipbuilding bounty is a printed brief from the mayors of Halifax and Dartmouth, and the presidents of the Boards of Trade in those places, to the Dominion Minister of Finance, entitled *A Bonus to Steel Shipbuilding in Canada: The Argument in the Case* (Halifax, 1906).

45 In 1894 Sir Charles Hibbert Tupper reported the purchase price of a new Clyde-built steamer for the lighthouse service to be $86,000; the Canadian tender for the vessel was $136,000, he said: House of Commons *Debates*, 20 July 1894, 6513.

In 1909 L.P. Brodeur, minister of marine and fisheries, listed seven vessels purchased from British builders since 1896 and compared the cost of two with tenders received from Canadian builders. The *Druid* was purchased from Fleming and Ferguson for $110,060; the tender from Collingwood was $170,000 and from Polsons $173,000. The *Lady Laurier* was purchased from Fleming and Ferguson for $184,000; the tender from Collingwood was $235,000 and from Polsons, $298,900. House of Commons *Debates*, 24 March 1909, 3196. But see also *Debates*, 17 and 18 May 1909, 6950.

In 1911 Brodeur reported tenders for the *Estavan*: British tenders were as low as $201,000, $219,000, and $227,000; Collingwood was $260,000 and B.C. Marine Railway was $455,000. The government gave the contract to Collingwood to "encourage this Canadian shipbuilding company": *Debates*, 31 March 1911, 6488.

46 Vessel registered in the United Kingdom but not built there were subject to duty, however: House of Commons *Debates*, 31 March 1911, 6488–9.

47 House of Commons *Debates*, 14 January 1907, 1462; 31 January 1907, 2389.

48 L.P. Demers of St John and Iberville, House of Commons *Debates*, 29 May 1906, 4088. On the costs of British jurisdiction over shipping see Ted L. McDorman, "The Development of Shipping Law and Policy in Canada:

An Historical Examination of the British Influence," LLM thesis, Dalhousie University, 1982.

49 Thus discussions between government and the steel industry on shipbuilding were sometimes initiated by government, not by the industry. Why was a government steamer not built in Nova Scotia, since "there is an industry in steel plate in New Glasgow"? "We consulted them about it," said the minister of marine and fisheries, "and we found they were not able to take such a contract." Sir Louis Davies in House of Commons *Debates*, 12 May, 1899, 2997.

50 I am indebted to David Frank of the University of New Brunswick for this information, from his unpublished paper on the campaign to set up steel shipbuilding in Halifax, entitled "A Past and Prospective Industry." "The steel plates are only a very moderate proportion of the total cost," said W.S. Fielding in 1901. "The real difficulty is in assembling the material, especially the machinery, and also in the importation of a large amount of skilled labour." House of Commons *Debates*, 21 May 1901, 5772.

51 The projected start-up cost was $1 million. Halifax City promised a bonus of $100,000 for the shipbuilding plant and a further $100,000 for a plant to produce boilers and other machinery, as well as certain tax exemptions. Hunter wanted a bounty of $5 per ton as well as $5 per indicated horsepower in each vessel, but soon the bounty desired went up to 10 per cent of the contract price for each ship. W.S. Fielding and his cabinet colleagues did not comply, and the project died. For all this information I am indebted to David Frank.

52 "I know of no other industry that gives so little employment of labour for the amount of money expended as the building of steel ships," argued J.H. Sinclair, MP for Antigonish, in House of Commons *Debates*, 26 February 1919, 54. See also William Duff of Lunenburg, House of Commons *Debates*, 23 March 1920, 632–4.

53 House of Commons *Debates*, 29 May 1906, 4087.

54 In reply to a question in 1907 the minister of customs listed the countries and the dates of orders-in-council admitting each country: Italy, 1873; Germany, 1874; Netherlands, 1874; Norway and Sweden, 1874; Austria-Hungary, 1876; Denmark, 1877; Belgium, 1879; Argentina, 1881. House of Commons *Debates*, 20 February 1907, 3369. Needless to say, Canadian shipowners had little interest in entry to the coasting trades of these countries.

55 J.B. Black in House of Commons *Debates*, 14 January 1907, 1446.

56 Coal consumers in Prince Edward Island were particularly concerned, and Parliament received a petition from eighty-one island shipowners and masters: House of Commons *Debates*, 4 May 1908, 7732–5.

57 One solution was to limit Norwegian coal-carrying vessels to those over

2,000 tons, on the erroneous assumption that they would not then compete with smaller Canadian vessels. In October 1914 the Shipmasters' Association of Halifax sent a telegram to the minister of marine and fisheries asking if a Norwegian steamer, then unloading coal from Sydney, was liable to seizure. The answer from J.D. Hazen read: "If steamer 'Ulabrand' over two thousand tons gross, is permitted to carry coal between Sydney and Halifax." National Archives of Canada, RG 42 vol. 438 file 190-2-5.

58 E.M. Macdonald in House of Commons *Debates*, 4 May 1908, 7748.
59 Letter of Ernest Wells, secretary, Ship Masters' Association No. 1 of Canada, to J.D. Hazen, MP, 21 April 1914, National Archives of Canada, RG 42 vol. 438 file 190-2-5. Letter of Thomas Cantley of Nova Scotia Steel to J.D. Hazen, 18 October 1913, in the same file.
60 Cantley to Hazen, 18 October 1913, ibid. He added that appropriate steamers used in the Great Lakes could not be brought through the canals.
61 Total foreign clearances in Canadian coasting (not including clearances on the lakes) were 1.35 million tons in 1910 out of a total of 26.8 million tons: Trade and Navigation Report, Canada *Sessional Papers*, 1911, no. 7.
62 House of Commons *Debates*, 14 January 1907, 1461–2.

CHAPTER NINE

1 C.R. Fay and H.A. Innis, "The Maritime Provinces," *The Cambridge History of the British Empire*, VI (New York: Macmillan, 1930), 663.
2 Peter McClelland, "Commentary: On Demand and Supply in Shipping and Regional Economic Development," in Lewis R. Fischer and Eric W. Sager, eds., *Merchant Shipping and Economic Development in Atlantic Canada* (St John's: Maritime History Group, 1982), 115.
3 Peter D. McClelland, "The New Brunswick Economy in the Nineteenth Century," PhD thesis, Harvard University, 1966, 231.
4 T.W. Acheson, *Saint John: The Making of a Colonial Urban Community* (Toronto: University of Toronto Press, 1985), 14–16.
5 Particularly important in this context are Ian McKay, "Industry, Work and Community in the Cumberland Coalfields, 1848–1927," PhD thesis, Dalhousie University, 1983; McKay, "Class Struggle and Merchant Capital: Craftsmen and Labourers on the Halifax Waterfront, 1850–1902," in Bryan Palmer, ed., *The Character of Class Struggle: Essays in Canadian Working-Class History, 1850–1985* (Toronto: McClelland and Stewart, 1986), 17–36; Richard Rice, "A History of Organized Labour in Saint John, New Brunswick, 1813–1890," MA thesis, University of New Brunswick, 1968; Bruce Archibald, "The Development of Underdevelopment in the Atlantic Provinces," MA thesis, Dalhousie University, 1971; T.F.

Baker, "The Underdevelopment of Atlantic Canada, 1867–1920," MA thesis, McMaster University, 1977; Robert J. Brym and R. James Sacouman, eds., *Underdevelopment and Social Movements in Atlantic Canada* (Toronto: New Hogtown Press, 1979); L.D. McCann, "The Mercantile-Industrial Transition in the Metal Towns of Pictou County, 1857–1931," *Acadiensis*, 10, no. 2 (Spring 1981), 29–64; Peter R. Sinclair, "From Peasants to Corporations: The Development of Capitalist Agriculture in Canada's Maritime Provinces," in John A. Fry, ed., *Contradictions in Canadian Society* (Toronto, 1984), 276–91; Graeme Wynn, *Timber Colony: A Historical Geography of Early Nineteenth Century New Brunswick* (Toronto: University of Toronto Press, 1981); Kenneth Donovan, ed., *Cape Breton at 200: Historical Essays in Honour of the Island's Bicentennial 1785–1985* (Sydney, 1985); Del Muise, "The Making of an Industrial Community: Cape Breton Coal Towns, 1867–1900," in Donald McGillvray and Brian Tennyson, eds., *Cape Breton Historical Essays* (Sydney, 1980), 76–94; Ken Pryke, "Labour and Politics: Nova Scotia at Confederation," *Histoire sociale/Social History*, no. 6 (November 1970), 33–55.

6 Although in Newfoundland, of course, merchants used political and legal powers to undercut many of the planters in the nineteenth century: see Steven D. Antler, "Colonial Exploitation and Economic Stagnation in Nineteenth Century Newfoundland," PhD thesis, University of Connecticut, 1975.

7 See especially Antler, "Colonial Exploitation," and Antler, "The Capitalist Underdevelopment of Nineteenth-Century Newfoundland," in Robert J. Brym and R. James Sacouman, eds., *Underdevelopment and Social Movements in Atlantic Canada* (Toronto: New Hogtown Press, 1979), 179–202.

8 Basil Greenhill and Ann Giffard, *Westcountrymen in Prince Edward's Isle: A Fragment of the Great Migration* (Toronto: University of Toronto Press, 1967), 92–3, 96.

9 Ibid., 90.

10 Letter of 10 June 1840 from Ward and Co. to Gibbs, Bright and Co., New Brunswick Museum, Ward Papers, packet 3.

11 Customs House Returns, New Brunswick House of Assembly *Journals*, 1861, 6.

12 Letters of 30 January and 28 April 1841 from Ward and Co. to Gibbs, Bright and Co., Ward Papers, packet 3.

13 Charlottetown *Daily Examiner*, 31 October 1878, reporting on Duncan's bankruptcy. The report also stated that Duncan owed $146,451 to the Merchants Bank of Prince Edward Island.

14 Pollock, Gilmour and Co. extended such credit to Harley and Burchill of Miramichi and drafts for materials to be supplied from the former's branch at Quebec: Burchill Family Papers, cited in McClelland, "New Brunswick Economy," 187 n 37.

15 A. Gregg Finley, "The Morans of St. Martins, NB, 1850–1880: Toward an Understanding of Family Participation in Maritime Enterprise," in Lewis R. Fischer and Eric W. Sager, eds., *The Enterprising Canadians: Entrepreneurs and Economic Development in Eastern Canada, 1820–1914* (St John's: Maritime History Group, 1979), 37–54; Richard Rice, "The Wrights of Saint John: A Study of Shipbuilding and Shipowning in the Maritimes, 1839–1855," in David S. Macmillan, ed., *Canadian Business History: Selected Studies* (Toronto: McClelland and Stewart, 1972).

16 Compare this with Norman Long and Bryan Roberts, *Miners, Peasants and Entrepreneurs: Regional Development in the Central Highlands of Peru* (Cambridge: Cambridge University Press, 1984), 236–7.

17 Fischer calculates that the balance was positive in twenty-six of thirty-two years between 1830 and 1870: Lewis R. Fischer, "Enterprise in a Maritime Setting: The Shipping Industry of Prince Edward Island, 1787–1914," unpublished research report, Maritime History Group, Memorial University of Newfoundland, 1978, 241.

18 Charlottetown *Patriot*, 22 July 1875.

19 Tonnage exported is tonnage transferred out of New Brunswick from the Saint John and Miramichi registries; the value of this tonnage is estimated at between £5 and £7 per ton in the 1820s and 1830s and between £6 and £8 thereafter. There may be an underestimate of transfers here because not all vessels exported under governors' passes are included.

20 This means $3 a ton after deducting costs including depreciation (see chapter 6). The annual average tonnage on registry in Saint John and Miramichi (excluding all vessels under 250 tons and excluding all vessels transferred within three years of first registry) was 139,000 tons.

21 "Annual Returns of Trade and Navigation for the Year 1864," New Brunswick House of Assembly *Journals*, 1865, 4.

22 Robert W. Fogel, *Railroads and Economic Growth: Essays in Econometric History* (Baltimore, 1964), 207.

23 David Hackett Fischer, *Historians' Fallacies: Toward a Logic of Historical Thought* (New York: Harper and Row, 1970), 17–18.

24 House of Commons *Debates*, 18 February 1878, 363.

25 *Eastern Chronicle*, 24 January 1854, cited in James M. Cameron, *Ships and Seamen of New Glasgow, Nova Scotia* (New Glasgow, 1959). 9.

26 Saint John *Daily Telegraph*, 2 October 1896.

27 Charlottetown *Examiner*, 19 August 1878.

28 McClelland, "The New Brunswick Economy," Table LXII, 241.

29 We know from various sources that wages accounted for about a third of the costs of building a ship. In 1863 W. Mitchell, New Brunswick's registrar of shipping, estimated the cost of building a 1,000-ton ship with a 7A classification as follows: frame, £1,480; planking and ceiling, £900; masts

and spars, £400; deck plank for two decks and houses, £500; fastenings (imported), £1,000; chains and anchors, £360; rigging, sails, and "making", £1,180; labour, £2,950; iron knees and straps, £650; castings, oakum, paint, carving, and cabin, £580; total, £10,000.

See also costs reported in McClelland, "The New Brunswick Economy," Table L, 191, where the labour for building three vessels accounted for 30 per cent of all costs. Some portion of the payments for materials would also, however, be a payment to the labour involved in providing those materials.

In 1854, Moses Perley estimated that half the cost of every ship was paid to labour and that, on average, ten days' labour was required for every ton built: T.W. Acheson, *Saint John*, 16. Since about 35,000 tons were built in New Brunswick in 1870, a low estimate of payments to labour would be $420,000 for the year, and an upper estimate (if Perley was correct) would be $700,000. This compares with the census estimate of $346,046 paid in yearly wages to shipyard hands. The census also estimated wage payments of $39,113 in ship material making. Total yearly wages in all industrial establishments were $3,869,360.

30 Total tonnage built in the province in 1863 was about 85,000 tons. If production costs were $36 per ton and wage payments were 33 per cent of such costs, then total wage payments would have been $1,009,800. If Moses Perley was correct and it took ten man-days for each ton built, and if the average daily wage was eight shillings, then total wage payments were £340,000, or as much as $1,652,400 if the exchange rate was $4.86 per pound. See Acheson, *Saint John*, 16; "Annual Returns of Trade and Navigation," New Brunswick House of Assembly *Journals*, 1863.

See also the reports on Saint John shipbuilding in the Saint John *Morning News*, 9, 14, 19, 21, and 26 January and 2 February 1863: these articles found 1,279 workers employed in twenty-one Saint John shipyards, not including those in ancillary trades outside the shipyards. I am grateful to Eric Lawson of Bowen Island, British Columbia, for calling my attention to this source.

31 According to A.G. Green, gross value added for New Brunswick in 1890 was $49.05 million; Peter McClelland estimated gross provincial product in 1870 to be 35.6 or $35.7 millions: McClelland, "The New Brunswick Economy," 272–3. If provincial product was proportionate to population, then GPP in 1860 would be 35.6 (252.0 / 285.6) = $31.4 millions, where 252.0 is the population in 1860 and 285.6 is the population in 1870.

32 McClelland, "The New Brunswick Economy," 275.

33 Total tonnage built in New Brunswick in 1870 was about 35,600 tons. The "value of articles produced" in shipyards, according to the census, was $1,086,714, which would mean that vessel prices were only $30.53 per ton.

34 If the tonnage built in 1870 (35,600 tons) is valued at $40 per ton, and if gross provincial product was $35.6 million, then shipyard output was 4 per cent of provincial product. The annual average tonnage built between 1850 and 1874 was 50,700 tons, or 5.4 per cent of provincial product in 1870, if the tonnage is valued at $38 per ton. In 1864, when 92,500 tons were built, shipyard output was 10.3 per cent of provincial product, if provincial product was $34 million. Needless to say, such estimates must not be taken as precise measures of reality.

35 W.E. Vickery, "Exports and North American Economic Growth: 'Structuralist' and 'Staple' Models in Historical Perspective," *Canadian Journal of Economics* 7, no. 1 (1974), 51.

36 This assumes that profits, as in most modern economies, were 10 per cent of gross product ($35.6 million). If we assume returns of 21 per cent, then profits after deducting costs (including depreciation) would have been about $840,000, or 23.6 per cent of $3.56 million. Assuming a slightly higher rate of return, we estimated shipping profits to be a third of provincial profits: see Lewis R. Fischer, Eric W. Sager, and Rosemary E. Ommer, "The Shipping Industry and Regional Economic Development in Atlantic Canada, 1871–1891," in Lewis R. Fischer and Eric W. Sager, *Merchant Shipping and Economic Development in Atlantic Canada* (St John's: Maritime History Group, 1982), 49.

37 See, for instance, Kris Inwood, "Economic Growth and Structural Change in Atlantic Canada, 1850–1910," in Lewis R. Fischer and Helge Nordvik, *Across the Broad Atlantic: Essays in Comparative Maritime History* (Oslo: Norwegian University Press, forthcoming, 1990).

38 Canada *Census*, 1871, 1881, and 1891. The 1891 census does not give a single category for "ship material making"; the figures for 1890 in Table 9.1 are the sums for block-making, masts and spars, and sails.

39 Once again these are not precise measures of reality but are employed here merely to show relative magnitudes. The 1871 census and the 1881 census give figures for "capital invested," whereas the 1891 census breaks down capital into "fixed capital" and "working capital." I assume that "capital invested" in 1871 and 1881 includes both fixed and working capital.

40 The figure for "working capital" ($410,360) in Nova Scotia shipyards in 1890 seems highly unlikely.

41 In 1890, fifteen Ontario shipyards produced articles valued at $584,200, or $38,947 per establishment; this compares with $9,866 per shipyard for the twenty-nine New Brunswick shipyards and $21,553 per shipyard for the seventy-nine Nova Scotia shipyards. Value added per employee was $734 in Ontario, and capital invested (fixed and working) per employee was $1,030: Canada *Census*, 1890.

42 This is the method of Phillip J. Wood, "Barriers to Capitalist Development

in Maritime Canada, 1870–1930: A Comparative Perspective," in Peter Baskerville, ed., *Canadian Papers in Business History*, I (Victoria: Public History Group, 1989), 33–57. Wood follows the method of Ernest Mandel, *Late Capitalism* (London: New Left Books, 1975). I assume that for each shipyard there was one salary, equal to the average annual wage for all shipyard workers; the calculation includes only 50 per cent of such salaries, in order that the results be comparable with Wood's estimates. Wood adds an important cautionary note: "The calculations are made in price terms rather than values. The relationship between values and prices is mediated by a complicated social process which may divorce commodity prices, within certain limits, from the values arising in the process of exploitation. The calculations presented here should therefore be considered to be indicators of s/v [surplus value] rather than fully adequate measures." See also Phillip J. Wood, "Marxism and the Maritimes: On the Determinants of Regional Capitalist Development," *Studies in Political Economy*, 29 (Summer 1989), 123–53.

43 On this subject see Phillip J. Wood, "Marxism and the Maritimes," *Studies in Political Economy*, 29 (Summer 1989), 123–53; and we await the important essay by Kris Inwood, "Economic Growth and Structural Change in Atlantic Canada, 1850–1910," in Fischer and Nordvik, *Across the Broad Atlantic*.

44 Richard Rice, "A History of Organized Labour in Saint John, New Brunswick, 1813–1890," MA thesis, University of New Brunswick, 1968, chapter 2. Rice suggests that collective action by shipwrights began as early as 1799, and there is evidence of ship carpenters' organizations in the 1830s and 1840s: Eugene Forsey, *The Trade Unions in Canada* (Toronto: University of Toronto Press, 1982), 9–10.

45 The breakdown of costs for a 1,000-ton vessel given in the "Trade and Navigation Returns," New Brunswick House of Assembly *Journals*, 1863, includes £1,000 currency for fastenings, £360 for anchor and chain, and £650 for iron knees or straps, which taken together amounts to 20 per cent of the final cost. McClelland presents costs of building three New Brunswick vessels: a 600-ton vessel in 1855, a 652-ton vessel in 1865/6, and a 1,302-ton vessel in 1868/9; for these vessels the average cost of iron, copper, chains and anchors, excluding metal in the outfitting, was 17 per cent. McClelland, "The New Brunswick Economy," 191.

46 New Brunswick duties on imported shipbuilding materials would add only £130 currency to the cost of a 1,000-ton ship in 1862, or 1.3 per cent of the final cost, according to the "Trade and Navigation Report," New Brunswick House of Assembly *Journals*, 1863, 17–18.

47 Eric Lawson's research on T.E. Millidge suggests that Millidge often fitted temporary anchors and chains until arrival of the vessel in England: Eric Lawson, letter to Eric Sager, 20 July 1987.

48 Imported materials for a 1,000-ton ship would cost £3,000 currency: ibid.

49 "Report of the Select Committee on the Causes of the Present Depression," House of Commons *Journals*, 1876, Appendix 3, 167.

50 The annual average tonnage built in New Brunswick in the 1870s was about 37,000 tons. Assuming that vessel production costs were $40 per ton and that metal costs were 20 per cent of final costs, this would mean an annual average demand for metal goods of $148,000. The value of output in metalworking industries in New Brunswick (foundries and machine working, blacksmithing, foundry working and fittings, nail and tack factories, and tin- and sheet-iron–working) was $1,691,000 in 1870 and $1,641,000 in 1880: McClelland, "The New Brunswick Economy," 194.

51 Ship materials output in Nova Scotia was valued by the census at $180,455 in 1870 and $234,623 in 1880; New Brunswick ship material output was $540,791 in 1870 (which may be an overestimate) and $155,450 in 1880. The category does not include rope- and twine-making. We may underestimate imported inputs because import tables in the *Sessional Papers* have a category for metal goods entering free of duty, separate from the category for ship materials, and metals include such things as "yellow metal for sheathing," which may also have been used in ships.

52 Samir Amin, *Accumulation on a World Scale: A Critique of the Theory of Underdevelopment*, I (New York: Monthly Review Press, 1974), 286–302. See also Ian McKay, "Class Politics and Regional Dependency: The Rise and Fall of the Working-Class Movement in the Coalfields of the Maritime Provinces, 1830–1930," paper presented to the Symposium on Canadian-Welsh Labour History, Gregynog, April 1987; McKay, "Industry, Work and Community in the Cumberland Coalfields, 1848–1927," PhD thesis, Dalhousie University, 1983.

53 Calculated from annual reports on trade and navigation in New Brunswick House of Assembly *Journals* and from trade and navigation reports, and shipping returns in Canada, *Sessional Papers*; see also McClelland, "The New Brunswick Economy," 159.

54 For three vessels analysed by McClelland built in 1855, 1865–6, and 1868–9, the average cost of timber was 25 per cent of the final construction cost. In 1876 Frank Killam stated that if a 1,000-ton vessel cost $45 per ton, inputs of wood cost $10 per ton: House of Commons *Journals*, 1876, Appendix 3, 165. The breakdown of costs stated in the "Trade and Navigation Returns," New Brunswick House of Assembly *Journals*, 1863, 17–18, suggests that for a 1,000-ton ship frame, planking, ceiling, and planking for deck and houses would cost £2,880 currency, or 28.8 per cent of the final cost.

55 Gross value of sawmill production in New Brunswick was $6,575,759 in 1870 and $6,532,826 in 1880; comparable Nova Scotia figures are

$1,397,937 (1870) and $3,094,137 (1880). From Canada, *Census*, 1871, 1881.

56 According to the census the total numbers in fishing boats and fishing vessels in Nova Scotia were 10,394 in 1851, 14,322 in 1861, 17,428 in 1871, and 24,636 in 1881. The number of fishermen per boat was 1.3 in 1851, 1.0 in 1861, 1.5 in 1871, and 1.4 in 1881 (or 1.5 if "shoremen" are included). The number of men in vessels was 4.5 per vessel in 1851, 6.3 in 1861, 7.7 in 1871, and 9.1 in 1881. The tonnage of vessels in fishing is given only in 1851; even if we allow for a 10 per cent increase in average tonnage from one census to the next, the number of fishermen per ton increases by 63 per cent between 1851 and 1881. Canada *Census*, 1871, 1881. The 1871 census includes the 1851 and 1861 censuses.

57 Capt. Moorsom, *Letters from Nova Scotia* (London, 1830), 50, cited in G.S. Graham, *Sea Power and British North America 1783–1820* (Cambridge, Mass., 1941), 53. On the extent of occupational pluralism see L.D. McCann, " 'Living a Double Life': Town and Country in the Industrialization of the Maritimes," in D. Day, ed., *Geographical Perspectives on the Maritime Provinces* (Halifax: St Mary's University, 1988), 93–113.

58 Joseph Howe, *Western and Eastern Rambles: Travel Sketches of Nova Scotia*, edited by M.G. Parks (Toronto: University of Toronto Press, 1973), 81, 83.

59 Ibid., 85. See also 98–9, where Howe notes the connections among access to the sea, local prosperity, and the ubiquitous "barter business" in Bridgetown.

60 If we add coastal entrances and seaward entrances and divide by population, we have the following estimates of tonnage per capita for 1880: Arichat, 27.7; Barrington, 14.2; Montreal, 12.0; and Shelburne, 15.7. The provincial figures are 3.8 tons per capita for Nova Scotia and 2.1 for Quebec. From Tables of Trade and Navigation in Canada *Sessional Papers*, 1881.

61 Taking tonnage entered inward from sea and dividing by population for 1870 gives the following tonnage per capita: Nova Scotia, 2.3; Quebec, 0.85. Of all tonnage entering Nova Scotia from the sea 35 per cent entered Halifax; 75 per cent of all tonnage entering Quebec came to Quebec City. Tables of Trade and Navigation, Canada *Sessional Papers*, 1871.

62 Mr Lefurgey, MP, in House of Commons *Debates*, 14 July 1908, 13056.

63 Value of industrial products for Ontario was $114.7 millions; for Nova Scotia, $12.3 millions; and for New Brunswick, $17.4 millions. Population figures were 1,620,851 for Ontario; 387,800 for Nova Scotia; and 285,594 for New Brunswick. Canada *Census*, 1871, III, Table LV. On railways and capitalist development in Canada see Paul Craven and Tom Traves, "Canadian Railroads as Manufacturers, 1850–1880," Canadian Historical Association, *Historical Papers* (1983), 264–6; Morris Altman, "Railways as

an Engine of Economic Growth?" *Histoire sociale/Social History* 21, no. 42 (November 1988), 269–81.

64 Among the guilty parties are Eric W. Sager, Lewis R. Fischer, and Rosemary E. Ommer, "Landward and Seaward Opportunities in Canada's Age of Sail," in Lewis R. Fischer and Eric W. Sager, *Merchant Shipping and Economic Development in Atlantic Canada* (St John's: Maritime History Group, 1982), 28 (a paper written mainly by the first-listed author).

65 Montreal–Britain grain rates are quoted intermittently in E.A.V. Angier, *Fifty Years' Freights* (London: Fairplay, 1920).

66 Douglass C. North, "Ocean Freight Rates and Economic Development 1750–1913," *Journal of Economic History*, 18 (1958), 550–2.

67 The excess subsidy paid to the Canadian Pacific Railway Co. appears to have been somewhere between $40 million and $61 million, depending on the assumed rate of return. P.J. George, "Rates of Return in Railway Investment and Implications for Government Subsidization of the Canadian Pacific Railway: Some Preliminary Results," *Canadian Journal of Economics*, 1, no. 4 (1968), 740–62; P.J. George, "Rates of Return and Government Subsidization of the Canadian Pacific Railway: Some Further Remarks," *Canadian Journal of Economics*, 8, no. 4 (1975), 591–600; L.J. Mercer, "Rates of Return and Government Subsidization of the Canadian Pacific Railway: An Alternative View," *Canadian Journal of Economics*, 6, no. 3 (1973), 428–37.

68 Sidney Pollard and Paul Robertson, *The British Shipbuilding Industry 1870–1914* (Cambridge, Mass.: Harvard University Press, 1979), 6.

69 I am indebted to David Frank for this information: see J.W. Carmichael in *Industrial Advocate*, 7 March 1899, and in Halifax *Herald*, 6 August 1898.

70 In producing output valued at $2,034,223, Ontario shipyards used $640,817 worth of materials (31.5 per cent). Manufacturing in the country as a whole used $601.5 million in materials to produce $1,165 million output (51.6 per cent): Canada, *Census*, 1911.

71 Again I am indebted to David Frank's unpublished paper on this subject; much of his information comes from the Letterbook of Harry Judson Crowe, Public Archives of Nova Scotia.

72 The technological transition was most complete in Ontario. In 1911 ten Ontario shipyards had a ratio of capital invested to number of wage-paid employees of $3,802; the average for all Canadian manufacturing was $2,648, according to the 1911 *Census*. In 1911, annual average wage payments in shipbuilding were $499 in Ontario and $695 in British Columbia; the annual average for Canadian manufacturing was $419. In Ontario shipyards, total wage payments were 28 per cent of the value of products in 1911; in all Canadian manufacturing, wage payments were 17 per cent of output.

73 According to the 1901 *Census* there were 4,469 manufacturing wage-earners in Halifax City and County and 21,010 in Nova Scotia. Since average wages in shipbuilding were relatively high, the potential increase in total wage payments was higher: about a third for Halifax City and County and about 9 per cent for the province.

74 The original government program produced sixty-three ships at a cost of $73 million (March 1918–March 1920). Of this amount about 12 per cent, or $9.1 million, was accounted for by Nova Scotia: "Annual Report of the Department of Marine and Fisheries," Canada *Sessional Papers*, 1922, LVIII, no. 21, 13. If we assume that Nova Scotia accounted for $24 million over two years, this would have been an additional $7.5 million a year over what was actually spent in Nova Scotia. About a third of the costs would have been direct wage payments.

75 Vessels built under the government shipbuilding program in 1918–20 cost $192 per ton on average. The cost of building a ship of 10,000 to 11,000 deadweight tons in a British yard was £203,200 in 1920, according to Lloyds, or about $90 to $99 per ton. These figures are from Canada *Sessional Papers*, 1922, LVIII, 6, 13. The cost of building the same ship in Britain in 1913–14 was about £74,000 or between $33 and $36 per ton. Pre-war Canadian-built steamship tonnage could cost between $60 and $100 per ton, depending on the type of vessel and location of shipyard.

76 "In view of our past experience with bounties, I doubt the wisdom of the policy. We have been heavily subsidizing the steel industry and after many years we are informed that without this prop it must come to the ground, and that we shall have, at no distant date, to continue a system which we had hoped would only be temporary, and to tell you the truth I am the worst opponent that you have to meet at Council." Laurier to Leighton McCarthy, MP, 24 February 1908, Laurier Papers No. 136676, National Archives of Canada.

CHAPTER TEN

1 Yrjo Kaukiainen, "The Transition from Sail to Steam in Finnish Shipping, 1850–1914," *Scandinavian Economic History Review*, 28, no. 2 (1980), 161–84; Basil Greenhill and John Hackman, *The Grain Races: The Baltic Background* (London: Conway Maritime Press, 1986); Georg Kahre, *The Last Tall Ships: Gustaf Erikson and the Aland Sailing Fleets, 1872–1947* (London: Conway Maritime Press, 1978).

2 S.G. Sturmey, *British Shipping and World Competition* (London: Athlone Press, 1962), 9.

3 Martin Fritz, "Shipping in Sweden, 1850–1913," *Scandinavian Economic History Review*, 28, no. 2 (1980), 154, 158. Norwegians also purchased used British steamers: Helge Nordvik, "The Shipping Industries of the

Scandinavian Countries, 1850–1914," in Lewis R. Fischer and Gerald E. Panting, eds., *Change and Adaptation in Maritime History: The North Atlantic Fleets in the Nineteenth Century* (St John's: Maritime History Group, 1985), 139.

4 Sarah Palmer, "The British Shipping Industry 1850–1914," in Fischer and Panting, eds., *Change and Adaptation*, 95–6; Robin Craig, *The Ship: Steam Tramps and Cargo Liners 1850–1950* (London: National Maritime Museum, 1980).

5 Simon P. Ville, *English Shipowning during the Industrial Revolution* (Manchester: Manchester University Press, 1987), 2–3, 149–54; Ralph Davis, *The Rise of the English Shipping Industry in the Seventeenth and Eighteenth Centuries* (London: Macmillan, 1962), 88–9. On ownership concentration see R. Craig and R. Jarvis, *Liverpool Registry of Merchant Ships* (Manchester, 1967), tables 24 and 25.

6 Peter N. Davies, "The Development of the Liner Trades," in Keith Matthews and Gerald Panting, eds., *Ships and Shipbuilding in the North Atlantic Region* (St John's: Maritime History Group, 1978), 175; see also Freda Harcourt, "The P&O Company: Flagships of Imperialism," in Sarah Palmer and Gyndwr Williams, *Charted and Uncharted Waters* (London: National Maritime Museum, 1981), 6–28. There are many histories of British liner companies.

7 Sarah Palmer, "The British Shipping Industry 1850–1914," 105.

8 William Page, *Commerce and Industry: Tables of Statistics for the British Empire from 1815* (London, 1919), 162; cited in Palmer, "The British Shipping Industry 1850–1914," 105.

9 This is from the so-called 1 per cent sample of the crew list archive, a project begun by David Alexander in 1979. Vessels of liner companies are inevitably underrepresented, since crew agreements for many major liner companies were retained in Britain and are not included in the Maritime History Archive at Memorial University.

The sample is a random sample, weighted by the number of sail and steam vessels on registry in the United Kingdom by decade. The computer file, which is normally accessed by SAS or SPSS-X programs, is available from the Maritime History Archive. For users of this file, Table 10.2 is from a table of gross tonnage by GEODES, or geographic description.

A voyage is the pattern of vessel movement from the opening to the closing of the crew agreement. The overwhelming majority of voyages, for both sail and steam, began in Britain. A North Atlantic voyage usually means a voyage from Britain or Europe to the eastern United States or eastern British North America and back to Britain or Europe; less often it means a voyage commencing on the western side of the North Atlantic. Similarly, most other voyages listed here refer to voyages beginning in Britain, going to the place stated, and returning to Britain, often with ports of call en route. There were 6,086 voyages by sailing vessels, and the sum of tonnage for these voyages was 3,813,365; there were 12,725 voyages by steamers (including auxiliary steamers), and the sum of gross tonnage for these was 24,071,118.

10 There is an important qualification here, as Robin Craig has reminded us: unknown proportions of the tonnage registered in other countries were owned by people residing in the United Kingdom.

11 Of course there were firms, such as the CPR, that had investments in land, the wheat economy, and shipping. But there were few such connections between capital in the shipowning heartland of the Maritimes and the wheat economy.

12 William D. Wray, *Mitsubishi and the N.Y.K., 1870–1914: Business Strategy in the Japanese Shipping Industry* (Cambridge, Mass.: Council on East Asian Studies, Harvard University, 1984), 7–8; see also Ryoichi Miwa, "Government and the Japanese Shipping Industry, 1945–64," *Journal of Transport History*, 9, no. 1 (March 1988), 37–49.

13 Wray, *Mitsubishi*, 8.

14 By 1876 Mitsubishi had 57 per cent of all steamship tonnage owned in Japan, and Wray concludes that the company had a monopoly in rapid long-distance shipping: ibid., 98–9.

15 Ibid., 13.

16 On state support see US Shipping Board Bureau of Research, *Shipping and the State* (Washington, DC, 1928); Edwin M. Bacon, *Manual of Ship Subsidies: An Historical Summary of the Systems of All Nations* (Chicago: A.C. McClurg, 1911); Royal Meeker, *History of Shipping Subsidies* (New York: American Economic Association, 1905).

17 A. Gomez-Mendoza, "Government and the Development of Modern Shipbuilding in Spain, 1850–1935," *Journal of Transport History*, 9, no. 1 (March 1988), 19, 35.

18 The law of 1881 granted a construction bounty of 60 francs per gross ton to iron and steel ships and from 10 to 20 francs for wooden ones. The carrying bounty was 1.5 francs per ton for each 1,000 nautical miles. With the franc equal to about $0.193 US, this means a bounty of about 6,000 francs, or $1,158, for a 4,000-mile voyage by a 1,000-ton vessel. The subsidy laws were revised in 1893, 1902, and 1906. See S.B. Clough, *France: A History of National Economics 1789–1939* (New York: Octagon Books, 1964), 240–1; Bacon, *Manual of Ship Subsidies*, 36.

19 S. Pollard, "*Laissez-faire* and Shipbuilding," *Economic History Review*, 5, no. 1 (1952), 111.

20 Ibid., 99–103; Sidney Pollard and Paul Robertson, *The British Shipbuilding Industry, 1870–1914* (Cambridge, Mass.: Harvard University Press, 1979), 201–29. Robin Craig argues in a personal communication of 24 June 1989 that the Admiralty had to be dragged into the era of steam.

21 Freda Harcourt, "British Oceanic Mail Contracts in the Age of Steam, 1838–1914," *Journal of Transport History*, 9, no. 1 (March 1988), 1.

22 Thus in 1892–3 the distributed profits and subsidies (the latter in brackets) of the major lines were as follows, in thousands of pounds sterling: Cie. Gen. Transatlantique: 80 (446); Messageries Maritimes: 120 (554); North German Lloyd: 30 (220); P&O: 140 (about 352); Cunard: 7 (about 63); Royal Mail St. P. Co.: 0.3 (90); Orient Co.: −43 (loss)(85); Pacific Steam Navigation Co.: −57 (loss)(20). From John Inglis, in *Transactions* of the Engineers and Shipbuilders of Scotland, 1893, cited in Pollard, "*Laissez-faire* and Shipbuilding," 114 n 5.

23 Ted L. McDorman, "The Development of Shipping Law and Policy in Canada: An Historical Examination of the British Influence," LLM thesis, Dalhousie University, 1982, 54. Mail subsidies and steamship subventions for ocean-going steamers in the fiscal year 1899–1900 amounted to $316,769 for Atlantic steamers and $194,666 for Pacific steamers: ibid., 94.

24 Canada, *Twenty-Fourth Annual Report of the Department of Trade and Commerce, 1925–1926* (Ottawa: Queen's Printer, 1926), 52; cited in McDorman, "Development," 54–5.

25 In a letter of 31 December 1909, Laurier wrote to J.H. Sinclair, who had urged the adoption of shipbuilding bounties: "I fear that your arguments are not absolutely sound from a pure economic point of view and if your dear father-in-law were still alive I think he would give you a strong lecture on your heresy. He would have to join me in it, for if your view is not sound economically I think it is sound politically, and I am a convert to it." Laurier Papers, National Archives of Canada, reel C-884, no. 164165.

26 Yoshida Toyo, cited in Wray, *Mitsubishi*, 21.

27 Clough, *France*, 240.

28 Walter Kresse, "The Shipping Industry in Germany, 1850–1914," in Fischer and Panting, eds., *Change and Adaptation*, 163.

29 Yrjo Kaukiainen, "The Transition from Sail to Steam in Finnish Shipping, 1850–1914," *Scandinavian Economic History Review*, 28, no. 2 (1980), 178.

30 Helge Nordvik, "The Shipping Industries of the Scandinavian Countries," in Fischer and Panting, eds., *Change and Adaptation*, 132.

31 J.S. Worm-Muller, *Den norske sjofarts historie* (Oslo, 1951), 229–300; Nordvik, "The Shipping Industries," 137.

32 Nordvik, "The Shipping Industries," 138. Studies of Bergen shipping argue that rates of return on capital invested in shipping in the 1880s and 1890s were higher than returns on financial assets or other industries: Lauritz Pettersen, *Bergen og sjofarten: Fra kjopmannsrederi til selstendig naering 1860–1914* (Bergen, 1981), 224–7; A. Thowsen, "Bergen og sjofarten IV 1914–1939," *Sjofartshistorisk Arbok* (Bergen, 1981), 44–58.

For an example of an investor who moved from textile manufacturing into shipping see Lewis R. Fischer and Helge Nordvik, "From Broager to Bergen: The Risks and Rewards of Peter Jebsen, Shipowner, 1864–1892," *Sjofartshistorisk Arbok* (Bergen, 1986), 37–68. The Aland Islands offer an extreme example: where there was capital, a seafaring tradition, and no landward opportunities, argues Basil Greenhill, "you may well develop into a major shipping community" if only because "there is nothing else you damn well can do." Basil Greenhill, "Aspects of Late Nineteenth Century Rural Shipowning in South Western Britain," in Keith Matthews and Gerald Panting, eds., *Ships and Shipbuilding in the North Atlantic Region* (St John's: Maritime History Group, 1978), 170.

Index